International
Politics
in Southern Africa

International Politics in Southern Africa

EDITED BY

Gwendolen M. Carter
and Patrick O'Meara

INDIANA
UNIVERSITY
PRESS

BLOOMINGTON

Library of Congress Cataloging in Publication Data
Main entry under title:
International politics in Southern Africa.

Proceedings of a conference held April 24-25, 1981
at Indiana University.

Bibliography: p.
Includes index.

Contents: The Communist states and Southern Africa/
David E. Albright—U.S. policy toward Southern
Africa/Robert M. Price—[etc.]

1. Africa, Southern—Foreign relations—1975-
Addresses, essays, lectures. 2. Africa, Southern—
Politics and government—1975- —Addresses, essays,
lectures. I. Carter, Gwendolen Margaret, 1906-

II. O'Meara, Patrick.
DT746.I59   1982   327.68   81-48325
ISBN 0-253-34285-6   AACR2
ISBN 0-253-20281-7 (pbk.)

Contents

Preface

This book is a direct outgrowth of our increasing awareness of the importance of analyzing the roles being played by major international powers in the Southern African region. We see it as a companion to *Southern Africa: The Continuing Crisis,* which we have revised and updated so as to appear at the same time as this volume. Both of these books are intended for broad audiences in this country and overseas, in the belief that the Southern African region is one of the most critical in the world today.

We hope that *International Politics in Southern Africa* will dispel some of the myths concerning major power involvement in the region and provide a sound basis for evaluating the complexities of international engagement.

In preparation for the book, we organized a conference at Indiana University on "Southern Africa: International Issues and Responses," on April 24 and 25, 1981, for the contributors to the work. We are indebted to The Lilly Endowment, Inc. for supporting the conference and thereby aiding in the publication of the book. The Cummins Engine Foundation, the Dean of International Programs, and the African Studies Program also provided encouragement and generous support. Those who participated in the conference as discussants or chairpersons included: Phyllis Martin, John Lombardi, Trevor Brown, William Siffin, Allen Maxwell, Edmond Keller, J. Gus Liebenow, Iliya Harik, Sheldon Gellar, and Harvey Starr. The lively interaction between contributors and commentators at the conference was an invaluable stimulus to the revision of the chapters.

We very much appreciate the assistance given this entire project by the staff of the African Studies Program, and in particular by Chloe Ann Miller, Sue Ann Hanson, Susan Domowitz, and Lisa McCullough.

GWENDOLEN M. CARTER
PATRICK O'MEARA

Introduction: International Politics and Rivalries in Southern Africa

The rich mineral resources of Southern Africa have long attracted Western capitalism from Europe and the United States. It is only since World War II, however, that international political interests and rivalries have brought that area into the arena of great power politics. The piecemeal ending of colonial control in Eastern, Central, and Southern Africa, in which a number of European states were involved, was more often marked by violence than had been the case in West Africa. Rival internal claimants for power and/or liberation movements sought outside support for their efforts to pressure or overthrow colonial authorities. The Soviet Union and Cuba early evinced their interest in gaining influence in areas from which they had previously been excluded. As tensions grew between the West and the East, they became reflected within Africa, and particularly in Southern Africa where the most recent stages of decolonization have marked the last decade. Today, international jockeying for power in Southern Africa between major international actors is reflected in the daily news, and gives rise to a host of questions about their motivations, activities, and likely effects.

The Impact of East–West Tensions

Are the countries which comprise the region and, indeed, the region itself mere pawns in the much larger configuration of East-West confrontation? Are the major powers, in fact, mainly involved in achieving their own particular goals and interests in the broader arena? Can we ascertain their real, as contrasted with the ideal, expectations of the major powers in the Southern African region? What, indeed, are their distinctions between long-range and short-range policies, symbolic and actual achievements, and between moral choices and ideological considerations?

A realist view of international politics tends to assume that the threat of conflict is always real and that well-designed diplomatic and military strategies are essential at all times, rather than the pursuit of what may be regarded as utopian or ideal goals. This dichotomy is to some extent reflected in the contrasting political concepts and even fortunes of the Republicans and Democrats in the United States; as Robert Price points out, Ronald Reagan's neorealist tilt marks a sharp break with the Carter human rights stance. Even sharper differences exist in Britain between Labour, its new challenger the Social Democratic Party, and the Conservatives. France's international position toward Southern Africa under Giscard d'Estaing was very different from that assumed by Socialist François Mitterrand. Thus, the approaches of the Western powers to the region can shift, perhaps radically, as a consequence of their own internal political changes, and thereby complicate efforts to maintain a common front. But equally, the congruence in the views of Reagan and Thatcher brings about a different and more conservative configuration in the actions promoted by the Western allies.

Conservatives tend to place a greater emphasis on the supposition that peaceful change can be induced in the most difficult situations, and for that reason the Reagan administration has supported a lessening of pressure on South Africa. It has emphasized the idea of "not pushing South Africa up against the wall" in order to secure incremental changes. In addition, it hopes to achieve a more conciliatory attitude on the part of South Africa toward moves for Namibian independence. As Price points out, the conservative hierarchy of interests tends to focus on South Africa's minerals, military-strategic importance, and anti-Communist stance. This position is enhanced by South Africa's extensive and richly funded propaganda network and lobby in the United States and elsewhere.

The liberal position and that of organized labor emphasize, however, that this view overlooks the fact that in the long range fostering indigenous political rights might ultimately be in the best interests of the United States and its allies, particularly because the alienation of the West's African allies by such policies is not in its own best interests. As Price points out, a sub-Saharan Africa embittered against the United States because of its "global" policies toward Southern Africa would have real, not just symbolic, costs for the United States. Price goes on to say that, to argue, as former National Security Adviser Richard Allen did, that the United States can and should have "normal" relations with South Africa while at the same time disapproving of their apartheid system, just as we have good relations with other countries whose domestic arrangements we do not admire (e.g., China, Bulgaria, etc.), misses the point entirely. He concludes that, because the strategy of global containment views everything through the prism of East-West conflict it distorts the nature of threats to American interests and obscures the existence of regionally based constraints.

Historical Time Depth of International Actors

Christopher Hill, in treating the complexities of Western European policies toward Southern Africa, makes clear the different degrees of intensity of involvement by major powers and their different time depths in that area. Britain, Portugal, and Germany have all had long and historic linkages with parts of Southern Africa, and these continue in the form of business, banking, and religious ties. All three countries are subject to the kith and kin sentiment because of long domiciled former compatriots in the region. For Britain, this sentiment has had enduring relevance particularly in regard to Rhodesia (now Zimbabwe) and South Africa.

British concerns in Southern Africa are not merely historical, however, for they include strong and continuing economic interests of major value to its own ailing economy. Politically, the United States is a relative newcomer to the region but it has had much longer economic ties through powerfully entrenched American mining and commercial companies. The Communists have had an even shorter level of involvement in the region, but as David Albright makes clear, the Soviet Union, the Cubans and East Germans, who work tacitly together in Southern Africa, and the Chinese, Rumanians, and Yugoslavs in their own individual ways have directly and actively sought to cement both political and ideological ties, first with liberation movements and subsequently, with varying success, within independent countries. Not to be underestimated is the deep concern for the region by Africa's most populous and wealthy nation, Nigeria, whose actions in pressing for political change in Rhodesia were particularly significant at certain points, as Olajide Aluko makes clear. Nigeria also plays a leadership role in the Organization of African Unity (OAU), as Colin Legum deftly describes. He also indicates the supportive positions adopted by the Arab states in the Middle East to strengthen African hands while Israel, now largely isolated except for its links with South Africa, formerly extended technical assistance and training facilities to African countries before they joined the Arab boycott.

South Africa as an International Power

In any study of international actors, South Africa with its advanced economy, military strength, and strong international ties must be seen as a potent power operating within the international and intraregional context. As such it dominates transportation links in the Southern African region, the delivery of goods and services, patterns of labor migration, and covert and overt levels of diplomacy. But, as Kenneth Grundy maintains, there are "absolute limits to the hegemonic potentialities of a white-ruled South Africa . . . a fact not always appreciated by Pretoria." He goes on to say that: "One of the more obvious features of the past decade has been the shrinkage in South Africa's northern hinterland, or at least in South Africa's virtually free access to 'its' hinterland, and in its ability to translate continued economic muscle into political leverage." Pretoria contends that within the region it is only defending itself against a Communist-inspired "total onslaught" and that it is the last bastion of civilization on the continent. On the other hand South African actions in pursuit of their own perceived goals and security must be seen as the major source of instability in the region. Its frequent incursions into Angola, its attempts to destabilize Zimbabwe, its raid on African National Congress houses on the outskirts of Maputo, Mozambique, and its own disruptive domestic policies are obvious impediments to even minimal Southern African unity.

Nonetheless, within the region, economic factors continue to override political or ideological differences. Thus the South African government coexists with pro-Marxist Mozambique because the use of the port of Maputo and of Cabora Bassa power are mutually advantageous. But while South Africa has economic hegemony, it should not be seen as the dominant partner in a one-sided relationship. It needs the African-controlled nations of the region almost as much as they need South Africa, and it, too, must make occasional diplomatic and political concessions.

In the future, the independent black-controlled nations of Southern Africa may become more adroit in bargaining with South Africa to their own advantage. Both sides are aware of one another's weaknesses and key interests. Robert Mugabe realistically summed up Zimbabwe's position after he became Prime Minister by saying: "We are not out to look for enemies. South Africa is a geographical reality, it is also an historical reality for us. We cannot get away even if we wanted to."[1]

SADCC as a Nascent Regional Force

To reduce South Africa's regional hegemony, as both Grundy and Horovitz point out, the independent African-ruled nations place increasing emphasis on national self-reliance and self-sufficiency, and also on mutual efforts to meet their own transport and other needs. A direct outgrowth of this goal has been the establishment of SADCC (Southern African Development Coordination Conference) at a summit meeting in Lusaka on April 1, 1980, by the leaders of nine Southern African states: Tanzania, Zambia, Angola, Mozambique, Zimbabwe, Malawi, Botswana, Lesotho, and Swaziland. As Richard Horovitz points out, SADCC is "a cooperative and interdependent grouping of countries" which is working together through an economic and political association to reduce "South Africa's economic stranglehold on the region."

The cooperative spirit animating SADCC has deep roots. In 1969, the leaders of independent African-controlled states in East and Southern Africa called on white-controlled countries in the Lusaka Manifesto to start the process of negotiated change but warned that the alternative was armed struggle. From 1974 on, the five Front Line States—Tanzania, Zambia, Angola, Mozambique, and Botswana—assumed their decisive role in aiding the Zimbabwean struggle for independence. Now that Zimbabwe is independent, Southern African states continue to work for the independence of Namibia, and for their own greater economic freedom.

sadcc is still at an early stage of its development. A preliminary meeting of Economic Ministers had been held in Arusha in July 1979 to review a series of well-designed research reports on needs and plans for moving toward greater economic self-sufficiency. In December 1980 an important donors' conference, focused on the vital area of transportation, was held in Maputo, Mozambique. A permanent secretariat has been established in Gaborone, Botswana, with a Secretary-General from Zimbabwe. Summit meetings are held annually in different capitals. With adequate international support and funding, sadcc holds considerable promise as a regional association, as Horovitz points out, but whether it can hope to counterbalance the pervasive economic power of South Africa remains an open question, as Grundy makes clear.

The Decisive Role of the Great Powers

Much depends on the policies of the great powers in Southern Africa. Chester Crocker, Assistant Secretary of State for Africa, has written, "The integrity and interdependence of the region as an arena for U.S. policy is not obvious, and is contested by many. But coherent policy toward the individual countries that comprise the subcontinent depends on our recognizing that the region's substantial potential rests on such integration and on rational economic policies. For understandable reasons, African-ruled states would prefer to reduce their dependence on rail lines to South Africa's ports, and they can be expected to move in this direction where possible. But unless outside aid flows into these countries in truly massive proportions—a most unlikely event—they recognize that their South African links can be moderated but not ended."[2]

What might change the attitudes and policies of the Western powers? Might it be a more deeply felt abhorrence of apartheid or fear of growing disorder and violence in South Africa? Could it possibly be a by-product of a future East-West detente?

While there are broad concepts that help to define the actions of the major powers—East-West confrontation, national interest, etc.— there is little concerted effort, even between allies, except on the future of Namibia. To bring it to independence has long been looked on as the responsibility of the international community but tacitly considered solvable only by the five Western powers—the United States, Britain, France, West Germany, and Canada—which conducted negotiations to that end throughout the Carter administration and have again resumed the responsibility. Frequently, however, policy tends to be either haphazard or responds to specific situations as they arise.

If there can be any unity shown in the Western position, it can be stated in simple terms. The West seeks to avoid large-scale violence in the region, and especially in regard to South Africa; therefore, it encourages a peaceful transition to a more acceptable system of race relations. There is a fundamental hostility by even the most conservative Western governments to the policies of racial discrimination in South Africa and a recognition by most Western powers that in the long run South Africa cannot survive without fundamental changes. Differences exist in regard to their willingness to act on these premises and their interpretation of the urgency of the situation.

All major powers have both ideal and real capabilities. As David Albright points out, Moscow's perceived interests in Southern Africa compete with what may seem more pressing ones elsewhere. Despite South Africa's propaganda, Moscow shuns direct confrontation in the region. The United States also finds conflicting goals between business interests and the Carter administration's human rights policy and commitment to fair labor practices by American companies abroad. It will not be easy for any great power to determine at a given time which of its interests is paramount and for what reasons.

The chapters in this book provide a vast array of material and bring insights into widely varied international policies toward Southern Africa. The search for constructive involvement in this increasingly important area is the responsibility of all of us.

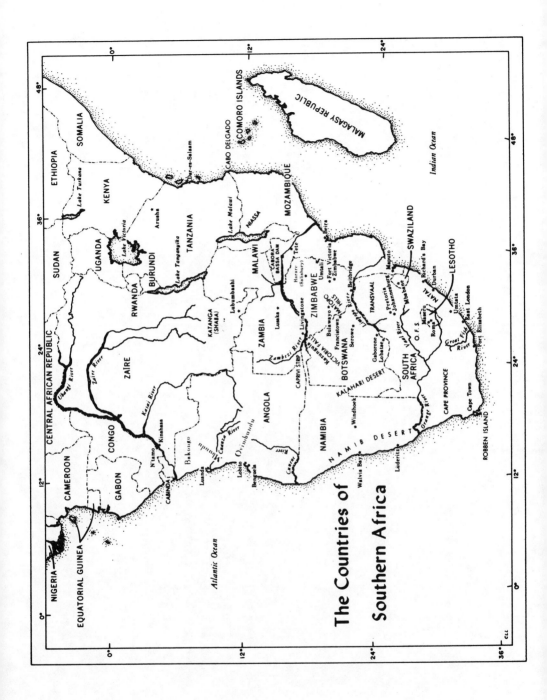

The Countries of
Southern Africa

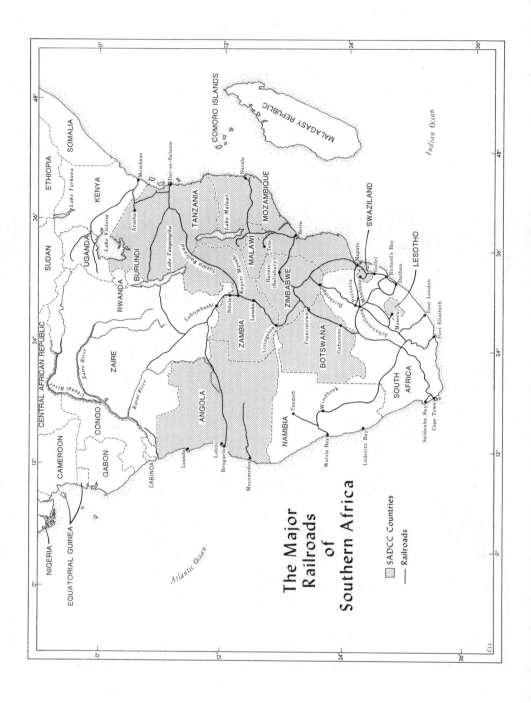

The Major
Railroads
of
Southern Africa

☐ SADCC Countries

— Railroads

1.

✳

The Communist States
and Southern Africa

David E. Albright

The 1970s witnessed a major increase in the involvement of the Communist states in Southern Africa. In the wake of the collapse of the Portuguese colonial empire in the mid-1970s, a number of Communist countries—the USSR, Cuba, the German Democratic Republic (GDR), Yugoslavia, Romania, and the People's Republic of China (PRC)—each assumed roles of some importance in the area.

From the outset, this multiplicity of significant Communist actors on the Southern African scene entailed considerable diversity of Communist response to the region and its circumstances, for the activities of the individual Communist states were often far from harmonious and mutually reinforcing. That situation continues to prevail in the 1980s. Indeed, each of these Communist countries has its own interests and purposes in the area. Thus, any serious attempt to depict the relationship between the Communist world and Southern Africa must adopt an all-encompassing perspective that takes account of the range of inputs, rather than focus on just one or even a few key Communist states. Such a perspective shapes the broad contours of this analysis.

Although elements of conflict have surfaced among the various Communist states that have taken on substantial roles in Southern Africa, it would be erroneous to suggest that the conflict has been of equal magnitude in all cases. On the contrary, three distinct groups

The views expressed in this chapter are those of the author and do not necessarily reflect the views of the U.S. government or the U.S. International Communication Agency.

3

of countries can be distinguished on the basis of the amount of strife that has characterized their relations with one another. These groups are (1) the USSR, Cuba, and the GDR; (2) Yugoslavia and Romania; and (3) China. In looking at the activities and goals of the individual Communist states in the Southern African context, it is useful therefore to order the assessment in terms of such clusters.

The "Quasi-Alliance" of the USSR, Cuba, and the GDR

During the course of the 1970s, there emerged in the Southern African context a close working relationship among three of the Communist states operating there. Although this relationship is difficult to label because of its complexity, perhaps "quasi-alliance" or "quasi-coalition" will suffice as shorthand. The group is composed of the USSR, Cuba, and the GDR, and it is their undertakings in the area which have undergone the most dramatic expansion over the last few years.

Early Activities

The recent enterprises of the USSR, Cuba, and the GDR with respect to Southern Africa did not spring forth unheralded. Indeed, in the Soviet case, contacts with the region date from the 1920s. During the early days of the Communist International, for example, Moscow not only maintained relations with the South African Communist Party, but also courted a number of black nationalists from South Africa, although it did not make much progress toward establishing close ties with any black leaders of the country until after the banning of the African National Congress (ANC) in the 1960s.[1]

In the early 1960s, the Soviets also forged links with the Popular Movement for the Liberation of Angola (MPLA) of Angola, and they furnished that organization with aid more or less continuously thereafter.[2] Subsequently they did the same with regard to the Mozambique Liberation Front (FRELIMO) of Mozambique, Southwest Africa People's Organization (SWAPO) of Namibia, and the Zimbabwe African People's Union (ZAPU) of Rhodesia.[3] Only in Zambia, however, did the USSR manage to create a formal presence, as a result of establishing diplomatic relations there after Zambia's attainment of independence in the mid-1960s.

Cuba's initial involvement with the region came in the early

1960s, when Havana first had contacts with the MPLA. But it was not until the mid-1960s that this involvement reached significant proportions. During the course of a three-month tour of Africa in 1964–65, Ché Guevara visited Congo-Brazzaville and conferred there with MPLA and FRELIMO leaders. These conversations seem to have resulted in a Cuban commitment to provide material assistance to both groups. In mid-1965, Cuban ships delivered a consignment of arms to Brazzaville, at that time the home base of the MPLA. By the late 1960s, moreover, there were Cuban instructors at a number of guerrilla training camps in Tanzania, where FRELIMO maintained its base of operations.[4]

As for the GDR, it established political ties with the MPLA and FRELIMO in the early 1960s. In 1969, FRELIMO became the first recipient of East German arms and military equipment in sub-Saharan Africa. Four years later, an agreement on military cooperation between the GDR and Congo-Brazzaville, where the MPLA had set up its guerrilla headquarters, enabled East Berlin to furnish similar aid to the MPLA.[5]

The Impact of Angola

Nonetheless, the demise of the Portuguese colonial empire and particularly the Angolan civil war of 1975–76 produced major changes in the regional activities of all three Communist states. These changes had both quantitative and qualitative dimensions. Not only did the scope and depth of involvement of the three countries increase, but the undertakings of the three also acquired a degree of coordination that had not existed previously.

It is important to remember, however, that this collaborative relationship only emerged gradually, rather than in one fell swoop. In fact, there were clear signs of differences in perspective between at least Cuba and the USSR for more than a year after the coup that toppled the Caetano regime in Portugal in April 1974 and paved the way for the independence of the Portuguese African colonies. Cuba, in accordance with its steadfast support of the MPLA since the mid-1960s, backed the MPLA to the hilt against its two Angolan rivals, the National Front for the Liberation of Angola (FNLA) and the National Union for the Total Independence of Angola (UNITA). This backing included the dispatch, in the spring of 1975, of more than 200 military advisers to Angola to work with the MPLA, and a later indication, in August 1975, when the MPLA found itself in deep military trouble, of a willingness to send additional help. The USSR, in contrast, wavered in its attitude toward the MPLA. For roughly six months after the coup in Lisbon, Moscow suspended aid to the main group within that organization, headed by Agostinho Neto, and furnished a small amount of material assistance to a competing faction, led by Daniel Chipenda. These actions reflected unmistakable Soviet doubts about the MPLA's general prospects. Subsequently, the USSR did resume arms supplies to Neto's forces, but it plainly endorsed efforts to bring about a coalition government embracing all three Angolan "national liberation" groups—an approach to which the three Angolan groups committed themselves in January 1975 under the terms of the agreement concluded at Alvor. Only after the attempts to form a coalition government broke down and the MPLA began to suffer major reversals on the ground against the U.S.- and Chinese-supplied forces of the FNLA-UNITA alliance did Moscow decide, in the late summer of 1975, to throw its full weight behind the MPLA. Even then, it consented to do so only on the condition that the other two Communist states would serve as point elements of the operation.[6]

This development set the stage for the joint Communist enterprise carried out in Angola on behalf of the MPLA in late 1975 and early 1976.[7] Soviet and Cuban planes airlifted Cuban combat forces and Soviet and East German advisers to Angola to aid the MPLA, especially after South Africa dispatched military forces to Angola in late October 1975 to assist the FNLA-UNITA coalition. At its peak in March 1976, the Cuban contingent alone consisted of 36,000 combat troops. The East German presence, though far less massive in terms of numbers, was second in importance only to that of the Cuban one. GDR instructors trained entire military units; moreover, East German personnel provided much of the medical treatment of casualties and supervised the air evacuation of MPLA wounded to the GDR for hospitalization. East Berlin also supplied many shiploads of "solidarity freight"—war matériel, including heavy weapons, and medical supplies. The USSR's contributions to the undertaking lay largely in the logistics realm. Not only did it commit many planes to the transfer of troops and advisers to the scene, but it transported vast quantities of weapons and military equipment—worth roughly $400 million—by air and sea to Angola. Among the arms were surface-to-surface missiles, the hand-held SMA-7 antiaircraft missile, 122mm "katyusha" rockets, T-34 and T-54 tanks,

PT-76 amphibious tanks, armored reconnaissance vehicles (BRDM-2), trucks, helicopters, gunships, heavy artillery, light aircraft, and even MIG-21 aircraft. To protect the supply operation, the USSR maintained a naval squadron off shore, with a base at Conakry, Guinea.[8]

Recent Undertakings

The success of this joint operation in installing the MPLA in power made a substantial impression on black elements in Southern Africa, and the USSR, Cuba, and the GDR all moved resolutely to capitalize on that advantage. Over the ensuing years, for example, Moscow has striven in a variety of ways to strengthen its links with the existing black governments in the area as well as with "national liberation" movements battling white-minority rule in Rhodesia, Namibia, and South Africa. In October 1976, the USSR entered into a long-term treaty of friendship and cooperation with the new MPLA regime in Angola, and the following spring, during a trip through Africa, Nikolai Podgornyi, then President of the USSR Supreme Soviet, signed a similar document with the new FRELIMO government in Mozambique.[9] Furthermore, the Soviet Union has endeavored to convince the rulers of these two states that these treaties amount to more than pieces of paper. For instance, in February 1981, after a South African raid on ANC facilities in Mozambique, Soviet leaders dispatched several warships to the Mozambican ports of Beira and Maputo as a sign of solidarity with the FRELIMO regime. (Nevertheless, Moscow has displayed a clear desire to limit its commitments to Mozambique. Not only did it confine itself to a simple show of force in the aftermath of the South African raid, but throughout the early months of 1981 it turned a deaf ear to the Maputo government's requests to join the Council of Mutual Economic Assistance [CMEA] which the USSR dominates.) Especially since 1977, when the ruling parties in Angola and Mozambique proclaimed themselves to be Marxist-Leninist, the Communist Party of the Soviet Union (CPSU) has fashioned a network of organizational ties with them. Even though Moscow rejects the claims of these parties to "genuine" Marxist-Leninist status (it classifies them merely as "revolutionary vanguard" parties) and by no means controls them, it has deemed it worthwhile to try to help them become effective institutions so as to minimize the chances for their displacement— and hence possible setbacks to Soviet interests.[10] Since the conclusion of the Angolan civil war, the USSR has managed to secure—at least temporarily—about a thousand key positions for Soviet officers in the military and command structure in Angola.[11] Not only has the Soviet Union continued to be Angola's chief arms supplier, but it has assumed a similar role with respect to both Mozambique and Zambia as well.[12] It has also established diplomatic relations with Botswana and Lesotho, two of the less ideological states in the region.

As for the "national liberation" movements, the USSR became, at least until the last phases of the guerrilla struggle, the primary source of arms for the ZAPU wing of the Patriotic Front in Rhodesia.[13] This close identification with Joshua Nkomo's group did, to be sure, cause a reversal in Soviet fortunes when Robert Mugabe, head of the rival Zimbabwe African National Union (ZANU), won the March 1980 elections that ended the guerrilla struggle, but the Soviets have managed to recoup some of their losses by reaching agreement with the Mugabe government in early 1981 to open up an embassy in Salisbury. In the case of SWAPO, the USSR has now assumed the role of its chief arms supplier. Moreover, after the temporary breakdown of the U.N.-sponsored talks on Namibian independence in January 1981, the Soviet Union emerged as the major great-power backer of the African initiative to impose an embargo on South Africa for refusing to accept the U.N. plan for elections in Namibia. Moscow, however, did not endorse an effort to set up an embargo under the auspices of the U.N. General Assembly after the Western veto of the African proposal in the U.N. Security Council. Had the independence talks not gotten back on track later in 1981, it is not clear whether the USSR would have moved toward such an endorsement. Finally, not only has the USSR reinforced its long-standing links with exile elements of the ANC of South Africa, but it has in addition sought to establish ties with members of the Black Consciousness Movement who have left the country more recently, although the latter effort does not appear to have been very successful to date.[14]

Cuba's attempts to exploit the new stature that it gained from the Angolan affair have focused on more limited targets in Southern Africa than have those of the Soviet Union. Of the independent black states in the area, Havana has concentrated largely upon Angola and Mozambique. As of the opening of the 1980s, an estimated 19,000 Cuban soldiers still remained in Angola to counter threats from UNITA insurgents and from South African forces trying to root out SWAPO bases in the southern portions of the country. Another 215 military advisers were at work in Mozambique.[15] Under agreements signed with the Luanda government after the end of the Angolan civil war, Cuba has had as many as 8,500 economic technicians in Angola at one time, although the figure dropped back to 6,500 in 1979. The number of Cuban economic technicians in Mozambique, by the same token, rose steadily from none in 1977 to 600 in 1979.[16] At the end of 1979, some 10,000 school-aged children from Angola, Mozambique, and other African states were studying on the Isle of Youth off the southern coast of Cuba.[17] On the organizational level, the Cuban Communist Party has forged fairly close ties with the ruling parties of both Angola and Mozambique.

Despite their concentration on Angola and Mozambique, the Cubans have not entirely neglected Zambia. For example, there have been a substantial number of high-level delegations exchanged between Havana and Lusaka.[18]

With respect to the "national liberation" movements in the area, Cuba has extended active support to all those engaged in full-scale guerrilla struggles. From 1976 until the Lancaster House agreement in late 1979 to terminate the conflict in Rhodesia, Cuban instructors provided training to ZAPU and ZANU forces at camps in various frontline states. This assistance laid the groundwork for the establishment of formal ties with the new Mugabe government after its formation in 1980. Since 1976, Cuban military advisers have furnished military training to SWAPO at camps in Angola.[19] In addition, Havana has offered moral backing to the ANC of South Africa, through the welcoming of ANC delegations and the like.[20]

The GDR's enterprises have been focused in much the same manner as those of Cuba. At the top of East Berlin's concerns among the independent black states have stood Angola and Mozambique. In 1979, Erich Honecker, General Secretary of the ruling Socialist Unity Party (SED) and Chairman of the State Council of the GDR, headed a large delegation to both countries, and during his sojourn in each he signed a 20-year treaty of friendship and cooperation with his hosts. These constituted the first such documents that the GDR had concluded with any state outside the immediate Soviet orbit.[21] As of the beginning of the 1980s, the number of East European military advisers in Angola had reached 400, and that of Soviet and East European military advisers in Mozambique, 525. The bulk of these in both cases came from the GDR. A fair portion of the 2,760 Soviet and East

European economic technicians in Mozambique at that time were likewise from the GDR.[22] Over the years, East German technicians have furnished the training for the security and intelligence services in the two African countries.[23] Other East German technicians are generally believed to have instructed the personal bodyguards of Samora Machel, Mozambique's president.[24] On a somewhat different plane, the GDR's ruling party, the SED, has entered into formal agreements of cooperation with the governing parties in both Angola and Mozambique. Although their specific content has never been made public, it is likely that these accords have sanctioned the posting of SED advisers to these parties.[25]

To the extent that the East Germans have paid attention to other black independent states in the region, Zambia has been the principal object of their wooing. Honecker's trip to Southern Africa in 1979, for instance, included a stop in Lusaka.[26]

As to the "national liberation" movements of the area, the GDR has become a major supplier of arms and training to those engaged in active guerrilla conflict. In the last half of the 1970s, the East Germans furnished both instruction and weapons to the forces of the ZAPU wing of the Patriotic Front of Zimbabwe, and during the final stages of the Rhodesian war, the East Germans apparently assumed primary responsibility for provision of arms and equipment to these forces. The involvement of the East Germans with SWAPO has also escalated during the last few years, particularly in the realm of military training. Although the GDR has stepped up its contacts with the ANC of South Africa (Honecker met with ANC representatives, for instance, during his stay in Lusaka in 1979), East German support has thus far been more symbolic than material in nature.[27]

Noteworthy Features of Recent Activities

Two specific aspects of these expanded Communist activities in the post-Angola period bear noting. First, their economic component has been quite limited. From 1976 through 1979, for example, the USSR extended only $20 million in economic aid to the countries of Southern Africa. This figure contrasted with Soviet extensions of $5,774 million of economic credits to the Third World as a whole. Similarly, annual Soviet exports to the region during 1976–78 averaged only 50.0 million rubles ($70.0 million), and annual Soviet imports from there, 11.7 million rubles ($16.4 million). By way of comparison, the

USSR's average annual exports to all developing countries during the same period amounted to a little more than 4 billion rubles ($5.6 billion), while its average annual imports from them reached roughly 3.7 billion rubles ($5.2 billion). The chief form of economic help that the USSR has provided appears to have been technical assistance. In 1979, Soviet and East European economic technicians in the area totaled 4,750, with most of them in Angola and Mozambique.[28]

Although a precise figure for GDR economic aid to states in Southern Africa is not available, it is clear that this figure, like that for the USSR, has been quite low. The GDR's trade turnover with the region has also stayed modest. In 1977, the turnover with East Berlin's two principal trading partners in the area, Angola and Mozambique, ran to just 260.9 million foreign exchange marks ($78.3 million), while in 1978 it totaled 364.2 million foreign exchange marks ($109.3 million). During the same years, the GDR's trade turnover with all developing countries came to 4,504.1 million and 5,027.7 million foreign exchange marks ($1,351.1 million and $1,508.2 million), respectively. As in the Soviet case, the major economic undertaking of the GDR in Southern Africa has been in the realm of technical assistance. A large percentage of the 4,570 Soviet and East European economic technicians in the region in 1979 were from the GDR.[29]

Cuba, as a developing country with a heavy dependence on outside subsidies to stay afloat and with only one major item (sugar) to export, has not possessed the wherewithal to furnish economic aid to Southern Africa or conduct any significant trade with it. Havana's undertakings, too, have lain essentially in the sphere of technical assistance. In 1979, Cuban economic technicians in the area numbered 7,100, all of them in Angola and Mozambique.[30]

Perhaps the most telling indication of the small part that economic endeavors continue to play in all three Communist states' enterprises in the area in the 1980s comes from the Zimbabwe Conference on Reconstruction and Development in March 1981. This gathering, called by the Mugabe government to elicit contributions to Zimbabwean development, drew representatives from 31 countries and 26 international organizations, and they pledged a total of $1.5 billion to the cause. But the member states of CMEA declined to attend.[31]

Second, and maybe more important, the enterprises in which the USSR, Cuba, and the GDR have engaged in the region have manifested a substantial division of labor among the three Communist states. The Soviet Union has served as armorer for the area. As already mentioned, Moscow has become the main source of arms for Angola, Mozambique, and Zambia, and it has furnished the bulk of the weaponry which the "national liberation" movements in Rhodesia (now Zimbabwe) and Namibia have received over the years. Cuba has been the chief supplier of personnel, both military and civilian, to the region. At the beginning of the 1980s, it still had an estimated 19,000 combat troops in Angola, and its contingent of economic technicians in Southern Africa in toto was considerably larger than those of either the USSR or the GDR. The GDR's primary function has been in the realm of security and intelligence. East German advisers have helped Angola and Mozambique set up and run services of this type.

Such clear evidence of a division of labor indicates that the coordination that emerged in the undertakings of the three Communist states during the Angolan civil war has persisted during subsequent years. Thus, it seems fair to characterize the activities of the three in Southern Africa as those of a "quasi-coalition."

Motivations of Cuba and of the GDR

Although the expansion of Soviet, Cuban, and East German enterprises in Southern Africa in recent years has been striking, it is impossible to gauge its meaning without understanding the motivations that have lain behind it. These, therefore, require detailed examination.

At the outset, it is essential to recognize that the subject of purposes cannot be dealt with simply from the standpoint of the coalition as a whole.[32] Arguments that Cuba and the GDR have simply been surrogates of the USSR do not hold up under scrutiny. Both have had perceived interests and goals in Southern Africa that have been quite distinct from those of the USSR.[33] Fidel Castro, for instance, has long viewed himself as a champion of "national liberation" and revolution in the Third World, and he has endeavored to project such an image abroad. Indeed, his government began to provide military advisers and other forms of aid to selected "national liberation" movements in Africa and elsewhere in the Third World as early as 1960–61, during the period when relations between Havana and Moscow were by no means close. By the same token, the Cuban Revolutionary Armed Forces, the most important institution of the Castro regime, have tended to favor activism in Africa for their own organizational reasons. They have regarded military engagements overseas not only as a means of enhancing their international prestige and their political influence at home, but also as a way of improving their military effectiveness and of upgrading the weapons systems they have at their disposal.

For its part, the GDR has felt a need to forge firm links with the existing and potential black governments throughout sub-Saharan Africa to further set itself apart from the Federal Republic of Germany (FRG). During the early 1970s, the GDR succeeded in gaining nearly universal diplomatic recognition as well as membership in the United Nations, but it did so at a price. It had to accept a special relationship with the FRG (i.e., to acknowledge that it was one of two German states within a single German nation) which greatly weakened the foundations of the division of Germany between East and West. Thus, East German leaders have been increasingly concerned to solidify the division in every manner possible in order to avoid domestic instability and to ensure internal security in the GDR. The leadership in East Berlin has also displayed a growing desire to guarantee access to the raw materials and minerals in Southern Africa as a hedge against reduction of supplies from fellow members of CMEA. Because the GDR does not possess a great many natural resources, it must purchase a large percentage of its raw materials, minerals, and food from abroad, and it has in the past obtained the bulk of these goods from other CMEA states, particularly in the USSR. But with the Soviet Union's mounting economic problems in recent years and Moscow's need to meet rising internal demand for such items, there has been growing uncertainty about how long this policy will prove viable.

Furthermore, both Havana and East Berlin have seen cooperation with the USSR in Africa as a means of enhancing their leverage on Soviet behavior in matters of more immediate concern to them than the continent itself. The present regimes in Cuba and the GDR each depend heavily on Soviet support to remain in power. Fidel Castro's government, for example, receives large amounts of economic assistance from the USSR, to say nothing of military supplies. The East German government, similarly, relies greatly on the Soviet Union to defend its diplomatic position in Europe and to ward off domestic challenges to its authority. Such levels of dependence create considerable dangers that Moscow will ride roughshod over Cuban and GDR interests unless Cuban and East German leaders can demonstrate to the USSR that retaining their goodwill has positive as well as negative aspects. Soviet actions during the USSR's drive toward détente with the West in the early 1970s afford a classic illustration. Moscow forced the GDR to evince more flexibility on matters such as Berlin than the East Germans were inclined to do, and it even engineered the ouster of Walter Ulbricht as First Secretary of the SED when he sought to resist Soviet pressure to follow the USSR's lead.

Even though Cuba and the GDR have had their own separate interests and objectives, however, it is not possible to maintain that they have functioned as entirely free agents on the Southern African scene. Neither, for example, has enjoyed many capabilities to operate independently there.[34] Both, it is true, have been able to provide military advisers to a number of governments and groups in the region, but each has lacked the air- and sealift units and the logistical backup capacity to project significant military power to the area on its own. Also, neither has possessed sufficient economic resources to have much effect on the region's economic situation. As already indicated, Cuba is itself a developing country, and it has required large infusions of Soviet aid to subsist. Moreover, its trade with other Communist states accounts for fully three quarters of its global two-way trade. Although the GDR is more industrialized and boasts a higher standard of living than any other Communist state, it has experienced mounting economic problems at home since the beginning of the rise of world oil prices in the wake of the 1973 Arab-Israeli war. As a consequence, it has been compelled to impose heavy restrictions on its economic help to, and trade with, all Third World countries. During 1976–78, for example, the GDR's trade turnover with non-Communist developing countries in toto averaged only 4,483.4 million foreign exchange marks ($1,344.9 million) a year. By way of comparison, its average trade turnover with non-Communist industrialized countries, whose exports have tended to dovetail with the most pressing East German needs, amounted to 22,657.3 million foreign exchange marks ($6,796.7 million) during the same period. It is worth mentioning, too, that the share of non-Communist countries as a whole in East German trade turnover dropped from 30.6 to 26.5 percent over these years.[35]

In addition, Cuba and the GDR have found themselves under other constraints in Southern Africa because of their desire to enhance their own leverage on Soviet policy that is more directly relevant to themselves. They have only been able to work toward this end through cooperating with the USSR in the region. Activities of too independent a nature in the area have run the risk of being counter-productive in the larger context. While each has had the option of seeking to persuade Moscow to follow a course in line with its own prescriptions, neither has managed to marshall major inducements in this regard aside from the force of the logic of its argument. There-fore, both Cuba and the GDR have had to tailor their concrete under-takings to the broad framework of Soviet policy. For this reason, as well as in their own right, Soviet purposes in Southern Africa demand careful analysis.

Soviet Purposes

In attempting to pinpoint the precise motivations behind Soviet undertakings in Southern Africa since the mid-1970s, it is essential to bear in mind that Moscow has not confronted a simple task in trying to define its objectives in the area. First, not all of the interests that it has perceived with respect to the region have been compatible. For instance, Soviet leaders have, on the one hand, had an interest in impeding Western access to the raw materials and minerals of South-ern Africa and in disrupting Western use of the sea lanes around the southern end of the continent. The region, and especially South Af-rica, has a great wealth of minerals, and these resources are plainly of significance to the West. Indeed, the area constitutes the major non-Communist source of supply of a number of minerals important to the West's advanced industrialized economies—e.g., chromium, plat-inum, and manganese. The sea lanes that lie around the region have equal value to the West. More than half of Western Europe's oil and well over 20 percent of the United States' oil travels through these waters on its way from the Persian Gulf to its ultimate destination.[36] Of these facts, Moscow has been exceptionally well aware, for Soviet commentaries have harped on them continually. The implication of the commentaries, moreover, has been that such circumstances reflect Western vulnerabilities.[37] On the other hand, Soviet leaders have seemed to believe that the USSR has an interest in avoiding an esca-lation of the racial conflict and guerrilla wars of the area into a nu-clear confrontation with the United States. They have likewise appeared to discern an interest in not taking actions in places like Southern Africa which would encourage the United States to try to regain strategic military superiority, an end which they fear Washington has the capacity to achieve if it actually set out to do so.[38]

Second, there has been a gap between some of the interests that Moscow has perceived in regard to Southern Africa and the capabilities at hand to fulfill them. As just mentioned, Soviet leaders have recognized the utility of denying the West access to the raw materials and minerals of the region and the use of the sea lanes around it. Yet the countries in the area have not been disposed to adopt such a course. Even Angola's self-styled Marxist-Leninist regime has permitted Gulf Oil Company to continue its operations in the Angolan exclave of Cabinda. Moreover, the USSR itself has not possessed the military means to eject the West from the area on its own. In fact, although Soviet capacities for the projection of force overseas have improved tremendously in recent years, the USSR has lacked the wherewithal, whether alone or in combination with its Cuban and East German allies, to mount a successful military push even against the white-minority government of South Africa in support of black forces attempting to topple it.[39] Similarly, Soviet authorities have given clear signs that they regard a radicalization of politics throughout the area as desirable. For example, Soviet sources describe the self-proclaimed Marxist-Leninists who rule Angola and Mozambique at present as merely "revolutionary democrats," maintaining that "there have been no irreversible processes" in these countries yet.[40] However, many local contexts have offered no more radical forces with which the USSR might collaborate than the existing governments. This has been particularly true in Angola and Mozambique.

Third, Moscow's perceived interests in Southern Africa have competed with its perceived interests elsewhere, and the USSR, because it has not had unlimited resources, has found itself unable to pursue all these perceived interests simultaneously. For more than two decades, Soviet leaders have sought to win recognition as a global power for the USSR, and especially since the early 1970s they have defined its interests in those terms. Indeed, there is virtually no place in the world now about which they do not articulate some type of Soviet interest. Yet they have also had to confront the USSR's lack of omnipotence. It simply cannot do everything at once that they might like it to do. Therefore, they have had to order their concerns in some fashion. Since the mid-1960s, they have relied essentially upon geopolitical considerations in this regard. On such a basis, Southern Africa has fallen fairly low on the list of priorities. Europe has stood at the top, East Asia has followed close behind, and the southern rimlands of the USSR—i.e., the countries forming an arc south of the Soviet Union, from South Asia around to North Africa—have occupied third place. The Horn of Africa also appears to have preceded Southern Africa in the rankings.[41]

In light of these various factors, the medium-term operational goals that the USSR has set for itself in Southern Africa have inevitably reflected compromises and choices. These goals have included:

(1) To stake out a Soviet role in the resolution of racial conflict in the area. Such a role would reinforce the USSR's claims to status as a global power. As Soviet leaders have been well aware, global power status does not flow from divine right or the consent of the international community; rather, it must be self-achieved, self-asserted, and self-sustained.[42] Hence, the more major international issues to whose resolution the USSR can show it is indispensable, the greater weight its contentions will have that it is a global power. And the racial conflict in Southern Africa has certainly qualified as a major international issue in Soviet eyes.[43]

(2) To promote the emergence of radical black governments in Rhodesia, Namibia, and South Africa. Although Moscow has displayed strong reservations about the Marxist-Leninist credentials of the current regimes in Angola and Mozambique, Soviet officials have been acutely conscious of the benefits of access and influence that the USSR has derived from the collapse of the Portuguese African empire and the rise to power of radical black governments in these two former Portuguese colonies in Southern Africa, and Soviet commentaries suggest that Moscow expects similar political transitions in the region to produce comparable results.[44] While the coolness toward the USSR of the new government of Robert Mugabe in Zimbabwe may have dampened this expectation somewhat, there is no indication that it has disappeared.

(3) To win local acceptance of the legitimacy of a Soviet political, economic, and even military presence in the area. For any country to validate its claim to global power status, it must demonstrate its global reach, and such a demonstration normally requires not just intermittent forays into distant regions but a sustained presence in those regions. Establishing this kind of presence in any given area is greatly facilitated by the cooperation of local governments there. Soviet lead-

ers have given ample signs in Southern Africa that they understand this fact. Not only has the USSR reached agreement with the black-ruled states there on many political, cultural, and economic activities that have brought Soviet personnel into the area, but it has also obtained the approval of them for certain types of Soviet military undertakings. The last have encompassed the supply of arms and military advisers, calls of Soviet warships at local ports, and the use of local airfields by Soviet planes for purposes of reconnaissance.[45]

(4) To weaken, though not to eradicate, the Western position in the region. In Moscow's eyes, the Soviet Union is engaged in a competition with the West for influence in Southern Africa, and this competition amounts to a zero-sum game. That is, gains for one side involve losses for the other side.[46] In such a framework, Western influence must decrease for the Soviet role in Southern Africa to grow. At the same time, Moscow believes that a precipitate departure by the West from the region would be undesirable from the Soviet standpoint. As it has pointed out in a more general context, "the Soviet Union's potential for rendering economic assistance is not infinite," and "of course, the Soviet Union cannot fail to be concerned for the well-being of its own people."[47] Thus, Soviet observers have more and more come to emphasize the need for "a long-term strategy" for "the industrialization of the former colonies and semi-colonies according to fundamentally different principles of social and international economic relations than those inherent in capitalism."[48] Even orthodox Soviet commentators have persistently argued that "socialist-oriented states" in the Third World should attract Western capital and work out "a system of regulation . . . that will guarantee the interests of the radical regimes and grant sufficient advantages to foreign investors to attract them."[49]

(5) To limit, and wherever possible reduce, Chinese influence in the area. Moscow has viewed the PRC as a threat to the USSR's efforts to establish itself as the chief patron of "national liberation" and revolutionary movements throughout Africa.[50] Soviet writers have repeatedly charged Beijing with seeking "to present Maoism as the only new and revolutionary liberation doctrine suited to African conditions" and "to undermine the solidarity of the three revolutionary trends in the modern world" by setting "the national liberation movements against the world socialist system and the international workers movement."[51] As evidence, they have cited in particular China's support,

in the Angolan civil war, of the FNLA and UNITA against the Soviet-backed MPLA.[52] In such a context, the struggle with China for influence in Southern Africa, too, has assumed the features of a zero-sum game.

Accomplishment of these objectives, Moscow has realized, constitutes a prerequisite for the pursuit of more ambitious ends. Indeed, Soviet officials have often betrayed a painful awareness that in a number of other places in Africa the USSR has suffered bitter disappointments because it has allowed itself to become carried away with optimism about what could be accomplished in the foreseeable future.[53]

To give these various goals an overall coherence, Moscow has adopted a simple strategy. Specifically, it has sought, whether acting alone or with Cuba and/or the GDR, to win recognition for itself as the prime supporter of "anti-imperialist" and antiracist forces in Southern Africa.[54] Not only does this strategy neatly integrate its individual goals into a concrete program, but that program has a great deal of potential appeal to local African peoples.

Yugoslavia and Romania

In Southern Africa, Yugoslavia and Romania have operated independently of each other; moreover, the former country has long maintained a stance of nonalignment in international affairs, while the latter is a member of the Warsaw Pact and hence a formal ally of the USSR. Nevertheless, there has been a high degree of parallelism in their enterprises in the region. More important, the undertakings of the two have in many ways run counter to those of the Soviet–Cuban–East German "quasi-coalition." Consequently, it is legitimate to treat the two states together in the context of the present discussion.

Early Activities

Neither Yugoslavia nor Romania is a recent newcomer to the Southern African scene.[55] Both have had links there since the 1960s.

Yugoslavia's connections with Southern Africa prior to the mid-1970s were of two sorts. As one of the key forces behind the organization of the nonaligned movement, Yugoslavia sought to enlist emergent black-ruled states of the region in this cause. Thus, the Belgrade government established ties with Zambia soon after the latter attained independence in the mid-1960s. Relations between them warmed considerably over subsequent years. President Josip Broz Tito visited Zambia in 1970 at the time of the Third Nonaligned Summit Conference. By 1972, trade turnover between the two states had reached 559 million dinars ($33 million), with Yugoslav imports from Zambia accounting for the great bulk of that figure.[56] In 1974, Tito even played host to President Kenneth Kaunda in Belgrade. Botswana, too, was the object of overtures from the Yugoslavs, although the extent of Belgrade's links with Gaborone never came close to approaching that of its ties with Lusaka.

Aside from these state-to-state connections with Zambia and Botswana, Yugoslavia also maintained contacts with a variety of "national liberation" movements of the area. These included the MPLA of Angola, both ZAPU and ZANU of Rhodesia, SWAPO of Namibia, and the ANC of South Africa. Indeed, Belgrade appears to have supplied substantial quantities of arms to the MPLA during the early stages of the Angolan civil war.[57]

Romania likewise operated on two fronts during the late 1960s and early 1970s. Although Romania belonged to the Warsaw Pact, Bucharest began a rapid expansion of its relations with the nonaligned world after Nicolae Ceausescu became First Secretary of the Romanian Communist Party in 1965. This effort succeeded in producing diplomatic links with Zambia not long after the African country gained its sovereignty, and the ensuing years brought a considerable increase of ties. In 1972, for instance, Ceausescu himself stopped in Lusaka for a stay on a trip around Africa. During that stay, he extended Zambia $50 million in economic aid.[58] In 1972, Romania opened up official relations with Botswana as well.

On the less formal level, Bucharest forged links with all three of the "national liberation" factions of Angola (the MPLA, the FNLA, and UNITA), with both ZAPU and ZANU of Rhodesia, with SWAPO of Namibia, and with the ANC of South Africa. Romania emerged as a particular champion of SWAPO. Not only did it join the U.N. Council for Namibia in 1972, but it also permitted SWAPO to open a permanent office in Bucharest in 1974.[59]

Recent Undertakings

Yet the breakup of the Portuguese African empire in 1974 and the civil war that ensued in Angola sparked both quantitative and qualitative shifts in the nature of Yugoslav and Romanian activities in Southern Africa. The years since these events have witnessed substantial growth in the depth and scope of Yugoslav and Romanian enterprises in the region. With regard to Zambia, Belgrade and Bucharest have sought largely to solidify their long-standing relationships. In 1979, during another of Ceausescu's tours of Africa, Romania concluded a treaty of friendship and cooperation and a number of economic agreements, including one to establish a joint company for copper exploration, with the Lusaka government. At the same time, it evidently refinanced the $50 million credit it had offered Zambia in 1972.[60] Belgrade's efforts have been less dramatic but nonetheless clear. Perhaps the signal aspect of them has had to do with trade. Although Yugoslavia was forced by the jump in world oil prices after the 1973 Arab-Israeli war and the global economic recession that this triggered to cut back its trade turnover with Zambia sharply in 1975–77, to barely half the peak level of 959 million dinars ($60 million) in the early 1970s, it increased the figure to 872 million dinars ($47 million) in 1978.[61]

The new regimes in Angola and Mozambique have become major targets of courtship for both Yugoslavia and Romania. Bucharest's undertakings in this regard have been particularly vigorous. After Angola and Mozambique obtained independence, Romania entered into diplomatic relations with both countries and also concluded various trade, economic cooperation, technical and scientific cooperation, and educational and training arrangements with them. Between 1976 and 1978, Bucharest's trade with at least Angola rose significantly. Its exports to that African country increased from 11.2 million lei ($0.5 million) to 36.8 million lei ($2.0 million) during the period, and its imports from there grew from 7.6 million lei ($0.4 million) to 59.5 million lei ($3.2 million).[62] Then in 1979 Ceausescu visited both Angola and Mozambique and signed treaties of friendship and cooperation with their leaders. Bucharest has formally promised to provide economic help to both states as well, but the precise figures remain unpublished.[63] Finally, the Romanians have established party-to-party contacts with the ruling bodies of the two African countries,[64] although these have apparently not involved the sort of ideological and organizational training characteristic of Soviet and East German party contacts with both African groups.

Belgrade has fashioned some of the same kinds of ties with these two African states, but the intensity of Yugoslav activities has stayed somewhat lower than that of Romanian enterprises because of friction between Belgrade and the Luanda and Maputo governments over the nonaligned movement. While Yugoslavia has tried to keep the movement free of identification with either East or West, Angola and Mozambique have endorsed Cuba's argument that the socialist countries are the natural allies of the nonaligned countries.[65]

Belgrade and Bucharest have even directed some additional attention to the more conservative states of the area. As one of the Front Line States, Botswana has assumed new importance in their eyes, and they have exchanged a few high-level delegations with it. Although Lesotho is obviously not of equal interest to them, they both at least now maintain formal diplomatic links with Maseru.

As for the "national liberation" movements of the region, Yugoslavia and Romania have labored diligently to strengthen connections with virtually all of them. During the years before the March 1980 elections in Rhodesia, there was a considerable increase in the number of visits by leaders of both ZAPU and ZANU to the two Communist countries, and high-level Yugoslav and Romanian officials made it a point to meet with the heads of the two organizations during any of their sojourns in the Front Line States. In 1979, for example, President Ceauşescu of Romania had talks with Joshua Nkomo of ZAPU in Lusaka and with Robert Mugabe of ZANU in Maputo. Both Communist states also supplied military aid to at least ZANU forces during the Rhodesian guerrilla struggle.[66] Such assistance stood Belgrade and Bucharest in good stead after Mugabe's triumph in the 1980 elections that ended the warfare, for both Yugoslavia and Romania have enjoyed cordial relations with the new Zimbabwe government. Moreover, Yugoslavia has sought to solidify these ties by pledging to contribute $4 million to the country's reconstruction and development.[67] Leaders of SWAPO and the ANC have likewise traveled to Yugoslavia and Romania more frequently in recent years than was the case in the early 1970s and other contacts between the two Communist states and these bodies have multiplied. In addition, it would appear that at least Romania has furnished SWAPO with military help.[68]

No less significant than the quantitative changes in Yugoslav and Romanian undertakings in Southern Africa, however, have been the qualitative ones. Belgrade and Bucharest have actively encouraged the resolution of internal conflicts and of the tensions between the black- and white-controlled states in the region in ways that would minimize the involvement of the two superpowers.[69] To be sure, both have steadfastly opposed any compromise on the principle of majority rule, and they have approved military struggle to achieve this end. At the same time, they have championed negotiation as a means of settling disputes; moreover, they have attempted to serve as conciliators in certain instances of tension or strife among groups in the area. Yugoslavia, for example, endorsed the decisions of ZAPU and ZANU to participate in the March 1980 elections in Rhodesia. Throughout the last half of the 1970s, furthermore, it had cultivated links with both bodies. And it applauded Mugabe's incorporation of non-ZANU elements into the new Zimbabwe government despite the decisiveness of his electoral victory. Belgrade has also agreed to supply a military contingent for the international forces that would supervise elections in Namibia under a plan advanced by the United Nations. Romania, too, supported ZAPU and ZANU when they agreed to field candidates for the 1980 Rhodesian elections. Like Yugoslavia, it had maintained good relations with the two wings of the Patriotic Front during the guerrilla struggle, and it backed Mugabe's move to create a coalition government after the elections. (Indeed, Bucharest had strongly favored the establishment of such a government in Angola until South Africa's military intervention on behalf of the MPLA's rivals.) In addition, Romania has played a major role, as a member of the U.N. Council for Namibia, in U.N. efforts to bring about a solution of the conflict in Namibia. At one juncture, it even expressed readiness to contribute troops to help police U.N.-supervised elections there, but it subsequently withdrew its offer when some African states doubted the wisdom of including forces from any countries with formal connections with either NATO or the Warsaw Pact.[70]

Purposes

The motivations that have underlain these enterprises in Southern Africa since the mid-1970s have run along similar lines in both the Yugoslav and Romanian cases.[71] They have entailed four goals.

To begin with, the two states have wanted to build up firm ties with existing and potential nonaligned governments in Southern Africa to reinforce their own independent stances in foreign policy. Yugoslavia has rejected the division of the world into military blocs since its own break with the USSR in the late 1950s, and it was a prime mover behind the convocation of the first Conference of Nonaligned States in the early 1960s. Romania, despite its membership in the Warsaw Pact, has insisted on following a distinctive foreign policy since about 1964, although this had roots in developments going as far back as the late 1950s. One facet of Bucharest's international posture has been an effort to identify itself with the developing countries of the nonaligned world. Yugoslavia and Romania have both seen it as imperative to have the strongest possible relations with nonaligned governments in the Third World. Such relations demonstrate that Belgrade and Bucharest do not stand alone in asserting their autonomy, and hence furnish them with a certain amount of protection.

Second, both states have sought to help resolve the racial conflict in the area in order to bolster their claims to be international mediators and brokers. Yugoslavia has long attempted to play such roles by putting forth proposals on East-West disarmament, on North-South issues, etc. Since the mid-1960s, Romania has pursued a similar course. For example, it has maintained ties with both Moscow and Beijing, and it has not severed its diplomatic links with Israel despite its own friendly attitude toward the Arab states and the Palestinians. In this context, then, Belgrade and Bucharest have viewed the racial conflict in Southern Africa as a good opportunity to affirm their credentials.

Third, both countries have desired to ensure access to the raw materials and minerals in the area and to open up new markets there, in order to bolster the economic underpinnings of their own foreign policy postures. Although each state is itself a substantial exporter of raw materials, each also imports major quantities of raw materials and minerals. During recent years, for example, fuels, materials, and semi-processed goods have accounted for more than 60 percent of Yugoslavia's purchases from abroad, while their share in Romania's purchases from abroad has hovered around 50 percent.[72] The more diversified the sources from which Belgrade and Bucharest obtain these items, the less risk they run of being caught in a dependence that could undermine their foreign policy positions. Such a consideration is particularly impelling since the USSR happens to constitute a major source for many of the items that Yugoslavia and Romania import in these categories. As for markets in Southern Africa, both countries must export goods to pay for the imports that they need to carry on their domestic development programs. Sales of raw materials and foodstuffs can cover only part of the bill, so Belgrade and Bucharest must also export some of the output from the new industrial facilities that they have built. Yet many of these products have not been competitive in Western markets.[73] Thus, if Yugoslavia and Romania want to avoid a trade dependence on the CMEA states and the dangers such a dependence entails, they must find Third World markets for these goods. Southern Africa, with its underdeveloped economies (except for South Africa) and potential for growth, has offered promising opportunities in this connection.

Fourth, both states have attempted to present themselves in the area as possible models of socialist development, although Romania appears to have felt a stronger urge in this regard than Yugoslavia. Belgrade has charted an innovative path for itself since the 1950s, and Bucharest took the first steps toward an autonomous course at the end of the same decade. Each has recognized that the greater international support that it can muster for the validity of its socialist experiments, the better the chance that they will survive such pressures as Moscow may decide to mount against them. Southern Africa, with a significant number of professedly Marxist-Leninist elements in power or in major leadership positions within "national liberation" movements, has seemed to the Yugoslavs and Romanians to afford potentially fertile soil in which to try to nourish such backing.

These objectives, it should be underscored, attest plainly to the geopolitical priorities of Yugoslavia and Romania. Their goals have derived far more from concern about their own situations in Europe than from their concern about circumstances in Southern Africa per se.

The People's Republic of China

China forms a category unto itself. Its uniqueness lies in the degree to which its undertakings in Southern Africa have conflicted with those of the Soviet–Cuban–East German "quasi-coalition" there.

Activities and Evolving Links

Developments of the mid-1970s in Southern Africa have had far less spectacular impact on China's enterprises in the region than on those of the Communist states already covered. In part, this fact reflects the high level of Chinese activities in the area during previous years.[74] Prior to the collapse of the Portuguese African empire in 1974, Beijing had established close relations with Zambia. Although diplomatic ties existed from the mid-1960s on, the big boost in this regard came in 1970, when the Chinese agreed to construct the massive Tanzania-Zambia railway. This "flagship" project involved the extension of $400 million in credits to the two countries, of which Zambia received more than half.[75] In the wake of this agreement, high-level contacts between Zambia and China multiplied rapidly. For example, Chinese leaders entertained the vice-president of Zambia in Beijing in 1972, and two years later they welcomed President Kaunda himself. During the 1965–74 period, China even provided the Lusaka government with a small amount of military aid, amounting to about $1 million.[76]

Beijing had likewise forged early and strong links with many of the "national liberation" movements in the region.[77] Its relations with FRELIMO of Mozambique, ZANU of Rhodesia, and SWAPO of Namibia were particularly intimate. To all of the three, the Chinese had supplied not only money but also military training at camps in Tanzania. While China could boast of only minimal contacts with Angolan nationalists before 1973, it had extended a modicum of aid to UNITA beginning in the mid-1960s. Then in December 1973, Holden Roberto of the FNLA visited Beijing to ask for substantial assistance from the Chinese, and the Chinese agreed to grant his request. Although China had also fashioned ties with the Pan-Africanist Congress (PAC) of South Africa and extended it at least token support, Chinese relations with this group were still fairly distant.

In part, the modest effect of regional events of the mid-1970s on recent Chinese undertakings in Southern Africa stems from the outcome of the Angolan civil war. Specifically, China found itself backing the losing horse. In June 1974, in accordance with the agreement reached with Holden Roberto the preceding December, 120 Chinese military advisers arrived in Zaire to work with FNLA forces based there; at about the same time, Beijing commenced shipment of arms to the FNLA. These activities continued even after the three nationalist movements signed the Alvor agreement to set up a transitional coalition government. Although China in July 1975 formally consented to respect the call of the Organization of African Unity for neutrality toward the three rival Angolan groups, it kept its military personnel at the FNLA's bases in Zaire until October 24, 1975. Moreover, in response to the MPLA's military offensive of June–July, Beijing in mid-July even reportedly authorized Zaire to release to the FNLA Chinese military equipment in the hands of the Zairian army. Not until after Cuban troops began to arrive in Angola in force and the South Africans intervened in behalf of the FNLA-UNITA side did the Chinese attempt to extricate themselves from the imbroglio. Even then, they may have expected the United States to salvage the situation for the FNLA-UNITA alliance, thereby permitting them to reengage without the taint of association with South Africa. But such was not to be. The MPLA, with the help of the Soviet–Cuban–East German "quasi-coalition," emerged triumphant.[78] As a consequence, China acquired the image of a "paper tiger," unable to deliver for its clients in a pinch. This image inevitably affected its opportunities in ensuing years.

Nevertheless, Chinese enterprises in Southern Africa have still intensified to some degree since the mid-1970s. With respect to Zambia, Beijing's primary concern has been to avoid erosion of its established position, and it has taken a number of steps toward this end. In 1976, for example, the Chinese announced that they were providing the Lusaka and Dar es Salaam governments with an outright grant of $55 million, half of which was to go to Zambia, to cover cost overruns on the building of the Tazara railway. Later in the decade, when Zambian personnel had trouble keeping the line running, China came to the rescue by sending its specialists back to help with operations.[79] During the last half of the 1970s, too, Beijing supplied Lusaka with about $20 million of new military aid.[80] In 1980, the Chinese again received President Kaunda for a visit.

China's support of the FNLA-UNITA alliance during the Angolan civil war and its endorsement of UNITA's later call for the withdrawal of non-African forces from Angola and for UNITA representation in the government have thus far effectively precluded ties with the MPLA regime, but Mozambique has been another story. The Chinese opened up official links with the FRELIMO regime soon after Mozambique obtained its independence in 1975. At roughly the same time, they extended a loan of about $60 million to Maputo.[81] By 1979, there were 100 Chinese economic technicians in the African country working on various projects.[82] During the first years after Mozambique won its sovereignty, Beijing also furnished it with about $5 million in military assistance, although Soviet offerings in this realm vastly exceeded what the Chinese could manage.[83] Last but not least,

China over the years has exchanged a considerable number of high-level delegations with Mozambique. Among the Mozambican visitors to Beijing has been President Samora Machel.

As for the other states in the region, China has entered into diplomatic relations with both Botswana and Lesotho. Moreover, Beijing has displayed something other than routine interest in the former, as one of the Front Line States. In 1976, the Chinese played host to President Sir Seretse Khama. That same year, they inaugurated an aid program to the Gaborone government with a small grant of military equipment for Botswana's new defense force, and they signed an agreement to provide the country with economic assistance. In 1978, they followed up on the 1976 aid accord by allocating $17 million of development credits to Botswana.[84] Since then, various delegations have passed back and forth between the two countries.

Before the March 1980 elections in Zimbabwe, China was the chief supplier of military training to ZANU forces at camps in Tanzania and Mozambique, and it constituted one of that group's major sources of arms.[85] This assistance paid off handsomely after Robert Mugabe's victory in the elections. China received an invitation to set up an embassy in Salisbury, and it proceeded to do so posthaste. Relations with the new government have proved to be quite cordial since then. The warmth of the ties has been enhanced by Beijing's expressed willingness to contribute $27 million to Zimbabwe's economic recovery and development and by its cordial reception of Mugabe on a state visit in May 1981.[86]

With respect to the remaining "national liberation" movements, there has been a general decline in Chinese undertakings since the mid-1970s. This state of affairs, however, has resulted more from circumstances over which Beijing has little control than from conscious design on its part. SWAPO, for example, has moved its main base of operations to Angola, with which China does not have formal ties. The PAC has fallen into substantial disarray and tends to be isolated from the new currents and groupings in South Africa itself.[87] Although the ANC would be accessible to the Chinese, they have made no overtures in its direction to date—possibly because of the legacy of mutual friction, but also possibly because they want to see whether other groups emerge to challenge the primacy of the ANC as the "liberation" vehicle in South Africa.

Motivations behind Undertakings

Like the USSR, the PRC has faced significant complexities in trying to lay out goals for itself in Southern Africa. In the first place, not all of the interests that Beijing has perceived in regard to the area have been entirely complementary. On the one hand, for example, Chinese leaders have considered it desirable to align China firmly with anticolonial and antiracist forces in the region so as to strengthen its identification with the Third World. Since 1974, Beijing has analyzed global affairs in terms of three worlds—(1) the superpowers, (2) other industrialized states, and (3) developing countries—and it has associated China with the last of these.[88] To be sure, events of the late 1970s and early 1980s, such as the Soviet interventions in the Horn of Africa and Afghanistan and the threat of Soviet intervention in Poland, have compelled Chinese leaders to take stock of the military realities confronting them.[89] Nevertheless, Beijing has continued to argue that "the rise of the Third World has brought about a radical change in the balance of power of the world's forces in favor of the people,"[90] and it has insisted that Third World countries can "preserve the stability and peace of the world" if they "join hands with all the justice-upholding countries and people in a resolute struggle to expose and thwart" the "aggressive design and war plan" of hegemonism, "the root cause of global unrest."[91] From this perspective, mobilization of the Third World under the Chinese aegis would afford China at least some protection against Soviet attack. To effect such a mobilization, however, China needs to be able to point to the commonality of its purposes and those of other Third World countries.

On the other hand, Chinese leaders have seen an interest in avoiding actions in Southern Africa that would generate undue friction between China and the United States and Western Europe. In recent years, Beijing has expended a great deal of effort not only to improve its political links with the United States and Western Europe, but also to expand economic ties and build a "united front" in the security realm with them. Indeed, the Chinese have made clear that the fulfillment of China's plans for modernization will require major imports of technology from the industrialized capitalist states, and perhaps long-term credits as well.[92] Because the United States and a number of West European countries have involvements in Southern Africa, unrestrained support of the anticolonial and antiracist forces in the area could run counter to at least some U.S. and West European interests, and thus fan tension between China and the Western powers.[93] This, in turn, might jeopardize the realization of Beijing's larger goals with respect to modernization and security.

Second, China has not possessed sufficient capabilities to pursue seriously some interests that Beijing has discerned in the region. For instance, Chinese leaders have evinced a wish to have a say in the resolution of the racial conflict in the area, in order to help establish China's credentials as a power with global concerns. Although Beijing has denied ambitions to become a superpower, China has long endeavored to win recognition as a global actor. Its sensitivity on this issue contributed to the rising friction between itself and the USSR in the 1950s.[94] Furthermore, Beijing refused to consider participation in the United Nations unless its representatives assumed the permanent seat on the Security Council that the U.N. Charter accorded China, and since PRC delegates first entered U.N. bodies in 1971, they have in low-key fashion asserted their concern with conditions in virtually every region of the world.[95] In this context, the racial question in Southern Africa has attracted particular attention from the PRC. The Chinese have constantly reiterated that "the South African racist regime is not only an insensate stone pressing upon the South African and Namibian peoples but also a catastrophe jeopardizing peace and stability in Africa."[96] Since the "signal victory" of antiracist forces in Zimbabwe, moreover, they have argued that "the days of colonialism and racism are numbered," and they have pledged that "the Chinese people will . . . firmly support the just cause for the total liberation of Southern Africa."[97]

Yet China's capacity to affect the situation in Southern Africa militarily has been exceedingly limited. Although the Chinese have three airborne divisions and some aircraft to transport them abroad, the aircraft could not negotiate the distances to Southern Africa without access to refueling facilities. Similarly, there are 38,000 marines in the Chinese armed forces, but the Chinese navy has lacked the vessels to carry out an effective sealift of them.[98] Furthermore, even if China could manage to get a few troops to the area, it would not have the ability to provide logistical backup for them. Thus Beijing has not had the capacity to project its own power into the region in any meaningful way. China does, of course, have an arms industry of its own, so it has had the capability of supplying at least a certain amount of weapons to antiracist forces in the area. The same has been true with regard to military advisers. Nonetheless, Beijing's ability to provide military assistance has been severely constrained by the demands of China's own security and the need to modernize China's military forces. Both factors have grown more pressing in recent years.[99]

Third, the interests that Chinese leaders have identified with respect to Southern Africa have competed with interests that they have perceived in other parts of the globe. As leaders of a state with pretensions to be a global actor, China's rulers have characterized its interests in accordance with such a role. While they may not have defined precise interests with regard to portions of the world most remote from them, their list of such places does not seem to have been lengthy. But China is far from all-powerful; hence, Chinese leaders have had to establish some sort of hierarchy of interests. This necessity has forced them to weigh China's interests in one region against those in others.

On Beijing's resulting ladder of geopolitical priorities, Southern Africa has occupied a low rung. During recent years, it has definitely fallen below Asia, the developed capitalist states of North America and Western Europe, Eastern Europe, and the Middle East, in that order. As an Asian power, China is subject to the effects of events in Asia more than it is to those in any other region. No less critical, the main security threats that Beijing has believed confront China have stemmed from China's neighbors in Asia. To the north and west lies the USSR; to the south, Vietnam; and to the southwest, India. Finally, China's main trading partner has been the economically dynamic Asian power to its east—Japan.

The significance of the developed capitalist states of North America and Western Europe in Beijing's eyes has flowed from two factors. To begin with, these states have possessed sufficient military strength to serve as useful counterweights against the Soviet Union. Links with them—however short of direct alliance these may be—can thus help to deter the USSR from attacking China. Indeed, the mere maintenance of NATO forces in Western Europe has prevented Moscow from concentrating its military might against China. Second, the developed capitalist states in Western Europe have been key sources of industrial goods and technology for China since the 1960s, and with the normalization of Sino-American relations in the late 1970s, the United States has become one, too. The major modernization drive that Beij-

ing launched in the late 1970s has given added weight to such relations. Eastern Europe's standing has derived from a couple of
considerations. Because the states of Eastern Europe are, like China,
engaged in "building socialism," Beijing appears to have felt a certain
affinity for them and their experiences. Perhaps more crucial, Beijing
has regarded it as desirable to encourage autonomous trends in Eastern Europe so as to focus the attention of the USSR on this region,
which Moscow itself deems of vital significance to Soviet security,
rather than on China. For instance, China has assiduously courted
both Romania and Yugoslavia since the late 1970s.

Since about 1977, Beijing has paid increased heed to the Middle
East because of a growing preoccupation with the geopolitical implications for Chinese security of Soviet military activities abroad.[100] For
example, it tried to bolster the Shah's government in Iran prior to the
February 1979 revolution there; it agreed in June 1979 to furnish
major quantities of weapons, including as many as 60 MIG-19's, to
Egypt,[101] and it has roundly denounced the Soviet invasion of Afghanistan and may be supplying some arms to the Muslim insurgents
there.

In view of these constraints, Beijing has fixed two specific objectives
for itself in Southern Africa for the medium term. They are:

(1) To convince the black governments and "national liberation"
movements in the area that there is a mutuality of purpose between
them and China. This mutuality of purpose, in the Chinese definition, has increasingly had both negative and positive aspects. Specifically, it has encompassed both the elimination of white-minority rule
and a readiness to do business with the West on the basis of equality.
Chinese commentaries on Zimbabwe since Robert Mugabe won the
March 1980 elections there, for instance, have stressed that Mugabe
desires to bring about reconciliation between whites and blacks, and
wishes to develop links with the West.[102]

(2) To induce the governments and "national liberation" movements in the region to oppose Soviet involvement there as self-
interested and aimed at creating hegemony. Chinese leaders have
badly wanted to curb the expansion of Soviet activities in Southern
Africa, for they have been well aware that these enterprises have had
deleterious effects on China's position in the region.[103] This desire
was manifest after the setback that the USSR suffered in the Zimbabwe elections. Beijing noted with ill-concealed glee that the "ambi-

tious superpower" which "has always coveted Zimbabwe and all of southern Africa" and which "tried to meddle in the affairs of Zimbabwe" was "unhappy about the London agreement and the new Zimbabwean government which will soon be formed." It then cautioned that "once there is a good opportunity," because of difficulties Zimbabwe might encounter, this superpower would not hesitate to "fish in troubled waters," and it warned that "this is a matter against which the Zimbabwean people should heighten their vigilance."[104]

These goals, it should be emphasized, have been highly hortatory in character. In essence, China has adopted a strategy of attempting to set itself up as Southern Africa's mentor.[105]

General Impact of Communist Involvement in Southern Africa

Despite the diversity that has marked the activities and purposes of the Communist states with respect to Southern Africa, it is still possible to offer a few broad observations about the overall effect of these states on the region in recent years.

On Politics

In the political sphere, the most salient feature of this impact has been the increased impetus that they have given to political change there. All the Communist countries have displayed a strong commitment to the eradication of colonial rule and of white-minority governments in the area, and they have thrown their weight behind those local elements working toward such ends. Their involvements in this cause have, in turn, generated new resolve on the part of such local elements to press their cases and have stimulated a sense of urgency on the part of many outside powers and even of previous local defenders of the status quo to bring about some sort of accommodation on these issues.

Beyond these issues, the Communist states have affected the region politically in a highly disjointed manner. This disorderliness has stemmed from both the fragmented Communist approach to the area and the varied susceptibilities and sensitivities of local actors. The Soviet Union and China, for example, have each clearly sought to produce political outcomes that would operate to the disadvantage of the other, and Yugoslavia and Romania have attempted to achieve political results that would strengthen their hands in dealing with the

USSR. By the same token, the MPLA regime in Angola, still smarting from Chinese backing of the FNLA-UNITA alliance during the civil war there, and remaining dependent on Soviet and Cuban military support to sustain it against UNITA and South Africa, has declined to open up diplomatic ties with Beijing, while the FRELIMO government in Mozambique, not troubled by such considerations, has carried on normal relations with China, even as it has evinced growing receptiveness to overtures from Moscow. As a consequence of these factors, the precise political effects of each of the Communist states involved in the region have differed from those of the other Communist states and also from one country to another within Southern Africa.

At the same time, not all the Communist states have proved equally successful in exerting political impact in the region, and this disparity has been of much greater significance in area-wide terms than the specific nature of these states' political effects in individual Southern African countries. The "quasi-coalition" of the USSR, Cuba, and the GDR has chalked up the best record by far in this regard, with China coming in a distant second and Yugoslavia and Romania bringing up the rear.

Basically, the explanation for the influence of the "quasi-coalition" has lain in its military presence in the region. Already by the early 1970s, the USSR had established permanent naval patrols in the waters off both the east and west coasts of Southern Africa. The civil war in Angola brought massive numbers of Cuban troops and Soviet and East German military advisers to that land. Even at the opening of the 1980s, an estimated 19,000 Cuban troops and 1,400 Soviet and East German military technicians remained there. Moreover, the "quasi-coalition" maintained at least another 740 military technicians elsewhere in the area.[106] Since the onset of the Angolan civil war in 1975, the "quasi-coalition," and particularly the USSR and the GDR, have poured hundreds of millions of dollars worth of arms and equipment into the region. Although it is impossible to arrive at a definitive total from available data, one figure points up the magnitude of the transfers. During 1974–78, the USSR provided Angola, Mozambique, and Zambia alone with $580 million worth of arms.[107] A military presence of these dimensions has inevitably caused all the governments and "national liberation" movements in the region to take the "quasi-coalition" carefully into account in their political calculations.

None of this, however, is to suggest that any of the governments or "national liberation" movements of the area have become political lackeys of the Soviet–Cuban–East German "quasi-coalition." To the contrary, even the MPLA regime in Angola, which confronts the most formidable pressure from the "quasi-coalition" members, has displayed a strong sense of political independence. For example, it, along with the other Front Line States, has prodded SWAPO hard to reach a settlement with Pretoria over Namibia, despite the fact that Moscow has encouraged SWAPO to continue to struggle to attain the group's maximum goals.

On the Economic Situation

As for the economic realm, the Communist states have barely affected the situation in Southern Africa at all except in a negative sense. Their promotion of various armed undertakings has, of course, helped to disrupt a number of economies in the region, although the precise extent of their impact in this respect defies measurement. In a positive sense, however, their influence has been slight.

Between 1975 and 1979, the USSR, China, and the East European states (including Poland, Czechoslovakia, Hungary, and Bulgaria) together extended only $246 million in economic aid to countries in Southern Africa.[108] By way of comparison, the United States alone extended $41.9 million just to Mozambique—hardly one of the prime American recipients in the area because of Congressional restrictions on assistance to it—during the same period.[109] Besides the United States, the West European nations, Japan, and Saudi Arabia have had substantial aid programs in the region. So too have such multilateral institutions as the World Bank and the African Development Bank.

Although conflicting statistics render impossible any precise discussion of trade for Southern Africa as a whole, it is clear that through the late 1970s the great bulk of the area's trade was with non-Communist, largely Western states. Even those countries with the most extensive trade links with the Communist world probably still carried on about 80 percent of their overall trade with non-Communist partners.[110]

The impact of the Communist states in the domain of technical assistance has been somewhat more substantial. In 1979, for instance, the USSR, China, Cuba, and the East European countries (again including Poland, Czechoslovakia, Hungary, and Bulgaria) among them maintained a total of 11,780 economic technicians in the region.[111] Nevertheless, the overall contribution of the non-Communist states, and especially the United States and Western Europe, still seems to have overshadowed that of the Communist countries even in this sphere, although adequate figures to measure the aggregate performance of the non-Communist states precisely are not at hand. Only in Angola, of all the countries in the area, would the level of technical aid of the Communist nations appear to have been genuinely competitive.

Both objective and subjective factors have helped to limit the effect of the Communist states in the economic realm. During the last half of the 1970s, every one of the Communist countries treated here experienced severe domestic economic problems. These derived from a variety of structural and policy deficiencies as well as from inflation imported from the outside world, but the ultimate result has been the same in all cases. Each state has found its capacity to engage in economic activities with developing nations quite restricted.[112] The extent of the restrictions, however, has differed among the countries, because of the relative sizes of their economies. Specifically, the GDR, Yugoslavia, Romania, and Cuba have felt the pinch more than have the USSR and China. During 1975–79, for example, the USSR managed to extend a total of $3,073 million in economic assistance to Third World states, while the PRC offered them $912 million. Thus, the magnitude of the economic help that the two proffered to countries in Southern Africa—sums of $23 million (for the USSR) and $50 million (for China)—plainly has had something to do with the geopolitical priorities of Moscow and Beijing in addition to their capabilities.[113]

In the Military Sphere

It is in the military domain that the Communist states have made their strongest showing in Southern Africa. They have had a major hand in the escalating militarization of the region. In 1974–78, for instance, the flow of arms from outside sources to the black-run governments of the area rose significantly over that of earlier years, reaching a total of $1,065 million. Of that amount, the USSR and China alone provided $605 million, with the USSR accounting for more than 95 percent of this figure.[114] Although there are no available statistics on the magnitude of arms transfers to "national libera-tion" forces in Rhodesia and Namibia in this period, the Communist countries unquestionably were responsible for the vast bulk of these transfers as well.

In response to this stepped-up flow of Communist arms to black elements of the region, the white-minority governments in South Af-rica and Rhodesia purchased some $620 million worth of arms from abroad in 1974–78.[115] The most telling, if indirect, evidence of the impact of the Communist states on the level of military preparedness in Southern Africa, however, has come from the size of the military buildup in South Africa since the mid-1970s. In 1974, Pretoria's standing armed forces numbered 47,450. These elements were equipped with some 120 tanks, roughly 380 combat aircraft (includ-ing 64 French Mirage III fighter planes) in both operational and training units, and 27 naval combatants. By 1980, the standing armed forces had grown to 86,050 men. Moreover, they possessed some 310 tanks, more than 400 combat aircraft (including 51 French Mirage III and 46 French Mirage F-1 fighters), and 33 naval combatants.[116]

The Communist countries have also displaced the Western coun-tries as the main source of arms for black elements in the area. An-gola, Mozambique, and Zambia now obtain the majority of their weapons and military equipment from the Communist world. So too did both wings of the "national liberation" movement in Rhodesia until the settlement of the conflict there and the emergence of a black Zimbabwean government under Robert Mugabe in 1980. SWAPO still gets almost all of its arms from Communist states.

This impact in the military sphere, of course, has been primarily the handiwork of the Soviet–Cuban–East German "quasi-coalition." While no overall figures for arms transfers from China, Yugoslavia, or Romania to Southern Africa are available, the data at hand do attest to the relatively low level of such transfers. In 1974–78, for example, China furnished only $25 million in military aid to the black governments of the region.[117] The USSR, in contrast, has supplied massive quantities of arms to the area. The sum of its military assist-ance just to the black governments of the area in 1974–78 alone reached $580 million.[118] For its part, Cuba during the mid-1970s dispatched as many as 36,000 combat troops to the region, and as of the beginning of the 1980s, an estimated 19,000 continued to operate there.

Prospects

There remains the question of the future. One point needs to be stressed at the outset. The involvements of the Communist states in Southern Africa since the mid-1970s have represented merely an intensification of long-standing efforts on their parts to inject themselves into the affairs of the region. Therefore, it is highly unlikely that the will of their leaders to carry out undertakings in the area will flag in the years immediately ahead, and the medium-term goals that they have been pursuing there will probably alter only on the margins, if at all. These factors, in short, ought to be regarded as essentially "givens."

Level of Communist Activity

The level of activity of the Communist countries in the region, however, is by no means foreordained. It will depend upon the constraints under which these countries have to operate and upon the opportunities that their leaders see before them. The former will have both internal and external aspects, and the latter will reflect circumstances outside as well as within Southern Africa. It is impossible to deal with these considerations from the standpoint of the Communist states as a group, for they will vary from state to state. Thus, assessment must be made on the basis of individual countries.

THE USSR

Since the extent of the enterprises in Southern Africa of the Soviet–Cuban–East German "quasi-alliance" has been in large measure a function of the level of Soviet undertakings there, it is logical to begin with the USSR. For at least the remainder of the 1980s, the USSR will face a difficult internal economic situation. Its overall rate of economic growth has declined appreciably in recent years, and the only way of remedying that situation in the long run is through increased productivity. To achieve gains in this sphere, however, will require the surmounting of vested bureaucratic interests in existing modes of operation, of a dropoff in the number of new entrants into the labor market, and of a likely energy squeeze that could force Moscow to reduce its exports of oil for hard currency and hence its imports of foreign technology. The magnitude of these impediments suggests that the USSR may well experience considerable economic strains in the years ahead. These strains not only would limit its capacity to provide aid to and to trade with Third World countries but might compel it as well to curtail its investments in improving its military capabilities.[119] Restrictions on military spending would probably reduce the funds available for enhancing Soviet capacities to project power to remote areas such as Southern Africa, for Moscow's primary concern in the military realm will undoubtedly remain the preservation of strategic parity with the United States. A political succession also looms on the near horizon in the USSR. Moreover, this succession will be an unusual one in Soviet history, for it will entail not just the replacement of the top leader but the turnover of virtually the entire upper echelon of the leadership, because of the age of those now in power. While the combination of the economic and succession factors could result in a Soviet policy of adventurism abroad—designed to extract sacrifices from the populace and to shore up the position of a particular leader or group of leaders—by far the more likely outcome is an increased focus on domestic matters.

Circumstances in the global arena tend to reinforce the probability that Moscow will eschew a wholesale policy of adventurism overseas. East-West relations have deteriorated drastically since the late 1970s, and the Western powers, especially the United States, have expressed a determination to carry out programs to enhance their military capabilities. The USSR itself has taken on a heavy new burden by intervening in Afghanistan to prevent the collapse of the Marxist government there. It could eventually have to accept enormous costs to preserve a Communist regime in Poland as well. At minimum, Poland will probably constitute a substantial drain on Soviet economic resources for some time to come.

As for opportunities, Moscow clearly seems to feel that those in Southern Africa have diminished as a result of the settlement of the Zimbabwean conflict. A resolution of the Namibian strife through negotiations—by no means unthinkable—would enhance this perception, for Soviet analysts have held that the political struggle in South Africa is likely to be protracted, in light of the formidable strength of the current white-minority government.[120] In contrast, Moscow has since the late 1970s seen the emergence of new opportunities in regions of higher geopolitical priority to the USSR than Southern Africa—particularly in the Persian Gulf.

Taken together, then, these considerations point forcefully to the conclusion that the USSR will probably maintain a holding action in Southern Africa in the years immediately ahead. While its activities in the area may not diminish, they are unlikely to expand significantly.

CUBA

Although Cuba and the GDR will have to work within the broad framework of the Soviet approach to Southern Africa if they hope to accomplish their particular goals, they will not be total prisoners of what Moscow decides to do. That is, they will enjoy some leeway for choice.

Of the two, Cuba may well cut back its undertakings in the region. At least, there will probably be plenty of incentives for it to do so.

The troubles that have plagued the Cuban economy with mounting intensity since the mid-1970s will not in all likelihood abate much, if at all, during the 1980s.[121] These have already spawned a high degree of discontent among elements of the Cuban populace and in 1980 caused the exodus of large numbers of people, primarily but not exclusively to the United States, when the government temporarily eased its controls on emigration. Thus, the Cuban regime may well have to pay greater attention to its domestic position, and less to its international role, than it did during the 1970s.

The heightened tension between Cuba and the United States in the 1980s, especially since the advent of the Reagan administration, could serve to reinforce such an imperative. In addition, Havana has discovered, in the wake of the Soviet intervention in Afghanistan, that too close an identification with the USSR entails serious drawbacks for itself in the Third World. Indeed, it cost Cuba the seat on the U.N. Security Council that Havana had coveted and had almost assured for itself prior to the Afghanistan invasion.[122]

Apropos of opportunities, the Castro government has discerned a decrease in recent years in those available to it in Southern Africa. By the late 1970s, the MPLA regime in Angola was evincing dissatisfaction with the quality of Cuban technical assistance.[123] Then there came the settlement of the conflict in Rhodesia and the election of Robert Mugabe, who has preached reconciliation between blacks and whites in Zimbabwe and has sought economic support from the West. Although the guerrilla struggle in Namibia goes on for the present, it too could end in some kind of compromise arrangement for the territory. At the same time, Havana has discovered new openings for

Cuba in the Caribbean and in Central America. Although exploitation of these possibilities entails certain risks in connection with the
United States, it does have certain advantages for Cuba vis-à-vis the
USSR. Havana is much less dependent on Moscow in operating in
this area than it is in more remote regions.

THE GDR

In contrast with Cuba, the GDR might conceivably intensify its
enterprises in Southern Africa to some degree in the years ahead. At
a minimum, it is unlikely to decrease them.

East Berlin, to be sure, will probably continue to encounter the
same sort of economic difficulties that have in the past impeded it
from aiding and trading with Third World areas such as Southern
Africa.[124] In fact, those difficulties could become more severe in the
wake of the military clampdown in Poland, if the West reduces its
economic ties with the GDR. Moreover, the GDR's preoccupation with
Europe has perforce increased with the growing tension between East
and West there and the evolution of the situation in Poland, for both
have implications for the GDR's security and internal stability.

Nonetheless, Southern Africa does offer some potential opportunities of which the East German leadership may wish to avail itself. East
Berlin, of course, plainly recognizes that developments in Zimbabwe
have represented a setback for the GDR, and it seems to be aware
that a negotiated settlement in Namibia could have a similar outcome.
Still, some black governments in the region have proved receptive to
East German assistance in the realms of security and intelligence. As
new and old governments endeavor to root themselves firmly in
forthcoming years, that number could grow. If it does, the East Germans will be strongly tempted to take advantage of the opening, for
at the moment no other area of consequence to them seems likely to
present them with a chance to play a comparable role.

YUGOSLAVIA

In all probability Yugoslavia will confront a highly mixed set of
considerations. Its capacity to interact with the states of Southern
Africa economically appears destined to remain fairly low in the
1980s. That Belgrade must import essentially all of its oil—which it
now gets from the USSR and the Middle East—has much to do with
the prospects in this regard.[125] Also, the Yugoslavs have directed the

bulk of their attention to internal affairs since the death of Tito in 1980, and they could feel it necessary to continue that emphasis if there are further outbursts of local nationalism such as that which took place among the Albanians of Kosovo in the spring of 1981. The persistence or even rise of prevailing tensions between East and West could bolster that feeling, for the Belgrade government fears that such circumstances might make the USSR more inclined to try to exploit national conflicts within Yugoslavia to undermine the country's independence.

Despite these constraints, however, Yugoslav leaders have unquestionably perceived potential opportunities for new Yugoslav undertakings in Southern Africa. Currently, these relate primarily to Zimbabwe, but Belgrade believes that similar openings could develop in Namibia. In addition, Yugoslav leaders see not only a desirability but also a chance of greater activism on the part of nonaligned states generally in a period in which there is heightened confrontation between East and West. They even took some steps after the Soviet invasion of Afghanistan to mobilize opposition to it among the nonaligned countries.[126]

All in all, then, the level of Yugoslav involvement in Africa will probably stay at least the same during the foreseeable future. It could even go up a bit.

ROMANIA

Like Yugoslavia, Romania will determine the dimensions of its enterprises in a complex framework, although Bucharest's handicaps will probably be somewhat more pronounced than those of Belgrade. Romania had an impressive record of economic growth during the 1970s and by the end of the decade was carrying on roughly 20 percent of its trade with developing countries, but there is serious question whether it can sustain that performance in the 1980s.[127] Thus, its ability to furnish assistance to and engage in commercial exchanges with states in regions such as Southern Africa will likely decline. Perhaps more important, deteriorating East-West relations and events in Poland in the early 1980s have caused Bucharest to focus its attention on Europe. Furthermore, the heightened tension on the continent tends to limit the degree to which Romania can safely attempt to project itself as a nonaligned country, a key element of its approach to Southern Africa since the mid-1970s.

At the same time, the Bucharest leadership plainly sees some new openings for Romania in Southern Africa. Romania moved quickly to try to solidify ties with Robert Mugabe's government in Zimbabwe, and it looks forward to a political transition in Namibia in the not too distant future. Although Bucharest at present appears to discern opportunities elsewhere in Africa, and in the Middle East, too, none of these seems to be any more attractive to it than those it deems available in Southern Africa. This consideration suggests that the level of activity of Romania in Southern Africa will remain roughly the same during the 1980s as it has been over the years since the mid-1970s.

CHINA

Of all the Communist states, China will probably have the most compelling reasons to scale down its involvement in the region from past levels. The Chinese drive for modernization that began in the late 1970s has resulted in the channeling of most of the country's economic resources into internal development or economic undertakings designed to further such development, and this situation seems unlikely to change in the 1980s. Indeed, the troubles that Beijing has encountered in trying to carry out modernization at the pace that it originally set indicate that, if anything, the task of modernization may require an even greater share of China's resources than was initially anticipated.[128] Under such circumstances, China will have quite limited capabilities to help and even to trade with Third World states such as those in Southern Africa.

Furthermore, not only does the Chinese military urgently need to be modernized, but Beijing since the late 1970s also has come to feel directly threatened by the USSR's military activities in Asia—e.g., Soviet intervention in Afghanistan, Soviet backing of Vietnam's invasion of Kampuchea, etc. Thus, China will in all probability find it hard to extend much in the way of military assistance to either governments or guerrilla forces in Southern Africa.

With regard to opportunities, Beijing does currently detect a few possibilities for expanded activities in Southern Africa. It has already sought to forge amicable ties with the Mugabe government in Zimbabwe, and it has some sense that political independence for Namibia might benefit China, unless achievement of that independence comes about through military means and through major Soviet aid. But such opportunities pale in significance beside the need that Chinese leaders now see to preserve and, if possible, strengthen the PRC's links with the United States, Japan, and perhaps even the states of the Association of Southeast Asian Nations (ASEAN). In the cases of the United States and Japan, such ties can facilitate China's modernization drive and help meet its perceived security needs.

In view of these factors, the level of the PRC's undertakings in Southern Africa may fall somewhat in the years ahead. Certainly, there is little possibility that it will rise.

The Communist Impact

If the foregoing speculations prove to be accurate, some implications for the broad situation in Southern Africa will flow from them. Specifically, the chances of any dramatic shift in the effects of the Communist states on the area in the foreseeable future will be virtually nil. If any changes do take place, they will probably occur on the margins and amount to a reduction, rather than an increase, of influence.

One caveat to this projection needs to be registered, however. A sudden and major conflagration in the area, particularly in South Africa, might induce the leaders of some or all of the Communist states to reassess their present calculations. Such reassessments could produce a new set of equations in the region. Whether a conflagration of this sort will occur, only time will tell.

2.

✳

U.S. Policy toward Southern Africa: Interests, Choices, and Constraints

Robert M. Price

As an arena for United States foreign policy, Southern Africa has represented an area about which there is neither consensus on the nature or extent of U.S. interests, nor on the general guidelines that ought to shape the relationship of the United States toward the region.

Consequently, between 1960 and the election of Ronald Reagan the United States has adopted no less than four distinct policy postures in respect to Southern Africa.[1] These can be labeled "benign" neglect, containment-confrontation, containment-crisis management, and accommodation.

Policies of Limited Engagement, 1960–73

The first of these postures—"benign" neglect—characterized U.S. policy from the end of World War II until 1975. Over this lengthy period there existed a basic consistency to policy: each presidential administration maintained good relations with the minority-controlled regimes in Southern Africa, while at the same time expressing, in general terms, American abhorence of apartheid and colonialism.

45

During the 1960s the United States demonstrated its disapproval of Portuguese rule in Mozambique and Angola and of white minority rule in South Africa and Rhodesia by supporting various limited actions within the United Nations. Thus the United States complied with a U.N.-sponsored embargo on arms sales to South Africa; it supported a variety of symbolic U.N. resolutions that condemned apartheid and colonialism; and, for a time, it adhered to the economic sanctions against Rhodesia mandated by the Security Council. At the same time, no American administration sought to directly project U.S. power into the Southern African region, or to use American influence to alter the situation of minority and colonial domination. That is to say, the United States did not act so as to restructure the political systems of the area. Indeed, the most salient feature of its policy toward the region over this lengthy period was, in fact, the limited nature of U.S. attention and commitment. It is this aspect of policy that has led observers to refer to the U.S. posture toward Southern Africa during this time as one of minimal engagement or "benign" neglect.[2]

To be sure, the styles of various administrations did differ. Most notably, the policy followed during President Nixon's first term involved a relaxation of the acts of "limited disaproval" toward minority rule that previous administrations had enacted. The arms embargo was partially lifted, U.N. resolutions condemning apartheid and colonialism were opposed rather than supported, and the Nixon administration provided tacit support for the Byrd Amendment in Congress which permitted American imports of Rhodesian chrome in violation of the U.N.-mandated economic sanctions. These and similar policies reflected a more explicit acceptance and acquiescence, if not moral approval, of the continuation of white rule in Southern Africa than had been shown by earlier administrations. At the same time, the change involved a "tilt" rather than a fundamental alteration in the "low-profile" approach of the U.S. toward Southern Africa. Minimal engagement could be said to still capture the essence of policy.

This posture of minimal engagement was conditioned by three closely interrelated factors. First, U.S. policymakers did not view Southern Africa as containing vital American interests.[3] The type of interests that the area did contain were viewed as being not of the kind whose damage would undermine the security of the United States. Second, Southern Africa fell outside the arena of East-West conflict because the presence of the Soviet Union in the area was insubstantial. Thus the situation in the region did not engage the primary concern of U.S. foreign policy in the post–World War II era. And third, the area appeared to be a zone of political stability, a condition guaranteed by well entrenched pro-Western regimes in South Africa, Rhodesia, Mozambique, and Angola. It is true that this barrier to Soviet "penetration" was constituted by two white minority governments and Portuguese colonialism, and that this fact posed potential problems in regard both to official statements abhorring racism and colonialism, and to U.S. relations with the newly independent states of Black Africa. But the dominant concern of U.S. policy in the twenty-five years after World War II was containment of the Soviet Union, and thus in that period the political status quo in Southern Africa was consistent with the goal of containment policy. Indeed, the Nixon "tilt" was based on the combination of an explicit recognition of the containment role played by minority-ruled regimes in Southern Africa, with a positive assessment of their basic stability.[4]

Containment Policies under Nixon and Kissinger, 1973–76

The years 1973–1976 were a watershed period for U.S. relations with Southern Africa. Three significant events clustered in this period which negated the factors that were the foundation for the policy of benign neglect. Chronologically the first of these events was the OPEC-orchestrated rise in petroleum prices in 1973 and relatedly the successful oil boycott launched by the Arab oil producing states during the Arab-Israeli war of the same year. Both events starkly highlighted the political and economic vulnerabilities attendant upon American import dependency and thus dramatically raised the salience, within the definition of U.S. national interests, of access to an array of industrially essential minerals. Because Southern Africa is a virtual treasure trove of such minerals, the actions of the oil producing countries propelled the region, in the eyes of many, from an area in which the U.S. stake was minimal to one in which it was vital.

At the same time that this change in perception was occurring, the Southern African region was experiencing major political upheavals. The Portuguese empire was collapsing; African insurgency within white-ruled Rhodesia was intensifying; and opposition of South African blacks to that country's apartheid regime was erupting in

Soweto, raising questions about the future stability of the Republic. In short, the demise of the Portuguese empire seemed to presage the collapse of the "old order" in Southern Africa.

To this mix of national interest and political instability was added the third ingredient: the effort by the Cubans and the Soviet Union in aiding the Marxist-oriented MPLA to seize and consolidate power in postcolonial Angola. The interaction of these three phenomena—the increased salience of access to minerals, the collapse of the "old" political order in Southern Africa, and the direct involvement of Cuba and the Soviet Union in Angola—drew Southern Africa into the vortex of international tension and propelled it to a top position on the U.S. foreign policy agenda. Benign neglect was dead, and America entered into a period of direct involvement in the political changes engulfing the area. That minimal engagement would no longer suffice seemed clear to most. What alternative posture should replace it seemed far less clear. Since the end of 1975 the U.S. position on Southern Africa might aptly be characterized as a policy in search of a long-term strategy.

The first effort to fashion a new posture toward the region was made by Henry Kissinger when he was Secretary of State. The occasion was the Angolan civil war, and the posture adopted has earlier been characterized as containment-confrontation. The struggle between political factions in Angola during 1975 held the possibility that a Marxist-oriented party might, with substantial Soviet assistance, consolidate political power in postcolonial Angola. Kissinger's interpretation of and preferred response to this situation involved the application to Africa of the containment security paradigm that had governed U.S. foreign policy globally since the war. The projection of Soviet power into Southern Africa through provision of military assistance and supplies to the MPLA of Angola was defined as a violation of the international "rules of the game."

Kissinger foresaw success for the Soviets in Angola as having three major negative consequences for the United States: it would undermine the stability of the postwar global order, in that now the USSR would be encouraged to spread its power elsewhere; it would also undermine the credibility of America's will and ability to act as a global power guaranteeing the stability of that order; and it would encourage radicalization of politics throughout Southern Africa to the detriment of the West.[5] To prevent such developments by making the cost of Soviet involvement in Angola prohibitively expensive, Kissinger sought to prevent an MPLA success by providing military assistance to the Angolan movements that opposed it. Thus the United States would confront and thereby contain the Soviet Union by assisting its own "allies" in Angola.

The effort at containment in Southern Africa through confrontation was short-lived. The U.S. Congress, weary of military involvements in the Third World in the wake of Vietnam, expressly forbade the president through the Clark amendment[6] to provide direct or indirect military assistance to Angolan factions. The MPLA, with assistance from Cuban troops and with Soviet material and logistical support, managed to consolidate its position in Angola.

For Kissinger the dangers of Soviet expansion in Southern Africa and the consequent need for a containment policy there did not cease with the Congressional action or the MPLA victory. Indeed they became more intense. By 1976, Joshua Nkomo's guerrilla movement based in Zambia and aided by Cuba and by the Soviet Union appeared to offer a serious military challenge to the white minority government of Rhodesia, and there were signs that a Soviet-backed nationalist movement, SWAPO (South West African People's Organization), operating out of southern Angola, had become a major factor in Namibia.

To the Secretary of State the situation in Southern Africa was ominous. He told the Senate Foreign Relations Committee that, having "imposed their solution on Angola," the Soviets and Cubans had entrenched their forces and "fresh opportunities lay before them. . . . Events in Angola," maintained Kissinger, "encouraged radicals to press for a military solution in Rhodesia." He foresaw that "With radical influence on the rise . . . even respectable African leaders began to conclude there was no alternative but to embrace the cause of violence. . . . The possibility grew of an emerging pattern of accommodation to the reality of Soviet presence and American inaction."[7]

After Angola it was thus the intensifying nationalist struggle for Rhodesia that Secretary Kissinger viewed as the vehicle for an expanded Soviet presence in Southern Africa. With a direct U.S. counterresponse precluded by domestic politics, the Secretary of State sought an alternative means of blocking the spread of Russian involvement and influence. If a "moderate" negotiated solution to the Rhodesian problem could be substituted for the growing guerrilla insurgency, then the vehicle for Soviet "advances" would be stopped and the need for a direct American counterresponse to the Russians would be eliminated. For this reason, beginning in the spring of 1976, Kissinger embarked upon a well-publicized and dramatic stint of shuttle diplomacy in Southern Africa. Its purpose was to use the influence of the United States both to end the guerrilla war and to displace Rhodesia's white minority regime, replacing it with a moderate government based upon majority rule. The primary motivation and goal of U.S. policy—containing the Soviet Union—was the same as it had been during the Angolan civil war. But the approach had now switched from direct confrontation to crisis management.

The strategy of managing the Rhodesian crisis rested upon one fundamental feature of the conflict engulfing that country. Both sides in the struggle were vitally dependent on the support of external actors within the Southern Africa region: the Rhodesian government upon South Africa, and the nationalist forces upon what were known as the Front Line States: Zambia, Tanzania, Angola, Mozambique, and Botswana. Kissinger's "moderate solution" to the Rhodesian crisis depended for its realization on convincing these external actors to put sufficient pressure on the particular groups they supported to force them to reach a compromise. The key feature of Kissinger's crisis management effort—the crucial role assigned to actors external to the Rhodesian conflict—proved the undoing of his strategy. The external actors were unwilling, at the time, to push their respective clients far enough to make a negotiated settlement possible. Kissinger proposed, and the Ian Smith government of Rhodesia accepted, a constitutional framework for majority rule within two years. But the proposal was rejected by the African nationalists and their supporters among the African states as leaving far too much real power in the hands of the tiny European minority. Consequently, when Secretary of State Kissinger left office at the beginning of 1977, to make way for the Carter administration, the war in Rhodesia continued unabated.

Accommodation Policies by the Carter Administration

The policy of the Carter administration toward Southern Africa contained elements both of change and of continuity in respect to its predecessor administrations. The Rhodesian conflict continued to be

the primary focus of attention, and the framework for crisis management initiated by Henry Kissinger, whereby regional states were
viewed as the key to producing a negotiated settlement, was maintained.[8] Indeed, it was extended to encompass the now growing military conflict over South African control of Namibia.

Although these elements of continuity are important, so too is the
manner in which Carter administration policy departed from the approach of the Ford-Kissinger period. Two elements of the new administration's policy stand out. First, a new posture was adopted toward
South Africa. The previous administrations of Presidents Nixon and
Ford were perceived in sub-Saharan Africa as relatively friendly
toward the white regime in South Africa. This was a reflection of the
early Nixon policy "tilt" toward white rule in Southern Africa and of
the belief that, as a "reward" for their cooperation on Rhodesia, Kissinger had offered the South Africans a sympathetic American approach both to terms for the settlement of the Namibian dispute and
against external efforts to destabilize the white minority-ruled Republic. The Carter administration broke clearly and dramatically with this
posture of sympathetic though troubled friend when, early in its
term, leading spokesmen pointedly criticized the apartheid regime
and called for the introduction of majority rule in South Africa. The
most significant of these early administration statements was that by
Vice-President Mondale, who, in a meeting with South African Prime
Minister Vorster, spoke of the goal of full political participation by all
South African citizens, subsequently interpreted as "one-man, one-
vote."[9] The effect of this and similar statements was, on the one hand,
to drive a wedge between Washington and Pretoria, and, on the other,
symbolically to align the government of the United States with the
long-term goal being pursued by the states of sub-Saharan Africa.

This development laid the foundation upon which the second difference between the Carter and previous administrations was constructed. During the Carter term the Front Line States played a much
more active and initiating role in respect to the settlement of regional
conflicts. In particular, they began to play a leading role in defining
the terms of acceptable settlements in Rhodesia and Namibia. The
U.S. adapted its position to their concerns, rather than constructing
its own framework and attempting to persuade others to accept it, as
had been done previously. The implications of this change in U.S.
posture from initiator to facilitator were twofold. African views and

interests would thereby play a more important role in the definition
of American policy in the region, and the United States would be
more willing to accept the process of radicalization in Southern Africa. Consequently some scholars have referred to the Carter administration policies as accommodationist.[10]

The accommodationist posture of the Carter administration rested
on several basic premises: that nationalist change in Southern Africa,
even when it brought to power "Marxist" parties associated with the
Soviet Union, did not necessarily threaten the interests of the United
States; that, therefore, Southern Africa could and should be insulated
from East-West competition and conflict; and that the only way in
which American influence and interests in Southern Africa could be
maintained and extended was for the United States to identify itself
with the aspirations of the African states in the region.

Within the Carter administration the accommodationist policy received its strongest support from U.N. Ambassador Andrew Young,
and from the State Department's Africa Bureau, with which he was
closely associated. Consequently this policy position came to be referred to as either "Africanist" or "regionalist." Although having an
important impact on policy, the Africanist tendency was not universally accepted or always consistently applied by President Carter and
his advisors. Another, and contrary, theme was also in evidence—one
that viewed an increasingly assertive Soviet Union as the primary
problem for the United States in Africa and thus the proper target of
policy.

Actions that reflected this latter tendency included certain dramatic
statements by the president and his national security advisor, Zbigniew Brzezinski, warning of the threat of Soviet expansion in Africa.[11]
The reaction to the 1978 Shaba rebellion against President Mobutu's
regime in Zaire is another example.[12] The Carter administration
chose to define what many Africanists consider instability produced
by a combination of ethnic conflict, economic collapse, and political
corruption as an instance of Soviet expansionism. Moreover, Washington's response to the Shaba rebellion was to provide U.S. assistance
to a French military intervention in support of the Mobutu regime.
Yet another example was the unwillingness of the Carter administration to officially recognize the Soviet-Cuban-backed government of
Angola, despite such action by all of America's allies. Because the
tendency that shaped these kinds of policies was primarily concerned

with the global political balance between the United States and the USSR, observers labeled it "globalist." While within the Carter administration this globalist perspective is usually associated with the views of Zbigniew Brzezinski and the National Security Council that he headed, it is not clear that officials of the Africa Bureau had completely abandoned globalist views.

The inclusion of both regionalist and globalist tendencies within the Carter administration undermined the credibility and longevity of the accommodationist policy toward Southern Africa. It prevented the emergence of a coherent justification for such a policy. Without a clear and forcefully articulated rationale to support it the policy of accommodation was a vulnerable target to attacks during the 1980 presidential election campaign. The Carter "Africanists" were criticized by Reagan partisans, both before and after the election, for being insensitive to the need to protect U.S. national interests and America's position of power within the global system. Their policy for Southern Africa was pictured as placing African interests above American interests and consequently as having failed to check the real and potential spread of Soviet power into Southern Africa.[13]

The Reagan Administration Policies: A Return to Containment?

The election of Ronald Reagan appears to presage a sharp alteration in United States policy. The new administration has defined Southern Africa as a region in which the activity of the Soviet Union threatens vital strategic and economic interests of the United States, and in which Soviet advances during the past half-decade have undermined the stature of the United States as a global power. It has signalled that henceforth the impact of regional events on the East-West power balance will be the primary consideration in shaping its policy. Although various members of the Reagan policy elite will, of course, differ on details, the basic thrust of the new administration's foreign policy in Southern Africa, as well as elsewhere, is an intention to break with the accommodationist policy pursued under President Carter and return to the traditional postwar American strategy of containing the Soviet Union worldwide.

The fundamental issue that this intention raises is whether a foreign policy paradigm developed in response to the global realities of the 1950s offers reasonable policy guidelines for the world of the

1980s. The debate between regionalists and globalists over Southern African policy poses the central questions that must be addressed in respect to this basic issue. 1) Does radical political change in the region *necessarily* threaten U.S. interests and enhance the position of the Soviet Union, or does the complexity of regional affairs defy definition in simple East-West terms? and 2) Can a global containment policy, one that responds to regional affairs primarily in terms of their perceived impact on the East-West balance, be successfully made operational in the contemporary context, or do situational constraints render such a policy counterproductive?

National Interest and U.S. Foreign Policy

The purpose of any foreign policy is to protect and further some national interest. Since 1975, when the large-scale involvement of the Soviet Union in Angola began, the American policy elite has been concerned with the potential threat to three U.S. interests in Southern Africa. "The stakes in the southern Africa power game . . . are breathtaking," write two prominent commentators on international affairs, "control of the most concentrated mineral wealth anywhere in the world on land; and control of the oil sea lane from the Persian Gulf. . . ."[14] This typical statement of the problem alludes to two of these interests: the economic interest in access to strategic minerals, and a military interest in the security of the sea lanes.

The third interest that Soviet activity in Southern Africa is seen to threaten involves the credibility of America's stature as a global power. While there are other interests of the United States in Southern Africa—a diplomatic interest in obtaining support through votes at the United Nations, and a "moral" interest in the existence of political systems that do not trample on human rights—it is threats to economic and military interests, and to global credibility, that dominate current concern and discussion in respect to Southern Africa. It is these latter matters that are seen as vital or strategic in that they have a direct impact upon the well-being of the United States as a nation. Thus they are the matters toward which foreign policy ought properly to be addressed. What are these interests, are they threatened by the Soviet Union's presence in Southern Africa, and what type of U.S. policy can best protect them?

U.S. Military-Strategic Interests in Southern Africa

The conception of a U.S. military-strategic stake in Southern Africa involves, primarily, a concern with possible Soviet access to naval bases in the area. Because the supertankers carrying the bulk of Western petroleum imports from the Persian Gulf are too large to navigate the Suez Canal, most of the oil bound for Europe and the U.S. travels south through the Indian Ocean, passing around the Cape of Good Hope into the Atlantic. Consequently, the security of these oil shipping lanes is of vital importance to the West. The possibility that the Soviet navy might obtain basing facilities in South Africa, and (to a lesser extent) in Mozambique, is viewed with great alarm by some, who see such bases as providing the means for the interdiction of the "Cape Route." Thus access to basing rights in Southern Africa is viewed as giving the Soviets the military means to rapidly apply an economic stranglehold on the Western alliance. As David Rees puts it in *Conflict Studies 77:*

> For nearly two hundred years the critical strategic importance of the Cape to the Western trading system has been generally recognized. . . . In the age of the Cape Oil Route, the strategic significance of the best intermediary position between Europe and India is even further enhanced. . . . Consolidation of Soviet influence in South Africa would almost certainly be the penultimate stage in the economic strangulation of the West. . . . South Africa's strategic integrity is thus clearly vital for the defence and even the survival of the West.[15]

Transposed to the political level, the Cape Route Doctrine defines radical transformation among the states of Southern Africa as a threat to the U.S. and the West, since such transformations are assumed to greatly increase the likelihood of Soviet access to military facilities. The specific policy implication of greatest significance that flows from this logic is that the United States must put aside whatever moral, or human rights, reservations it may have regarding the domestic arrangements within South Africa, in order to help insure the survival of a reliable regime in Pretoria. At present this means, at the very least, avoiding actions that would encourage or assist radical destabilization in the country, and in the long run it means a willingness to assist the white minority government should it be threatened by an insurgency supported by the Soviet Union.[16]

Such a policy will certainly have ancillary costs of a diplomatic and economic nature, but if a strategic threat is posed within the framework of the Cape Route Doctrine the payment of considerable costs can be justified to protect the vital oil lifeline. The problem, however, is not with absorbing costs to protect vital interests, but with the validity of the Cape Route Doctrine as a basis for policy. Does the doctrine point to a valid threat? Careful analysis of the political, military/technical, and strategic suppositions upon which the Cape Route Doctrine is based reveals that it is hopelessly flawed, and that the significance of Southern Africa as a base for interdicting the oil lanes ranges from marginal to nonexistent.

While military/technical flaws are the most significant in undermining the Cape Route Doctrine as a basis for U.S. policy toward Southern Africa, its political flaws are also worthy of some comment. Its core political notion is that a radical regime coming to power in Africa with aid from the Soviet Union will as a matter of course be so subject to Soviet influence that it will allow its ports to be used as bases for offensive naval operations against the West. This view discounts almost entirely the nationalism which is, after all, the primary political orientation of the African movements that have been assisted by the Soviets. Moreover, it overlooks entirely the instrumental aspect of the link between these nationalist movements and their Soviet supporters. It is precisely because the Soviet Union was willing and able to supply material support for African nationalism in Southern Africa that the "radical" movements and regimes value their ties with the Russians.

To view the political parties that now rule in Angola, Mozambique, and Zimbabwe, or the SWAPO guerrillas operating in Namibia, as Communist satellites created by Moscow, tied to the Soviet Union by a vision that the USSR is a model for their own country's development, and thus effectively little more than Soviet puppets, distorts reality beyond all recognition. On the contrary, considerations of domestic and foreign politics make these regimes especially concerned with projecting an image of self-reliance and sovereignty. Nothing undermines such an image more effectively than the establishment by a foreign state of a large and permanent military installation.

The empirical evidence is far more consistent with the view that the radical transformation of Southern Africa has brought into existence regimes with a strong nationalist orientation concerned with guarding their own autonomy than it is with the view that these regimes are products of Soviet subversion which once in power will be Moscow's agents. No Soviet military or naval facilities have been constructed in Mozambique or Angola during the years of their independence; the heads of state of both countries have publicly stated their intentions to stay clear of military bloc politics; and the government of Zimbabwe would not even permit the USSR to open an embassy in Salisbury until ten months after independence.

To point to the erroneous nature of the assumption that radical regimes will automatically make their territory available for Soviet military purposes is not to argue the reverse; that such regimes will never enter into a military arrangement with the USSR. Under circumstances in which a regime finds itself highly vulnerable to attack by hostile and more powerful neighbors the dictates of survival may well suggest a strategy of close association with a militarily potent patron-state. Such an association would then be seen as consistent with, rather than a violation of, a nationalist commitment.

Such a dynamic can be seen at work in Southern Africa, where military raids by white-ruled states on their African-ruled neighbors led to increased military association between the Soviet Union and both Zambia and Mozambique. In the former case, persistent raids by the Rhodesian military on bases of the Zimbabwe African People's Union (ZAPU) within Zambian territory, culminating on Easter weekend 1979 in their dramatic daylight attack on ZAPU headquarters in Lusaka, Zambia's capital city, led that country to negotiate for and eventually sign a military assistance pact with the Soviet Union.[17] A raid by the South African military on the African National Congress headquarters in Mozambique in February 1981 was followed soon after by a visit of four Soviet warships at the port of Maputo. In both cases it was the revelation of their utter inability to cope with external attack that led these African regimes to seek a closer military relationship with the Soviets.

What is significant about these parallel events is not their magnitude in regard to constituting a military threat to the West. In this respect they are very minor developments. Rather, they are important in what they indicate about potential future trends and the dynamic which is likely to underlie them. The significant fact is that the closer military association between the two Southern African states and the Soviet Union was stimulated by a regional problem, the continuation of white rule, and the conflicts that follow from it. To interpret these events as a by-product of a global East-West conflict, as do most proponents of the Cape Route Doctrine, is to miss the nationalist dynamic in the situation.

The policy implications of these different interpretations are profound. If the Zambian, and, more importantly, the Mozambican, developments are viewed through the global East-West prism, then the policy implication is to counter the Soviet advance by closer support for and cooperation with South Africa, the one avowedly pro-Western and anti-Soviet power in the area. The opposite view is that given the regional dynamic to the Mozambique-Soviet tie such a policy will have an effect directly opposite to its intention. It will likely increase Soviet military presence in the region because Mozambique will then perceive a greater need to seek the protection of a powerful patron.

Even granting the political suppositions incorporated in the Cape Route Doctrine, its military/technical assumptions render it implausible. Assuming the "worst," that the Soviets should gain free and complete access to the Simonstown naval facility on the Cape in South Africa, would they use it to interdict Western oil supplies? This seems highly unlikely. If the Soviets are intent on stopping the flow of oil to the West there are means available that would be more effective and far less costly than implementing a naval blockade in the vastness of the Indian Ocean from Southern African bases. Bombing the Persian Gulf oil fields, seizing them by commando raid, or, most especially, blocking the narrow Strait of Hormuz at the mouth of the Persian Gulf would all halt oil suppiles more swiftly, easily, and with greater effect. Southern African bases, given their distance of nearly 6,000 miles from the Persian Gulf, would be irrelevant to such operations.

Even if Soviet leaders are not persuaded by the technical deficiencies of an Indian Ocean–Cape of Good Hope blockade launched from South African ports, other considerations render such an action highly irrational from the Soviet vantage point. Important strategic considerations add to the difficulties of such an operation. To deploy their submarine fleet so as to interdict Western shipping from South African bases, the Soviets would have to accept a fundamental weakening in their navy's capacity to carry out one of its primary strategic responsibilities: to provide defense of the Soviet heartland from sea-launched nuclear attack.

This fact becomes especially clear when the notion of a Soviet move to interdict Western oil supplies is put in realistic international perspective. Since such a move would be considered a major act of war directed against all the Western industrial states, Soviet strategists would have to confront the likelihood that it would be a prelude to a major conventional (and quite possibly nuclear) war. Under such circumstances, at least two considerations would become paramount to them: (1) Europe would be a major, if not the primary, theater of any conventional war fought between the USSR and the West, and (2) since there could be no guarantee that the enemy would remain within the bounds of conventional warfare, the Soviet defense against nuclear attack must be on alert. The first consideration—the possibility of a ground war in Europe—would necessitate the deployment of Soviet naval power in the North Atlantic and Mediterranean to prevent supplies originating in the United States from reaching U.S. and allied troops.

The second consideration—the expansion of a conventional war into a nuclear conflict—enters because, however much Soviet strategists may believe that a conflict sparked by their action to interdict oil supply lines can be prevented from "going nuclear," they cannot ignore the possibility. Thus they must be concerned with deploying their navy for the defense of the Soviet heartland in the areas from which a U.S. sea-launched nuclear attack would be initiated, i.e., the Mediterranean, the North Atlantic and North Sea, and perhaps the Arabian Sea, not thousands of miles away in the Indian Ocean and off the Cape of Good Hope in search of oil tankers. Therefore, even assuming the unlikely possibility that the Soviet Union would be willing to run the grave risk of major conventional war (or even nuclear conflict) in order to interdict Western oil shipments, to attempt to do so from bases in Southern Africa would, from the Soviet vantage point, be strategically untenable. Thus, the argument that pro-Western governments in Southern Africa are vital to the security of the West because of the proximity of these areas to the oil shipping lanes cannot be sustained.

Vital Economic Interests

In contrast to the military dimension, where U.S. strategic interests turn out to be largely illusory, there can be little doubt that the United States has a very tangible and vital economic stake in Southern Africa. The United States and its allies—Western Europe and Japan—are dependent on imports for a variety of mineral resources that are essential to the production process of highly industrialized econom-

Table 1

U.S. Import Dependency on Southern Africa[a]

Mineral	% of Needs Imported	Major Southern African Supplier (% of U.S. Imp.)	Major Non-Southern African Source (% of U.S. Imports)
Chromium	90		
Chromite Ore		South Africa (35)	USSR (24)
Ferrochrome		South Africa (38)	
		Zimbabwe (20)	
Vanadium	36	South Africa (57)	USSR (8)
			Chile (28)
Antimony	52	South Africa (44)	China (18)
Platinum Group	89	South Africa (42)	USSR (26)
Manganese	98		
Ore		South Africa (9)	Gabon (36)
Ferromanganese		South Africa (30)	
Industrial diamonds	100	South Africa (81)[b]	Zaire (11)
Cobalt	97	Zambia (7)	Zaire (42)

[a] Data from different "authoritative" sources varies in some cases by as much as 10 percent. Figures presented in Tables 1 and 2 represent a mid-point in this variation.
[b] Includes diamonds reexported by Ireland, the U.K. and Belgium.

Sources: U.S. Congress, Senate, Sub-Committee on African Affairs, "Imports of Minerals From South Africa by the United States and the OECD Countries," September, 1980; U.S. Congress, House, Subcommittee on Mines and Mining, "Sub-Saharan Africa: Its Role in Critical Mineral Needs of the Western World," July 1980; U.S. Department of State, *The Trade Debate*, May 1978; U.S. Bureau of Mines, *Mineral Industries of Africa*, 1976; U.S. Department of the Interior, *Mining and Minerals Policy*, 1977; U.S. Bureau of Mines, *Commodity* Data Summaries; *Africa Confidential*, v. 18, n. 5, (1977), p. 8.

ies. In respect to these minerals Southern Africa, and especially the Republic of South Africa, possesses a major share of the world's known reserves, and produces a significant proportion of the world's supply. Tables 1 and 2 provide a general overview of the magnitude of Southern African mineral reserves, the degree of U.S. import dependence, and the significance of Southern African states as suppliers. It should be noted that the reliance of the EEC countries and Japan on imports from Southern Africa is similar.

Table 2

Southern African Reserves and Production of
"Essential" Minerals

Mineral	Major African Producer	% of World Reserves	% of World Production
Chrome	South Africa	68	34
	Rhodesia/Zimbabwe	31	23
Vanadium	South Africa	64	39
Antimony	South Africa	7	21
Platinum group	South Africa	86	46
Manganese	South Africa	41	24
Industrial diamonds	Zaire		39
	South Africa	7	17
Cobalt	Zaire	31	52
	Zambia	16	9
Uranium	South Africa	17	13

Sources: U.S. Congress, Senate, Sub-Committee on African Affairs, "Imports of Minerals From South Africa by the United States and the OECD Countries," September 1980; U.S. Bureau of Mines, Commodity Data Summaries.

It is the top four minerals listed in Table 1 that give Southern Africa, and particularly South Africa, its vital significance for the United States. These minerals have four features in common: they are essential in a core industrial activity (chromium, vanadium, and antimony are vital to the production of anti-corrosive steels, and platinum is a key element in anti-pollution technology); they are found in insufficient quantity, or not at all, in the industrial countries; there are no known feasible substitutes for them; and the only major reserves of them outside of Southern Africa are found in the USSR, with the exception of antimony, which is found in substantial quantities in China. Thus if the United States and its allies were to be cut off from access to Southern African minerals their only alternative source for these vital industrial raw materials would be two Communist countries.

This fact involves a serious twofold strategic risk. The first risk is the obvious one that a traditional rival would be in a position to withhold vital resources to achieve political ends. The second risk is less obvious, but perhaps more significant. It relates to the structure of the Soviet and Chinese economies. Since these are not export-oriented economies, government investment policies cannot be counted on to expand production of the minerals in question so as to keep pace with world demand. Consequently, there is a real danger of insufficient productive capacity to meet external demand should the industrial world become solely reliant on the Soviet Union and China for its supplies of chromite, vanadium, and antimony. This would not be the result of malevolent political design, but rather of the internal logic of the political economies of the two countries. It would seem, then, that U.S. national interest dictates continued importation of materials essential to the production of specialty steels from sources other than the planned economies, and that means from South Africa and Zimbabwe.

In sum, the complementarity between the essential ingredients of modern industrial production, on the one hand, and the unusual mineral endowment of Southern Africa, on the other, creates a very real U.S. national interest in maintaining continuous and secure access to Southern African minerals. Moreover, since the flow of minerals depends upon the continuous development of reserves, it is also necessary, from the Western point of view, that there be a continuous application of capital and technology to at least certain sectors of the region's mining industry.

POLICY IMPLICATIONS OF MINERAL DEPENDENCE

The United States thus has a national interest in continued Southern African production of essential minerals, and in access to that production. Less clear, however, are the policy implications of this fact. The conventional wisdom on the subject is that the United States should prevent radical political transformation of the political systems which control the supply of critical materials, especially when such transformations are assisted by the Soviet Union. The assumption is that the Soviets would then be in a position to deny critical minerals to the West. Accordingly, the political changes that have occurred in Southern Africa over the past several years are viewed with alarm and the need is stressed to maintain a non-radical pro-Western re-

gime in South Africa. Thus, shortly before he became Secretary of State, Alexander Haig told a subcommittee of the House of Representatives that the United States is already engaged in a "resources war" and that Southern Africa is its primary theater. He said that if "future trends, especially in Southern Africa, result in alignment with Moscow of this critical resource area, then the USSR would control as much as 90 percent" of key minerals vital to the economies of the United States, Europe, and Japan.[18] The subcommittee before which he testified concluded that "America has a vital interest in the survival of South Africa as a Western ally."[19] And, echoing the same theme, President Reagan stated in a major interview: "We cannot abandon a country [South Africa] that is strategically essential to the free world in its production of minerals we must have."[20]

Many observers on the "left" also share this perception of the threat to mineral access following radical transformation of Southern Africa. They either share the view which is currently dominant in the policy elite that radical regimes will use their resources as a political weapon in order to undermine the Western political economy, or presume that such regimes will adopt economic strategies which seek to break their ties to the capitalist economies. Either way they see an interventionist strategy in support of political "stability" in Southern Africa as consistent with the interests of the U.S. capitalist system. Liberals too see a threat to U.S. economic interests in the political conflicts surrounding the South African system. Agreeing that the United States has a vital stake in access to South Africa's minerals, but unwilling either to call for support of the status quo or to accept a loss of these interests in the future, they favor strong efforts to undermine the present South African regime so as to ingratiate the United States with the African government that would presumably come to power there.

It can also be argued, however, that all of these perspectives are erroneous because they are based on a fallacious proposition: that radical political transformation in Southern Africa will jeopardize the West's access to essential minerals. Despite its nearly universal acceptance, neither logic nor experience supports such a notion.

Let us examine the situation with regard to the most important case in economically strategic terms—that of South Africa—and let us assume the "worst," i.e., that a radical movement backed by the Soviet Union will take power from the present minority government.

One of the primary and fundamental structural aspects of the South African economic system is the production of minerals for export. The mining sector is significant not only in terms of its contribution to GDP (contributing approximately 18 percent) and employment, but also because the export of a large proportion of its product earns the necessary foreign reserve to finance the essential importation of technology and of industrial and consumer goods. No South African government, however radical, could afford to forego the revenue earned by mineral exports, and the only significant market for South African minerals is the United States and its allies.* Thus any government in power in South Africa, whatever its ideological slant, would be locked into selling its industrial raw materials to the West just as the West is locked into buying them.

This would be especially true for a radical African regime, which would almost inevitably, as in Zimbabwe, attempt to satisfy the social welfare demands of the population to a greater degree than does South Africa's present minority government. The resources to pay an enlarged welfare bill—for education, health facilities, housing, and the like—would have to come out of overall economic expansion, and given the nature of the South African economy such as expansion would entail an increase in export earnings as one of its crucial elements. Thus a radical regime in South Africa, interested in increasing its foreign reserve flow, would be motivated to *expand* the export of its minerals and not the reverse.

This has implications for government policy in the area of foreign capital and technology as well. The domestic need to increase mineral export earnings and thus to maintain and even increase mining production, combined with the need to expand overall industrial production as a basis for increasing welfare and employment, would place a radical regime in South Africa in the position of seeking external capital, technology, and management resources. Even the present economic system, controlled by the dominant white minority, relies heavily on external capital and technology. How much more reliant would a new regime be—having to answer to a much larger support base and therefore more earnestly in need of economic expansion? This external dependence would be not only for capital and technol-

*Gold dominates the South African mining sector with respect to contribution to GNP, employment, and revenue earned. However, for over a decade the relative position of non–gold mining in all of these categories has been steadily increasing (see Republic of South Africa, Department of Statistics, *South African Statistics* [annual]).

ogy, but also for management and technical know-how, as a black government sought to remove economic control from the old dominant minority. Since the Soviet Union demonstrates neither the capability nor the willingness to take on the task of subsidizing an economy like South Africa's (as it has the less developed and less sophisticated Cuban economy), there would simply be no alternative open to a new government of South Africa but to turn to the West for the supply of needed capital, technology, and management.

The above argument applies with equal—if not greater—force to the other mineral-rich countries of the Southern African region. Angola, Mozambique, Zambia, and Zimbabwe each require access to external capital and technology if their ambitions in respect to economic development are to be realized. All except Mozambique already have significant mineral and mining sectors, and Mozambique has plans to create one. In Angola, petroleum exports are reported to supply up to 80 percent of foreign reserve earnings and over 60 percent of total government revenue.[21] In Zambia, copper exports are the base of the economy and, indirectly, of the political regime as well. The mining sector in 1980 contributed fully 90 percent to export earnings, 30 percent to government revenue, and 20 percent to GNP.[22] Zimbabwe with its more diversified economy relies less heavily on mineral exports overall, but the minerals sector generates more income than any other sector. Ninety percent of Zimbabwe's mineral production is exported.[23]

Given the contribution of the mining sector to foreign reserves, to government revenue, to employment, and to Gross National Product—and given the development and welfare goals pursued by African governments—there is simply no way that the countries of Southern Africa can forego selling their minerals abroad. And the only substantial customers available are found in the industrial West.

The case regarding the compatibility of African radicalism and Western economic interests does not rest solely on the structural logic presented above. An examination of the policies adopted by "Marxist" governments in Southern Africa reveals the empirical reality of this logic and further exposes the questionable character of an automatic linkage between radicalism and Soviet influence on the one hand, and secession of economic intercourse with the West on the other. The governments of Angola, Zimbabwe, and Mozambique have sought to expand their minerals production, to encourage direct private foreign investment by multinational corporations, and have entered into joint-venture agreements with Western firms. In other words, their policies in respect to relations with Western economic interests look very much like those followed by African countries that lack the ideological commitments and external ties of these "Marxist" states.

Angola is the litmus test of the notion that the expansion of Soviet influence in Southern Africa threatens U.S. and Western economic interests, and particularly their access to minerals. The Soviet and Cuban presence is far greater in Angola than elsewhere in the region. With some 20,000 Cuban troops still in the country, the existence and survival of the current regime owes a good deal to that presence. This does not, however, greatly affect Angola's relationship with Western economic interests. Reliance upon Soviet and Cuban military and technical assistance has coincided in fact with an emphatic pursuit of a policy of economic nonalignment.

From its very outset in 1976, Angola's MPLA government declared its intention to seek foreign capital involvement in its economy, particularly in respect to developing its rich mineral endowment of oil, diamonds, iron ore, copper, lead, cobalt, silver, and uranium.[24] These intentions have been reinforced by government delegations traveling in Europe and the United States and by the promulgation of investment laws whose terms for the private foreign investor compare quite favorably with those available elsewhere in Africa.[25] There have been talks with nearly a dozen U.S. and Western European oil companies concerning the opening of a large area of Angola's coastline to oil exploration.[26] During 1979 oil prospecting agreements were signed with Elf-Aquitaine (France), Total (France), Petrogal (the Portuguese national oil company), and Texaco.[27]

Gulf Oil, which has traditionally dominated oil production in Angola, has worked out an amicable working relationship with Angola's Marxist government. Soon after the civil war of 1975–1976 Gulf had production back up to prewar levels and the export sales of its petroleum were providing the majority of Angola's foreign exchange and government revenues. The American company and the Angolan government successfully negotiated a partial nationalization of the Gulf facilities, which left Gulf with a 49 percent equity stake.[28] This represents a larger foreign equity involvement than is permitted in the minerals sector by other more "conservative" African governments such as Nigeria and Zambia. While current U.S. security doctrine posits a Soviet threat to American economic interests in Angola, firms from Europe, Brazil, Japan, and the United States itself compete to expand their presence in the country. The fact that the U.S. government has refused to open diplomatic relations with the MPLA government, while all U.S. allies have done so, would appear to be a greater impediment to American economic interests than is Marxism, or Soviet and Cuban influence.

The ultimate irony in regard to the Soviet/Cuban threat to American economic interests in Angola lies in the fact that Cuban troops have provided security for the sixty-man expatriate crew at the Gulf facility, protecting them from a local insurgent group that seeks autonomy for the Cabinda enclave in which the facilities are located. Not surprisingly, the realities of the Angolan situation are perceived quite differently by American companies "on the ground" than by the "globalists" operating from Washington. "The surface indications aren't always as real as they seem," a senior Gulf executive told the *Wall Street Journal.* "The Angolans adopted a pragmatic approach toward us. . . . They're interested in seeing their resources developed and want the best technology and services."[29]

This evidence on the structure of the Southern African economies, and the related content of government policy, contradicts the notion of a simple inverse relationship between Soviet-supported radical regimes and U.S. economic interests. While fundamental transformation in a country's political arrangements might well create a transition period of reduced mineral production, a farsighted program of Western stockpiling, some of which already exists, could meet this difficulty. The Critical Materials Stockpiling Act of 1946 provides the authority for government stockpiles in the United States. In 1976 the president approved new guidelines which call for stockpiles of critical materials to cover three years' use.[30] There are indications that the Reagan administration is committed to this type of program. With this protection of immediate vital economic interests, there seems little reason to fear they will be threatened by the expansion of Soviet influence in Southern Africa.

The "Psychological" Concern for the U.S. Image as a Global Power

The public debate over U.S. policy in Southern Africa is couched in terms of oil sea lanes and critical materials; that is, in terms of threats to certain tangible interests. But during three successive presidential administrations policymakers have been concerned with another kind of threat emanating from Southern Africa. The ease with which the Soviets and Cubans have expanded their role in the region, especially in Angola, is viewed by many as a threat to the credibility of America's determination to act as a global power. Since the subject of this concern is the manner in which the United States is *perceived* by others, this "credibility problem" might be considered a threat to a psychological interest.

Speaking before a Senate Committee in support of U.S. assistance for one side in the Angolan civil war, then–Secretary of State Henry Kissinger spelled out this concern about America's image of determination and resolve:

> America's modest direct strategic and economic interests *are not the central issue. The question is whether America maintains the resolve to act responsibly as a great power.* . . . A stable relationship with the Soviet Union . . . will be achieved only if Soviet lack of restraint carries the risk of counteraction. The consequences [of inaction] may well be far-reaching and substantially more painful than the course we have recommended.[31]

What worried the Secretary of State about the lack of a direct U.S. response to the Soviets in Angola was the erosion of the very core of the global containment strategy that had guided U.S. foreign policy since the 1950s. The ultimate purpose of this strategy was to avoid a situation where a threat to vital U.S. interests led to a direct confrontation with the Soviet Union and thus made nuclear war likely. The mechanism for avoiding such a confrontation was convincing the USSR of America's will to defend its interests through forcefully countering the expansion of Soviet influence outside the USSR and Eastern Europe. Thus the U.S. would demonstrate its will and determination, the credibility of its power, in "peripheral" areas where the interests of the superpowers were minimal and thus costs and risks were assumed to be correspondingly low.

Failure to demonstrate U.S. credibility in the face of the spread of Soviet influence is seen within this security perspective as leading an inherently expansionist USSR to an increasingly bold foreign policy. Thus, Alexander Haig, operating within this perspective, states that "if the United States had acted in Angola, the Russians would not have acted so brazenly in Ethiopia, Yemen, and Afghanistan."[32]

Moreover, once inaction has undermined the Soviet belief in America's will to use its power, so the argument goes, the USSR would eventually be tempted to challenge some vital U.S. interest, and a direct and dangerous confrontation would ensue.[33] This is the meaning of Secretary Kissinger's warning to the Senate in 1976 that inaction in Angola would lead to "far-reaching and substantially more painful" consequences.[34]

Reagan's Priorities in Southern Africa

Concern with the effect of Soviet involvement in Southern Africa on America's military and economic interests and on the credibility of its stature as a global power has, to a greater or lesser extent, characterized the four administrations of Presidents Nixon, Ford, Carter, and Reagan. As already noted, what is distinctive about the early period of the Reagan administration is the intensity of its anxiety over all three elements of the interest "triad"—security of the sea lanes, access to strategic minerals, and maintaining credibility as a global power—and also the explicitness of its commitment to containment as the cornerstone of its policy toward the region. While various members of the administration may differ on specific tactical questions, there appears to be overwhelming consensus that limiting the Soviet role is the top priority for U.S. policy in Southern Africa, as elsewhere.

Global Containment Strategy: The Implications

At the most general level, applying a global containment strategy to Southern Africa entails formulating specific policies for the region in terms of the East-West conflict ("expansion of Soviet influence"). It also involves shaping the American relationship with individual states in respect to that primary consideration. Considerable evidence exists that an important, if not dominant, element within the Reagan foreign policy establishment views this posture as requiring a significant shift in policy toward Angola, Namibia, and South Africa.

Angola is central to the Reagan containment strategy because to many in the foreign policy elite the absence of an effective counter to the Soviet/Cuban involvement there in 1975–76 represents a major failure for the United States as a global power, with ominous implications for the expansion of Soviet power elsewhere.[35] Moreover, the continuing presence of some 20,000 Cuban troops in Angola is seen as a glaring symbol and reminder of that failure. In contrast to the Carter administration which, however inconsistently and unclearly, sought an accommodation with what it viewed as a *fait accompli* in Angola, the Reagan administration apparently seeks to "roll back" the Cuban and Soviet presence there.[36]

Documents released to the *New York Times* in May 1981 revealed an intention by the Reagan administration to force the withdrawal of Cuban troops from Angola and the inclusion of a pro-Western element, UNITA (the largest political opposition movement), within a new coalition government through a combination of economic blandishment and political destabilization.[37] An official memorandum, attributed to Assistant Secretary of State Chester Crocker, stated that the Soviet-backed government of Angola would be told that Washington could help it economically but only after "the Cubans leave and they cut a deal with Savimbi" (the pro-Western leader of UNITA). "If they won't play," states the memorandum, "we have other options."[38]

The other options refer to increasing assistance to the UNITA insurgents, who have an ethnic base in the southern third of Angola, and who have managed to maintain some level of armed resistance to central government control during the last four years.[39] Such assistance could be provided directly, or through third parties. The South Africans, who are already supporting UNITA, could be encouraged (and helped) to increase their military involvement in Angola. Either way the cost of Cuban/Soviet involvement in Angola would be increased both for the external powers and the Angolan government itself. Even if the effort to dislodge the Cubans failed, the price of Soviet "intervention" would be raised and the U.S. determination to counter Soviet "advances" will have been demonstrated. Thus, the credibility of the United States would be enhanced.

This Reagan strategy was concretely manifested in the administration's request that Congress lift the Clark Amendment, which prohibits U.S. military assistance to Angolan political factions, and by its announcement of a willingness to have senior officials meet with UNITA leader Jonas Savimbi.[40] Neither of these steps commit the Reagan administration to any concrete action. Nevertheless, they are signals to the region of the administration's thinking and likely intentions.

On Namibia, the application of global containment also implies a departure from the approach followed by the previous administration. The Carter administration sponsored a cooperative effort by the United States, Canada, Britain, France, and West Germany (the "Western Contact Group"), the Front Line States, and Nigeria to secure the implementation of a United Nations-sponsored framework for ending South African control of the territory and preparing the way for it to become an independent state. While this effort seemed to provide the best hope of ending the armed conflict over Namibia, the plan for U.N.-supervised elections had two basic flaws from the perspective of the new Reagan administration. One was that it appeared to necessitate increasing the pressure on the South African government, something that runs counter to another aspect of Reagan policy. The second flaw was that SWAPO, the Soviet-backed insurgent movement, was likely to emerge with a clear majority and thus unlimited power from U.N.-supervised elections based upon one-man, one-vote. Through the prism of East-West conflict the United Nations plan for Namibia appeared to be a mechanism for Soviet expansion through peaceful means.

The Reagan administration therefore sought an alternative formula for Namibian independence which embodied at least two key elements: agreement prior to an election on a constitution containing political guarantees for the white minority and the anti-SWAPO political parties; and a prohibition on the use of Namibian territory by movements seeking to overthrow the South African regime.[41] This formula could have the twin effect of meeting the South African government's concerns over security, thus reducing its resistance to Namibian independence, and of limiting SWAPO control within an independent Namibia.

In respect to South Africa, the Reagan administration has publicly stated its intent to pursue closer and more friendly ties than those that existed during the Carter administration. According to Assistant Secretary of State for African Affairs Chester Crocker, "the political relationship between the United States and South Africa has now arrived at a crossroads of perhaps historic significance." After twenty years of worsening relations, "the possibility may exist for a more positive and reciprocal relationship between the two countries based upon shared strategic concerns in southern Africa, our recognition that the government of P. W. Botha [the Prime Minister] represents a unique opportunity for domestic change, and willingness of the Reagan administration to deal realistically with South Africa."[42] The remarks of the Assistant Secretary reveal the two basic ways in which the administration is thinking of altering U.S. policy. First, a shared concern with the "strategic threat" in Southern Africa posed by the Soviet Union will become the basis for a "reciprocal" relationship between Washington and Pretoria. Concretely this would manifest itself by relaxing trade restrictions imposed by previous administrations, renewing U.S. cooperation in the South African nuclear energy program, and exchanging military attachés.[43] Moreover, a sense of shared security threat could manifest itself in military cooperation of various kinds, such as U.S. use of South Africa's naval facility at Simonstown and of its substantial communications monitoring capacity in the South Atlantic. Second, the new administration has appeared far more receptive than its predecessor to South African claims about its commitment to genuine reform in the apartheid system. The Reagan administration posture, articulated by the president himself as well as by his assistant secretary of state, is that Pretoria's commitment to change is substantial and genuine and that it should be encouraged through the relaxation of external pressures.[44] Thus some dramatic new domestic reform in South Africa could well provide the context for the Reagan administration to implement a reciprocal relationship between Washington and Pretoria.

Beyond shifts in policies toward Angola, Namibia, and South Africa, the specifics toward which U.S. policy is leaning in Southern Africa are less clear. The fundamental premise that U.S. relations with individual states will be shaped by Washington's perceptions of how their actions affect the East-West balance will probably determine the dispensation of American economic assistance. The provision of aid will probably be "tuned" to the willingness of a given state to help the U.S. "resist Soviet expansion." A sample of this type of policy may well be found in the contrasting stance which has been taken in respect to economic assistance for Mozambique and Zimbabwe. In mid-March 1981, the administration cut off U.S. food aid to Mozambique in retaliation for its expulsion of six U.S. diplomats on charges of spying. Washington publicly interpreted these expulsions as the work of Cuban advisors, and thus this practically unprecedented cut in food assistance can be interpreted as an especially firm countermeasure to a display of Soviet/Cuban influence. In contrast, one week later, the administration announced backing for an effort to triple

U.S. economic assistance to Zimbabwe. Significantly, the political leadership in Zimbabwe has not been reluctant to show its displeasure and distrust in respect to Moscow for having supported its rivals during the Rhodesian war.

Although Washington may view the central problem in Southern Africa as Soviet intervention and expansion, there are obviously other actors with an interest in the situation who may see things differently. And, their perspectives may affect both the ability of the U.S. to implement a policy based upon global containment, and the costs of doing so. In other words, the regional context in which policy is implemented cannot be ignored since ultimately it will determine the policy's costs, feasibility, and likelihood of success.

The Regional Context

In the intraregional politics of sub-Saharan Africa one issue has emerged upon which there is unanimous agreement: the need to complete the process of removing white minority rule from the continent. Continent-wide attention is thus focused on the last vestiges of this rule, first in Namibia, and then, most importantly, in South Africa. The histories of colonialism and racial rule have made this a natural issue around which the otherwise divided states of Africa can unite in common cause. Indeed, the symbol of African identity in world affairs has become *active* opposition to white supremacy in Southern Africa as a first priority of foreign policy. A country like Nigeria, which aspires to a leadership role in continental affairs and also has a position of weight in international forums, seeks to establish its legitimacy to "speak for Africa" through its tough stance on South Africa's apartheid regime.

The implications of this fact for the United States are twofold. First, a policy that can be interpreted as lending support to the current political arrangements in South Africa and Namibia will be viewed as opposed to African interests. Indeed, given the sensitivity of African states on the issue of South Africa, a neutral stance would not be sufficient; in order to be perceived as a friend in sub-Saharan Africa, a posture of active opposition to the apartheid regime is probably required. This reality has not been altered by Pretoria's recent promises of domestic change. The states of sub-Saharan Africa completely discount these claims. They point out accurately the fact that these recent "reforms" are not directed toward the type of political restructuring that would significantly diminish the strength of white supremacy. In any case, African states view continued pressure on Pretoria as an essential ingredient to produce such politically significant reform.

To argue, as National Security Adviser Richard Allen has, that the United States can and should have "normal" relations with South Africa while at the same time disapproving of their apartheid system, just as it has good relations with other countries whose domestic arrangements it does not admire (e.g., China, Bulgaria, etc.),[45] misses the point entirely. The issue is not the relationship between America's morality and its foreign policy, although this point is often made, but rather that the countries of Africa are making U.S. relations with South Africa the touchstone of their relations with America. Like it or not, the United States is in a position where it must choose. Thus, a policy of repairing the "damage" in Washington-Pretoria relations that resulted from Carter administration policy, as the Reagan administration appears to desire, would have a very serious negative effect on U.S. relations with the rest of the African continent.

The second implication of the primacy of the minority-rule issue is that the definition of regional political conflict and change in East-West terms will have limited credibility within Africa. African states will evaluate local political movements as well as the actions of outsiders—be they Cubans, Russians, or Americans—in terms not only of aid provided, but more particularly in respect to their role in furthering the demise of local white rule, especially in its real and symbolic bastion, the Republic of South Africa.

This is the lesson of the U.S. experience with Soviet and Cuban involvement in the 1976 Angolan civil war. Once the South African government became an active backer of the UNITA faction, ultimately sending the South African Defense Force into Angola against the MPLA, the Angolan civil war came to be seen as part of the overall struggle against white minority rule, and the Cuban/Soviet assistance to the MPLA was viewed in that light. Consequently, what the United States chose to call aggression, intervention, and imperialism was accorded a significant modicum of legitimacy by many African states. The foreign minister of Kenya, regarded as among the most pro-American African countries, commented in mid-1978: "The Cubans have changed the history of Africa. . . . On the question of racial subjugation in southern Africa, no one can convince me that the Azanians [Black South Africans], Zimbabweans, and Namibians should not get assistance from elsewhere if they are denied assistance by the West."[46]

The lesson in the Angolan conflict of 1976 is directly relevant to the policy choices facing the United States in 1982. The MPLA is recognized as the legitimate government of Angola by practically all African states, despite the Cuban troops there. Its support for SWAPO, which uses Angolan territory to launch operations against South African troops inside Namibia, places it at the very forefront of the continuing fight against white rule in Southern Africa. In contrast, the UNITA opposition, because of its initial collaboration with South Africa in 1976 and because it has continued to rely on logistical and material support from that source, is generally considered to be an agent of the South African regime. For the U.S. government to provide support for UNITA, or even threaten to do so, in order to defend self-determination and counter the Soviet/Cuban presence, would be counterproductive. Within Africa, the United States would be perceived as destabilizing a legitimate African government, as striking a severe blow at the effort to remove Namibia from South African control, and as aiding South African domination of Southern Africa generally. In contrast, the Cubans and the Soviets would once again be viewed as defenders of Africa's interests and as opponents of those who practice racial rule.

There is little doubt that should external assistance to UNITA be increased significantly the size and importance of the Cuban/Soviet presence in Angola will also increase, and that this will be approved of by most African states. Moreover, barring a direct U.S. or South African military intervention in Angola, the likelihood of UNITA's dislodging the Cuban force there is very slim. Consequently, the provision of assistance to UNITA in the name of stopping Soviet/Cuban expansionism, to which the new Reagan administration appears, in principle, to be inclined, can be expected to have rather paradoxical results. Its consequence is likely to be an increased role and status for the Soviets and Cubans in Africa, while the influence and standing of the United States are diminished.

A sub-Saharan Africa embittered against the United States because of its "global" policies toward Southern Africa would have *real*, not just symbolic, costs for the United States. The most obvious potential cost is in terms of access to Africa's minerals, and particularly its petroleum. It is often pointed out that Nigeria is second to Saudi Arabia in supplying oil to the United States, and that Nigerian leaders have frequently hinted about using the oil weapon against countries they deem to be supporting white minority rule.[47] The earlier discussion of the structure of import dependence indicates, however, that costs to the United States are not likely to lie in the area of mineral denial. In the case of Nigeria, for example, the petroleum sector accounts for 90 percent of exports, 80 percent of federal revenues, and 25 percent of GDP.[48] The government's very ambitious economic development plans, its considerable social overhead expenditures, and the financing of decentralized political institutions within its elaborate federal system all require maintaining oil exports at a high level. While Nigeria may be America's second largest supplier of petroleum, the U.S. market also happens to represent Nigeria's single largest customer, accounting for some 40 percent of her oil exports. Except under very unusual circumstances—e.g., war in the Persian Gulf—Nigeria could not easily and rapidly find alternative customers, and thus a boycott of the United States would wreak havoc on both its economic and political system. Consequently, public political rhetoric to the contrary, Nigeria is highly *unlikely* to cut its oil supply to the United States in reaction to U.S. foreign policy.

There are, however, less self-damaging actions that Nigeria could and likely would take. In periods of international oil shortage, preference could be given to others. More significantly, American companies might well be discriminated against in the offer of investment opportunities and in the award of lucrative contracts for construction, engineering, and equipment supplies which are a part of Nigeria's oil-fed industrialization effort. The big winners here would be the European and Japanese multinational corporations which are the main competitors to the U.S. firms. While Nigeria is the single most important market in Black Africa, this type of undermining of America's competitive business position can be generalized throughout sub-Saharan Africa should the continent become embittered toward the United States. This is where the long-term economic cost of a "globalist" policy toward Southern Africa may lie.

By 1970 the United States had become significantly import dependent, with negative trade balances not only for unprocessed minerals but also for basic manufactures. This trend has continued and is unlikely to be reversed.[49] In order to pay for a growing volume of required imports, it must cultivate export markets and generate revenue inflows from foreign investments and service contracts. In a world of intense competition between U.S. companies and their European and Japanese counterparts, a foreign policy that ignores the repercussions of diplomatic positions on export markets and investment access places the long-term economic strength of the United States in jeopardy. The kind of foreign policy that flows from the global containment perspective seems particularly insensitive to and thus inappropriate for this reality, at least as far as Africa is concerned.

An Africa embittered toward the United States would be costly in diplomatic as well as economic terms. Experience suggests a number of areas in which U.S. interests have required cooperation on the part of the states of the region. Angola, for example, has played an important role in furthering two U.S. interests in Southern Africa. It clamped down upon the Zaire insurgents which twice invaded Shaba Province from its territory and brought the U.S.-backed Mobutu regime in Zaire to the brink of collapse; and it has used its leverage over swapo to help bring the Namibian conflict toward a negotiated end. Similarly, Nigeria, Tanzania, and Mozambique, along with Angola, offered vital cooperation to the United States and Britain in bringing the Rhodesian war to a negotiated settlement, which, in turn, dealt a significant blow to the expansion of Soviet influence in the region.

These efforts were based upon a degree of trust that the Carter administration was able to establish for the United States in Africa. Should the Reagan administration reverse the policies upon which this trust was based in order to "confront the Soviet Union," it is extremely hard to imagine that the requisite cooperation will be forthcoming in the future.

Finally, and perhaps most important, the commitment of the United States to the Rapid Deployment Force (rdf) in the Indian Ocean so as to provide security in the Persian Gulf requires military cooperation from at least several states on the East African coast. In the kind of embittered atmosphere which a "globalist policy" switch in Southern Africa would create such cooperation would become highly problematic. Even in so pro-Western a state as Kenya, a U.S. policy that was identified with supporting racial rule in Southern Africa could well generate significant domestic political pressure for the termination of the RDF-related military arrangements that have recently been negotiated. Thus the repercussions of a tilt toward South Africa could place in jeopardy a major element in America's post-1980 security system.

South Africa, U.N. Sanctions, and the United States

The question of a "globalist" tilt toward Pretoria aside, the centrality of South Africa in the dynamics of African regional politics poses a major policy dilemma for the United States and its Western allies. How can their substantial economic interdependence with South Africa be reconciled with their desire for good relations with the other states of sub-Saharan Africa? This "contradiction" in the relations of the West and Africa has increased in salience as African states, as well as anti-apartheid groups within the industrial countries, have called for the use of economic leverage as a means to force the South African regime to change. Within the United Nations African states have called for mandatory economic sanctions (a trade embargo), modeled on those imposed on Rhodesia after 1965, in order to force South Africa to accept independence for Namibia under majority rule. Once the Namibian issue is settled it is quite possible that a similar call for sanctions will be made in order to force a change in the apartheid system within South Africa itself. The United States and the European members of the Security Council have opposed economic sanctions against South Africa and they are likely to maintain that opposition in the future. Several elements of national economic and diplomatic interest dictate this position.

Mineral Dependence

As the earlier discussion of the U.S. stake in Southern Africa indicated, the United States, Western Europe, and Japan are dependent on South Africa for a number of essential industrial minerals, with chromite being the most important. Stockpiling could provide a buffer for a short disruption in supply, but experience with trade sanctions elsewhere indicates that a lengthy rather than short period of self-denial would be required. Moreover, Europe's and Japan's dependence on South African minerals goes beyond the industrially essential minerals that are both vital and cannot be obtained readily elsewhere. For example, South Africa is an important, and expanding, supplier of the world's coal. In 1979 it was the EEC's second largest coal source, accounting for 23 percent of the common market's coal imports, and it was expected soon to pass Poland and become the EEC's primary source of foreign coal.[50] Given the industrial world's effort to turn away from petroleum-based energy, and the serious questions being raised about a commitment to nuclear power, South Africa's substantial coal reserves and the technological capacity of its mining industry will increase its importance as a supplier to the industrial world. Thus, the dependence of the industrial West and Japan on minerals from South Africa makes it a matter of national interest to oppose sanctions that would prohibit trade with that country. Moreover, mineral dependence also dictates an interest in South Africa's increasing production so as to maintain supplies. Since increased production requires the application of capital and technology to the mining industry, Western economic interests would run counter to an effort that sought to deny them to South Africa's minerals sector. Moreover, South Africa's strong position as a supplier of essential minerals to the industrial countries limits the options as far as selective embargoes are concerned, because it provides means for costly countermeasures. Should mandated trade sanctions be limited to items deemed nonessential, South Africa could decide to retaliate by denying those items that are vital.

Export and Investment Stake

Although for the United States the importance of South Africa as an export market and as a site for investment is marginal relative to its overall economy, the export and investment involvement of several West European countries is substantial. In particular, Britain and West Germany are heavily involved and a cut in economic relations with South Africa would have serious repercussions on their own economies, as indicated in the next chapter.

Enforceability

The potential for an effective implementation of economic sanctions against South Africa is not high. The large number of countries and even larger number of individual firms with a significant interest in continuing business with South Africa makes it inevitable that efforts at evasion would be numerous. The experience of U.N.-mandated sanctions in Rhodesia shows that trade embargoes can be successfully circumvented for considerable periods. Given South Africa's far more extensive and sophisticated worldwide business linkages, efforts to undercut an embargo could be expected to be far more widespread. Finally, South Africa's extensive coastline means that short of a naval blockade a fully effective trade embargo is highly unlikely.

Although total effectiveness is not required to make an embargo costly to the South Africans, "leaks" would be the source of continuous diplomatic costs to the United States and its Western allies. They would be constantly placed in the position of failing to enforce or actually undermining United Nations policy, and thus would be viewed as being opposed to Africa's interests.

Economic interdependence and consequent difficulties of enforcement may make it unlikely that industrial countries will agree to formal international sanctions against South Africa, but they do not preclude the use of other forms of economic leverage. After the Soweto "uprising" of 1976 South Africa found that the terms of its access to international capital and technology markets had severely deteriorated. Under pressure from both governments and domestic political lobbies, multinational corporations and international banks became less ready than they previously had been to do business in and with South Africa. Access to goods embodying advanced technologies was also hampered as the United States and other governments expanded their definition of products with a potential military usage whose export was prohibited.

Statements and actions of South African government leaders indicated the concern with which they viewed these developments. Recognizing that international opposition to racial rule threatened to undermine their country's long-term economic future, the leaders of South Africa's ruling National Party committed themselves to changes within their domestic system and to international negotiations on Namibia. Many observers of the South African scene have exaggerated both Pretoria's willingness to give up its control over Namibia and the significance of the changes embodied in its domestic reform effort. The latter does not, for instance, alter the white minority's total domination of South Africa's political system. Recent reforms should properly be viewed as an effort to render the exercise of political domination by a racial minority more palatable to world opinion. Nevertheless, the experience of the last several years *does* show that

Pretoria is highly sensitive to leverage applied through the international economic system, and may modify its policies in response.[51] Although it is doubtful that any external economic leverage could, by itself, force the South African government to abandon minority control, it may produce modifications in the system whose long-term significance for change is far greater than Pretoria had originally intended. The extension of trade union rights to black workers, which occurred during 1979, and which was a response to combined domestic and external pressure, is an example of a reform whose intent was essentially conservative but whose unintended consequences for change could be substantial.[52]

An extension and refinement of policies followed by the United States and other industrial countries in the wake of Soweto may therefore offer a strategy toward South Africa which is both responsive and realistic: responsive to the concerns of sub-Saharan Africa, and to the moral standards which the West so often professes; and realistic in that it does not require states to do what historically they have rarely, if ever, done, that is, to sacrifice vital national interests for principles of morality.

This kind of strategy would involve the United States in adopting, and urging others to adopt, a variety of measures that would maintain the pressure for change on the regime in Pretoria. Such measures would include discouraging investment in or bank loans to sectors of the South African economy that are not involved in producing critical minerals; limiting the transfer of new technologies through export prohibitions on a broadly defined area of dual purpose (civilian and military) goods; encouraging the development of alternative sources for goods now imported from South Africa; and similar actions.

As an alternative to United Nations economic sanctions this type of strategy, although less dramatic, has certain advantages. First, it can be applied so as to avoid major threats to the economies of the "sanctioning" countries. This includes not only the industrial countries which depend on a South African supply of critical minerals, but also the states of Southern Africa, whose own economies apart from Angola are enmeshed with and to varying degrees dependent on the economy of South Africa. As is revealed in chapter 7 of this volume, the patterns of transportation infrastructure, labor supply, and trade in the Southern African region are such that severing their economic links with South Africa would cause the economies of Lesotho, Botswana, Swaziland, Zimbabwe, Mozambique, Malawi, Zambia, and Zaire to suffer serious short-term harm, and in some instances disastrous consequences.

A policy of general economic sanctions emanating from the United Nations would have great symbolic significance. But neither the political process nor the institutional procedures that characterize the U.N. organization are conducive to the design of flexible policy instruments. The results in the area of a sanctions mandate are predictable. Evasions will be commonplace as states which supported sanctions for symbolic reasons find that the policy does harm to themselves. In contrast to an international organization, a sovereign government can fashion strategy of economic pressure on South Africa that has the requisite flexibility to take cognizance of this potential harm to non-target states.

A policy of the U.S. government, in contrast to one emanating from the U.N., is also capable of greater nuances in respect to actions taken by South Africa. Government policies can be modified, pressures increased or relaxed, in direct response to specific actions undertaken by Pretoria. For example, pressure could be heightened if South Africa engages in military attacks on the territory of its neighbors, or intensifies its coercion against domestically based dissidents. In other words, a government-fashioned and implemented policy can focus on, constrain, or encourage specific behavior on the part of the target state, while international sanctions demand a general change which, in any case, is unlikely to occur.

A second set of advantages of a government-based strategy of economic pressure over U.N.-mandated sanctions is that the former is much less likely to galvanize a response of nationalist cohesion within the white population of South Africa. From the South African government's vantage point, the disruption that sanctions would entail is certainly worth trying to avoid, but, once imposed, sanctions create a wartime mobilization atmosphere in which nationalism is an important ingredient in dealing with, and overcoming, disruption. That is why the threat of sanctions may provide more political leverage than the sanctions themselves.

The basic point of this position regarding economic pressure on South Africa can be summarized as follows. A policy of U.N.-mandated general economic sanctions is inconsistent with the national interest of the United States and ought, therefore, to be avoided by the U.S. government. On the other hand, a U.S. government policy of economic pressures on South Africa to force change domestically and to constrain military policy externally is consistent with U.S. national interests and is practical. It ought, therefore, to be pursued.

But can such a policy meet with sufficient approval within sub-Saharan Africa to persuade the states of the region to forego their calls for sanctions within the United Nations? This is essential for a successful U.S. policy toward Southern Africa, for, should the periodic calls for U.N. sanctions continue, and should the United States continue to veto them in the Security Council (or violate them should they be mandated by a majority vote of the General Assembly), America will be symbolically identified as a friend of racial rule and an enemy of Africa, specific policies notwithstanding.

The willingness of African states to accept bilateral pressures on South Africa as an alternative to U.N. sanctions is enhanced by the reality that several African countries, especially those in the southern region, will suffer greatly should sanctions be imposed. Thus a number of African states also have a national interest in finding an alternative to U.N.-mandated general sanctions. But whether this complementarity in national interest between the United States and African states can be made operative, or whether the states of Africa opt instead for a symbolic victory in the United Nations, to the detriment of the United States, depends on their perception of the availability of a genuine alternative to sanctions. And this depends largely on the nature of U.S. foreign policy toward the region.

U.S. policy must involve two things to be convincing in the sub-Saharan African regional context. First, policy measures that have an impact on capital, technology, and trade flows must actually exist. Second, the United States through its actions must provide symbolic evidence of its alliance with the states of Africa in opposition to the apartheid regime in South Africa. The latter position is necessary to create and maintain the basis in trust that in turn will provide the necessary time for policy instruments to be fashioned and to have an impact.

What should be obvious is that the "globalist" orientation that is identified with the Reagan administration is singularly unsuited to the above task. Even if the specific policies that finally emerge from the transitional policy review do not in fact involve a major move to improve U.S. relations with Pretoria, the signals that have been transmitted by a variety of actions during the early months of the new administration have undermined African trust and confidence in America's commitment to assist in the demise of racial rule in Southern Africa.

Consequently, the imposition of a global containment posture on Southern Africa may well enhance the likelihood of frequent U.N. votes on sanctions. These will continuously place the United States in opposition to the countries of Africa, eroding America's diplomatic and economic position on the African continent, and enhancing the status and influence of the USSR. In other words, the result of policies that emerge from viewing Southern Africa through the prism of East-West conflict is exactly the opposite of what the policies are designed to achieve.

Political Change, Political Violence, and U.S. Policy toward South Africa

The "sanctions issue" represents an immediate, short-term, dilemma for U.S. policymakers. Another dilemma, more long-term and fundamental in nature, concerns the stance of the United States toward black insurgency within South Africa, that is, toward movements that deploy political violence in an effort to end white minority rule. The traditional U.S. position has been to condemn on moral grounds both apartheid and those who would seek to remove it by violent means, and to gear policy toward "encouraging evolutionary change." This type of posture has recently been reiterated by spokesmen for the Reagan administration. "As a democracy," writes Chester Crocker, "we cannot endorse situations or constitutions that are racist in purpose or effect; nor can we endorse the abuse of Western norms by people of whatever race dedicated to seizing or holding power through violence. . . . we must act in ways that permit the supporters of evolutionary change to gain and hold the initiative.[53]

A posture in opposition to violence and supportive of peaceful change is at first glance highly laudatory. All other things being equal, no decent and reasonable person favors violence and warfare. However, in the complex reality of South African politics it may not be tenable to maintain a position that is genuinely opposed both to white supremacy and to the political movements that would remove it by violent means. A policy that opposes political violence and revolutionary movements in South Africa in the name of "American" or "democratic" values suffers from several philosophic flaws and practical liabilities.

In the first place, the notion that America should oppose revolutionary groups in South Africa because "as a democracy, we cannot endorse the abuse of Western norms by people . . . dedicated to seizing or holding power through violence,"[54] represents a rather peculiar reading of political theory and political history. A commitment to democracy may well carry with it opposition to the use of political violence within a democratic political order, but it has no such implication with regard to systems that lack a framework for democratic participation. The South African political system denies the right of political participation to over eighty percent of its population, and sustains this situation at a high level of legally sanctioned political repression (state violence). Under such conditions, it is a strange application of democratic norms to insist that the majority of the population utilize legal means to change the system—means which are in any case legally denied to them—and to correlatively oppose the use of violence to wrest political power from the racial minority who hold it.

Because opposition to violence in a situation in which peaceful change is precluded lacks the force of logic (except within the terms of a pacifist philosophy) most of those who advocate a U.S. policy of opposition to revolutionary groups in South Africa are at pains to show that opportunities for evolutionary change do in fact exist.[55] President Reagan thus commented shortly after assuming office, "There's been a failure, for political reasons in this country, to recognize how many people, black and white, in South Africa are trying to remove apartheid, and the steps they've made. As long as there's sincere and honest effort being made . . . it would seem to me that we should be trying to be helpful. Can we take any other course?"[56] The problem with this line of reasoning is that the claim that South Africa is currently undergoing change toward significant political participation by the black majority is a highly tenuous one. While it is true that the South African government has, since 1978, both promised and implemented real changes in the apartheid system, and that its critics have been extremely reluctant to recognize or admit this, it is equally true that these changes do not in any significant way realize, or even imply, an increase in the black majority's political power or political rights within the South African system. The white government has steadfastly maintained its determination to keep the power to allocate resources in the hands of the white minority. Thus, while aspects of apartheid have certainly been modified, the issue of white supremacy has not yet been addressed in speech or action by the Botha government. Indeed, a case can be made that the reforms being initiated have the precise purpose of shoring up white supremacy in the face of external and domestic assault, not doing away with it.[57] So the assertion that the current government's pragmatism offers an opening for evolutionary change, and thus a viable and superior alternative to the use of political violence, is a rather tenuous basis for the shaping of foreign policy.

The practical implications of the above analysis are twofold. In the first place, increasing levels of political violence can be expected in the South African system in the near to medium term. This does not mean that the South African system will soon succumb to a revolutionary onslaught, as many of its opponents have been predicting for half a decade. The current organizational and military capacity of the black opposition relative to that of the South African security system makes that a very low probability in the immediate future. Nonetheless, the system is vulnerable to sabotage and other forms of sporadic political violence directed at the apartheid regime. Most observers, including South African government officials themselves, see this type of activity, particularly in the urban areas, as very likely to increase dramatically.

In the second place, such attacks on the apartheid regime will be widely supported within sub-Saharan Africa and beyond as morally and politically justified. Herein lies the long-term dilemma for the United States. A policy that is hostile to groups deploying violence against the South African government and that actively seeks to thwart the achievement of their goals, out of preference for a hypothetical and doubtfully achievable "moderate" alternative, will in effect place the United States in a position of supporting the maintenance of racial rule. This need not, of course, be the intention of the policymakers. But it will nonetheless be the result of their policy in both appearance and reality. This is especially true under circumstances in which South Africa's minority government is dealt with sympathetically and in which "destabilization" is viewed as threatening to vital Western interests.

The implication of the argument above is that, if the United States is to avoid a long-term process of estrangement in its relations with the states of Africa, with all its attendant economic and diplomatic costs, it must develop a policy posture toward South Africa that recognizes two things: (1) that increasing violence employed by revolutionary movements is the inevitable result of the structure of that country's sociopolitical system, and (2) that such movements, should they attain power, do not necessarily threaten vital U.S. interests. Such a policy posture represents a substantial departure from what has been the customary postwar American world view, but it is nevertheless consistent with both the facts of the situation and with America's long-term national interests.

Conclusion

Vital economic and military/strategic interests of the United States are threatened neither by the radical political change nor the expansion of Soviet influence that has occurred in Southern Africa during the past half decade. What would threaten U.S. interests is a foreign policy strategy that is insensitive to the dynamics of regional affairs. Global containment is such a strategy. Because it views everything through the prism of East-West conflict it distorts the nature of threats to American interests and obscures the existence of regionally based constraints on the achievement of policy objectives. A policy posture toward Southern Africa that is oriented primarily to the region as an arena of East-West confrontation will directly or indirectly align the United States with the maintenance of racial rule. The result will be a loss for the United States in terms of its diplomatic and economic position throughout sub-Saharan Africa, and a substantial gain in prestige and influence for the Soviet Union. It is hard to imagine how credibility of the United States as a global power would be enhanced in such circumstances. The demonstration of the will to use power translates into enhanced credibility only when the goals toward which power is directed are accomplished. When, however, the environment in which power is exercised is resistant to such accomplishment, credibility is undermined.

The costs attendant upon a switch to a global containment policy in Southern Africa may result in the Reagan administration's ultimately adopting the type of policy followed by its predecessor. That is, the constraints on American action inherent in the regional situation may be recognized, and the resultant policy will end up looking much like the Carter policies which the new administration has so severely criticized. While such pragmatism would be less damaging to U.S. interests than a policy which refuses to recognize the reality of a constraining environment, it would not be cost free. Globalist rhetoric will tend to undermine the confidence and trust African states have in the United States, even if actual policy diverges, since the rhetoric will raise doubts about the depth of America's commitment to these policies. Moreover, the gap between globalist rhetoric and a regionally realistic policy would indeed call into question the ability of the United States to effectively exercise its will. What is need is a strategic perspective that is adapted to contextual realities, one that avoids raising imaginary threats that cannot be countered and avoids defining tests of credibility that cannot be passed. The Southern Africa context has revealed that only by accepting a complex and variegated notion of U.S.-Soviet relations can the United States hope to mesh its policies with the pluralistic reality of regional politics and thereby maintain and expand upon its own interests.

3.

The Western European States and Southern Africa

Christopher R. Hill

Between the countries of Western Europe and those of Southern Africa exist bonds of long standing, forged by decades of political and economic interaction. The United Kingdom (here designated as Britain), Germany, and Portugal each controlled territories in that region in earlier times. Britain has particularly long and deep associations with the Republic of South Africa, whose rich mining resources and easily accessible strategic position at the foot of the continent have attracted a century of massive investment and exploitation by British and America capital. France had no colonial possessions in that part of Africa, but its long and continuing political and economic interests in West and Central Africa have assured it a special concern for any developments within the continent. The Netherlands retains its distinctive links with South Africa as the original home of the Afrikaners who form the majority within the ruling white minority in that country.

Each of these countries has distinctive interests within Southern Africa, but, in addition, they are members of a loose multi-state post–World War II association known as the European Economic Community (EEC), or simply the European Community (EC). This association is serviced by the European Commission sited in Brussels, and has a Council of Ministers and an elected Assembly representing its ten members: Britain, West Germany, France, Italy, Ireland, Belgium, the Netherlands, Luxembourg, Denmark, and, since 1 January 1981, Greece. The principal concern of the member states of the EC is with their own common agricultural program but they also relate to Third World countries through the Lomé Convention, which will be described below.

Outside the framework of the EC, but under the aegis of its Council of Ministers, is what is termed European Political Cooperation (EPC). This quasi-technical term is used to describe the process through which the members of the EC seek to align their foreign policies and sometimes, as noted later, take steps toward the formulation of a single joint foreign policy.

By far the major proportion of foreign political and economic policies continues, however, to be in the hands of individual states. The particular interests in Southern Africa and distinctive policies of Britain (long the foremost colonial power in the region), West Germany, and France will be considered in detail before discussing the issues and ways in which the EC and EPC have played particular roles that affect Southern Africa.

Britain

The burden of history weighs more heavily on Britain in modern Southern African affairs than on any of the other former colonial powers in the region. British rule in South Africa came formally to an end in 1910, although many an elderly Afrikaner dates the achievement of genuine independence to 1961 when Prime Minister Hendrik Verwoerd took what had just become the Republic of South Africa out of the Commonwealth.

In the carving up of Africa in the late nineteenth century, Britain not only gained paramountcy over South Africa but also much longer enduring colonial, or quasi-colonial, control over many other parts of Southern Africa. These included the three High Commission Territories of Bechuanaland (renamed Botswana when it achieved independence in 1966), Basutoland (since 1966 Lesotho), and Swaziland (independent in 1968), as well as Northern Rhodesia (since 1964 Zambia), Nyasaland (since 1966 Malawi), and Southern Rhodesia (now Zimbabwe). In all these states, the British connection has remained close and they have become members of the Commonwealth. This is particularly remarkable in the case of Zimbabwe, whose present leader, Prime Minister Robert Mugabe, had long headed a guerrilla struggle against the white-minority Rhodesian regime. In September, 1979, however, he agreed to British-sponsored negotiations at Lancaster House, London, which hammered out the terms of the constitution under which peace was achieved and free elections held.*

Over the years, a formidable and varied pool of expertise has grown up in Britain, nourished by Britain's long association with the region. Missionaries, travelers, businessmen, philanthropists, colonial civil servants, and diplomats have all played their parts in creating a pool both deep and wide of highly informed specialists in the region. Their knowledge has been concentrated in such bodies as the Royal Geographical Society, the London Missionary Society, the now more or less defunct British Institute of Race Relations, the Royal Institute of International Affairs (Chatham House) and the United Kingdom South Africa Trade Association (UKSATA). In addition, some businesses, notably the banks with their wide-spread branches, have their own private intelligence services. Moreover, the academic world includes many outstanding scholars representing a variety of approaches, ranging from the Marxist to the severely pragmatic, to Southern African issues.

There is a considerable and growing interaction between British government departments (commonly known as Whitehall from their concentration on and near that street), business, the churches, the universities, and some outstanding journalists on questions affecting Southern Africa. A vast amount of information, advice, and informed opinion is available to any British government, particularly when the Conservatives are in office, since the business community generally has closer ties to a Conservative than to a Labour government.

Broadly speaking, the "establishment" view is that the tide is running toward change in South Africa, though perhaps not strongly enough, and perhaps too late. The West's vital interests there are

*Colonial independence conferences have traditionally been held at Lancaster House, in London. The Zimbabwe conference was convened on 6 September 1979, and resulted in independence on 17 April 1980. The Commonwealth (a loose but effective association of states which grew out of the former British Empire) played a considerable part in the settlement of the Rhodesian question, which had persisted since Prime Minister Ian Smith made a unilateral declaration of independence in 1965.

The Commonwealth Secretariat, based in London, plays an active role in both political and economic relations between the widely separated members of the Commonwealth while the Southern Africa Committee of the Commonwealth Group, composed of all their High Commissioners (the equivalent of Foreign Ambassadors) and a representative of the British Foreign Office, acts as a powerful pressure group in British and Commonwealth Affairs. Commonwealth states tend to operate through other groupings, such as the Organization of African Unity and the Front Line States (see glossary), over Namibia and South Africa.

such, the argument continues, that not much more can be done than to encourage the trend toward change, though without seeking to set any precise agenda or timetable, which are matters to be decided by the peoples of South Africa themselves.*

Such a moderate view is probably acceptable to most of the very large number of British people who have links with South Africa, through kinship, friends, business relationships and so on. Such links play a great, though unquantifiable, part in the formation of public opinion. Among nonspecialists they probably incline people toward the view that South Africa is a bastion of conservative (or at least non-Communist) common sense in an unstable world. That view is well represented in both Houses of Parliament and cannot be ignored by any British government, particularly a Conservative one. On the other side, the "establishment" hope that change is on the way in South Africa, is rejected by many others in Britain, notably its vocal Anti-Apartheid Movement, as a reckless and culpable evasion of the real issue, which is to destroy apartheid.

While South Africa's strategic importance carries some weight in Britain, as in the United States, the economic ties are far more significant. Dr. David Owen, when Foreign Secretary in the last Labour administration, put British investment in South Africa at £5,000 million, and a subsequent estimate by the Foreign and Commonwealth Office (FCO) is that 7% of all Britain's overseas investment is in South Africa; in 1977 Britain exported goods worth £581 million (1978 £667 million, 1980 £1,002 million) and imported £880 million. To that must be added the "invisible" contributions of banking—difficult though they are to disentangle, since so many loans are multilateral, but estimated by the FCO at £1,100 million—and of shipping, insurance, and so on. Such figures give the business lobby great power, as does its interpenetration with the political elite. For example, Lord Carrington, Foreign Secretary in the Conservative government and formerly Minister of Defense, brings to his understanding of Southern Africa the experience of several years' service as director of a number of companies with very large interests in the region. These

---

*Compare the much more radical line taken in the Netherlands, where there has been pressure in Parliament for a unilateral oil embargo against South Africa, which the government has refused to carry out. In Sweden a start has been made on a policy of disengagement. But neither country has interests in the Republic as significant as those of Britain, France, or Germany. Thus, though they may provide models for the future, these developments are of relatively little current importance.

companies include Barclays Bank and the international mining house Rio Tinto Zinc, which has important uranium interests at the Rössing mine in Namibia. Another former Minister of Defense, Lord Shackleton, a Labour peer, is the Rio Tinto group's deputy chairman.

Examples of this interpenetration of business with government and the civil service could be multiplied; for instance, the Director of UKSATA was formerly a senior British diplomat. The importance, therefore, for a British government, particularly a Conservative one, of carrying business opinion with it can hardly be exaggerated. But business opinion is itself not homogeneous: many company chairmen may themselves be convinced of the necessity of change in South Africa, unlike their white senior employees on the spot, many of whom are locally recruited rather than expatriates sent out from Britain. Others, relatively unconcerned about change per se, may believe that their overall concern should be with carrying on a successful business, and adapting to whatever changes may occur.

The weight of investment and trade leads to the conclusion, which Marxists would share, that the essential aspect of relations between Britain and South Africa, and therefore with Southern Africa as a whole, is that South Africa is an integral part of the world capitalist system. Conceivably Britain could survive the loss of its trade with and investment in the Republic, but it is virtually impossible to suppose that any British government would voluntarily take steps calculated to lead to such an outcome. In some quarters it has been suggested that if trade (not investment) were diminished, the effects on the British economy could be withstood with relative ease, but in the current parlous state of the economy no government is likely to run the risk, unless of course it can be convinced that it will otherwise encounter a worse danger, like the loss of trade with Black Africa, and particularly with oil-rich Nigeria, which leads its anti-apartheid front (see chapter 6).

Germany, Portugal, and Belgium

Although far less successful in their colonial relationships in Southern Africa and particularly in the manner of their termination than was Britain, three other Western European states—Germany, Portugal, and Belgium—controlled substantial territories in or on the boundaries of Southern Africa for considerable lengths of time, and in each case developed important economic links with them. Thus while they developed neither the depth of relationship nor extent of informational channels that Britain possesses, they retain special interests that are reflected from time to time in their economic and political decisions.

Germany's colonial experience in the region was with South West Africa (now Namibia); it established a protectorate over the territory in 1884, which was recognized by the British in 1890 when the boundaries were settled. Germany lost all its colonial possessions at the end of World War I through the Versailles settlement; they were turned into mandates under League of Nations supervision, and South Africa was designated as the mandatory power for South West Africa. Failure to bring Namibia to independence as all other such territories have been remains an international issue in which Western European states are involved (see below).

Many Germans had already settled in South West Africa and today they form a quite wealthy community of some 18,000. Moreover, the German and Finnish Lutheran Churches remain the strongest evangelical bodies in the territory, which is often said to be the most Christianized in Africa.

Portugal was the earliest colonial power in the region, building on the irregular contacts it had made as a seafaring country on both the Atlantic and the Indian coasts since the end of the fifteenth century. Spasmodic forays into the interior in the nineteenth century brought what became Angola and Mozambique under Portuguese control. Like that of the Germans in South West Africa, however, Portuguese rule was exploitative and harsh and, from the early 1960s, liberation movements fought inside the two colonies (which the Portuguese called overseas territories) to eject the Portuguese army and to take over the Portuguese economic interests that dominated them. After extended fighting, the 1974 coup in Lisbon by the disillusioned, war-weary, and socialist-minded army brought into office a regime that soon conceded independence to both territories.

In the meantime, however, Portugal had worked closely with white-controlled Rhodesia and South Africa on security and economic projects. It strengthened arrangements for South African use of Mozambique's major port, Lourenço Marques (now Maputo). Beyond this arrangement, which was related to provision of migratory labor for the Witwatersrand gold mines, Portugal entered into two major dam-building projects with South Africa. The larger one resulted in the Cabora Bassa hydroelectric scheme on the Zambezi River in Mozambique's Tete Province to provide power for the South African electric grid. The other, smaller power development, on the Cunene River in southern Angola, was designed to provide power to Namibia's mines, white farms, and nascent industrial centers. Thus when Mozambique became independent in 1975, it found itself tied tightly into South Africa's economic system, while Angola, though much less closely involved with South Africa, has a special concern for Namibia's achievement of independence.

The Belgians, who acquired their control of the Congo (now Zaire) in the nineteenth century, were ejected in the early 1960s by internal upheavals and revolt. They have, however, been more successful than the Portuguese in reestablishing their economic activities there which center in the rich copper mining areas in southern Zaire, adjacent to those of Zambia.

None of these three Western European states has been able to establish the close ties with existing black regimes in Southern Africa that Britain maintains with its former possessions, but, as will be seen in the succeeding sections, their historical contacts continue to have meaning today.

Comparison of British, French, and German Relationships with South Africa

It is clear that the Federal Republic of Germany (henceforth referred to simply as Germany, unless the context requires otherwise) lacks the extensive historical links with South Africa possessed by Britain; it also has a much smaller pool of expertise upon which to draw. The major historical connection lies, as already noted, in the occupation by Imperial Germany of South West Africa until World War I. There are still 18,000 ethnic Germans in the territory, whose rather reactionary influence in Bonn, exerted via the Conservative Opposition there by the Interessengemeinschaft der Deutschen Sud-Wester (IG), an organization of German settlers in Namibia, has sometimes somewhat embarrassed the German team in the Contact Group (see below). However, at the Geneva Conference on Namibia, early in 1981, the IG at the instigation of the German government held talks with SWAPO, although apparently without any definite result.

There exist also extensive cultural links with Namibia and South Africa through the South African Council of Churches (the Lutherans are, as we have seen, especially strong in Namibia), which has received significant funding from Germany; through the schools in South Africa, subsidized by the German government, to which many of the 60,000 ethnic Germans there send their children; and, to a lesser extent, through the trade unions and a modest program of government scholarships.

The presence of these colonies of ethnic Germans could potentially raise issues in German domestic politics, since if they were to be repatriated questions of social security and other benefits would arise. These questions, to which the German government naturally hopes it will not be necessary to find the answers, are of personal interest to Herr Hans-Dietrich Genscher, who was Minister of the Interior until his move to Foreign Affairs in 1974 and so is keenly aware of the potential legal and social problems.

It was after Genscher's move to Foreign Affairs that steps were taken by the government to remedy its relative lack of expert knowledge about Southern Africa. Genscher, alarmed by the turmoil in Angola, was instrumental in setting up teams of researchers in a number of institutes, for example in West Berlin and in Ebenhausen, near Munich. These teams have since been working intensively on the problems of the region and the expertise generated is beginning to work through to a wider audience. Further contributions to the debate, which still goes on within only a small public, are made by such bodies as the German Justice and Peace Commission, which is producing a series of books on Southern Africa, the foundations associated with the various political parties, the churches, the increasingly active Institut für Internationale Begegnungen in Bonn, and the Informationstelle Südliches Afrika. The last named is the research body associated with the German Anti-Apartheid Movement (AAM). It produces serious research, but the AAM has a largely left-wing membership and suffers from suspicions that it derives funds from East Germany. There is also a small but increasingly well-informed group of members of the Bundestag (Parliament) who take an interest in the region.

Although Germany has nothing like the wealth of informed pressure groups and interest groups that exists in Britain, the debate about policy goes on, and is reflected in the lack of unanimity on

Southern African issues among German officials and ministers. Some of the latter have already judged that the South African problem cannot be relegated to the long term, but will become pressing soon after the question of Namibia has been settled. Others still believe that a far longer time scale is possible, during which it will not be necessary to choose between commitment to black- or white-controlled Africa.

Despite these differences, the close involvement of Germany in Southern Africa, thanks originally to the accident of history and then to the fortuitous circumstance of Germany's membership on the Security Council until 1978, has led to a growing awareness in political circles that the country needs a Southern Africa policy. There is also a fairly widespread feeling that this foreign policy should have a moral basis, no doubt in reaction, at least among older people, to the remembered horrors of the Hitler period. Moreover, Genscher has a keen interest in the Third World, and believes that Southern Africa is a region in which Germany can make a distinctive contribution.

In France there has until lately been little public interest in Southern Africa, since the historical connections have been largely with the north and west. There has been, therefore, a dearth of informed comment (though this may slowly change under a socialist president) except in the business world, where there has been considerable, and growing, interest in trade with the Republic.

France and West Germany: Investment and Trade

South Africa's total foreign liabilities rose from R3,828 million in 1966 to R5,818 million in 1970 and R19,929 million in 1976. While David Owen's estimate of total British investment at £5,000 million has already been noted, it must be added that reliable investment figures are difficult to obtain, and that since 1973 the South African statistics have concealed investment by individual member states of the European Community in a total EC figure. Table 1 includes estimates by the Centre Français du Commerce Extérieur (CFCE), Paris, of total French and German investment by 1975 (R736 million and R1,800 million respectively), but no explanation is given of how the figures were reached. By contrast with those made by the CFCE, German estimates of total investment—including direct, indirect, pre-1952 investment, and reinvestment profits—make no pretense of exactitude. In September 1978 the German-South African Chamber

Table 1

French and German Investment in South Africa

(in R millions unless otherwise stated)

	1966	% total	1975	% total
Total foreign investment	3,826		16,450	
Investments by France—				
direct	96		139	
indirect	105		597	
	201	5.3	736	4.5
Investments by Germany	115	3.0	1,800	11.0

of Trade guessed at between DM4,000 million and DM12,000 million and opted in December for the lower figure, as does the Chamber's director. On the other hand, the Chamber's chairman went for the upper end of the range, while both the South African Reserve Bank and the CFCE, in the figures used in Table 1, are near the lower end.

INVESTMENT

Great difficulty attends the compilation of German direct investment statistics. Records have been kept since 1952 of the outflow of capital, but not of reinvestment of retained profits, nor, of course, of capital raised in third countries by South African subsidiaries of German companies—especially Euro currency loans or those obtained in the "grey" market. All this being said, German officials estimated German direct investment as ± DM650 million early in 1979.

In 1979 a further measure became available which includes the book value of subsidiaries abroad. This yields a total book value of direct investment of DM998 million at the end of 1976. The Deutsche Bundesbank, which published the figures, warns that they may be on the low side, and that comparisons between countries must be imperfect, since accounting practices are not uniform. They add, however, that no better figures are likely to become available.

French figures are even harder to obtain than are German. We have seen (Table 1) that CFCE estimated total French investment at R736 million in 1975, of which R139 million was direct and R597 million indirect, giving 4.5 percent of total foreign investment in South Africa. The French Anti-Apartheid Movement (Centre de Recherches et d'Information sur l'Afrique Australe: CRIAA) makes a rather higher estimate, giving France 6 percent of the total. It appears likely that there has been little change in French investment in the period since 1978, but if the efforts of the Conseil National du Patronat Français (generally known as the Patronat) are successful it should increase over the next few years, unless such a development is discouraged by the new socialist government.

TRADE

Trade figures are far easier to obtain than are those for investment and in the French case the figures published by the Ministère du Budget are ample, though not complete, since they exclude sales of military equipment and of licenses for local manufacture in South Africa of military hardware. French exports to South Africa in 1978 totaled Fr2,742 million or 81% of imports, and four principal categories (ships, boilers and mechanical appliances, electrical goods, and vehicles) accounted for 75% of this total. By contrast with these highly sophisticated exports, imports consisted largely of raw materials, 85% of the 1978 total of Fr3,400 million being accounted for by coal and anthracite, inorganic chemical products, precious stones and metals, metal ores, wool, and fruit. The adverse trade balance gives some cause for concern in French business circles where it is also realized that the large "one-off" contracts of the past can hardly be repeated, so that a diversification of exports is desirable.

As may be seen from Table 2, Germany's trade with South Africa is greater in absolute terms than is that of France; indeed, it has now outstripped Britain as South Africa's most important trading partner. As one would expect, there is an imbalance (as in the French case) between the kinds of goods imported and exported. In 1978, 28% of South Africa's exports to Germany were finished products, compared with 96% of its imports.

POLITICAL AND CULTURAL ATTITUDES

At the political and cultural levels there are numerous differences between French, German, and British attitudes to and connections with South Africa, in addition to those which have already been mentioned.

Table 2

French and German Trade with South Africa

(in millions)

Year	French Imports	French Exports	German Imports	German Exports
1973	Fr 980[a]	Fr 1,071[a]	—	—
1974	Fr 1,203[a]	Fr 1,678[a]	—	—
1975	Fr 1,234[a]	Fr 1,815[a]	—	—
	R 93[b]	R 245[b,c]	R 427[b]	R 1,034[b,c]
	or		or	
	R 115[c]		R 445[c]	
1976	Fr 1,538[a]	Fr 2,320[a]	—	—
	R 148[b]	R 256[b]	R 473[b]	R 1,059[b]
	or	or	or	or
	R 158[c]	R 255[c]	R 489[c]	R 1,058[c]
1977	Fr 2,470[a]	Fr 2,438[a]	DM 2,555[d]	DM 2,598[d]
	R 214[b,c]	R 240[b,c]	R 517[b]	R 933[b]
			or	or
			R 529[c]	R 930[c]
1978	Fr 3,400[a]	Fr 2,723[a]	DM 2,455[d]	DM 3,082[d]
	R 296[c]	R 475[c]	R 682[c]	R 1,275[c]
1979	R 351[c]	R 471[c]	R 910[c]	R 1,309[c]

Sources: [a] Conseil National du Patronat Français
[b] Centre Français du Commerce Extérieur
[c] 1980 Annual Report, German/South African Chamber of Trade and Industries
[d] Bundesamt für Statistik

It is, for example, apparent that, although France is not prepared to take the lead in Southern African policy, but may, rather, choose to follow where Britain leads, France is nevertheless seeking to extend its influence in areas of Africa outside its traditional sphere of influence. In Paris (as, indeed, in Bonn and at the European Commission in Brussels) persistent overtures are made to the South-West African People's Organization (SWAPO), the largest African political party in Namibia, which has been recognized by the United Nations General Assembly as the one authentic representative of the Namibian people. In Lusaka, a French instructor has joined the United Nations Institute for Namibia, and the Institute's Director, Gottfried H. Geingob, has been presented with a decoration, the Palmes Acadèmiques, as a symbol of French interest in the struggle for Namibia. There are also persistent stories of French attempts to use Francophone Africa as a conduit for influence in Southern Africa.

At a perhaps more significant level, France maintains a strong embassy in South Africa with a career diplomat at its head, whereas in the former colonies in West Africa the tendency is to appoint ambassadors who carry political weight at home. Within the Contact Group on Namibia it was noticeable that, despite Anglo-French rivalry elsewhere in Africa, France followed Britain in its recent rather softer line (a product of changed political circumstances in Britain rather than of altered underlying realities) which contrasts with the somewhat tougher German attitude and is closer to the current movement by the United States toward a policy less antagonistic to South Africa.

The French government's pragmatic attitude toward South Africa has been assisted by the lack of influential pressure groups in France. This attitude also existed in Britain before its change of government in May 1979 but has been fortified by the Conservatives' accession to power. Despite the view held by at least some French officials that without a dramatic gesture in the direction of change very soon, Afrikanerdom cannot have a long-term hope of survival in anything like its present position, there has until lately seemed to be a basic difference (amounting to more than a difference in emphasis) between the dominant strand in French thinking about South Africa and the emerging consensus in Britain and Germany. It appears now, however, that Socialist President François Mitterrand is stimulating a dramatic change to a more active policy of support for the Third World and outspoken criticism of South Africa.

Under the former president, Giscard d'Estaing, it was possible to sum up the French attitude as "wait and see," combined with a determination to let Britain, assisted by Germany, take the lead in the formulation of foreign policy—a lead which France was prepared to follow to the extent that French interests permitted it. In Germany and Britain, on the other hand, the fundamental political judgment has been made that if South Africa is to change peacefully, it must do so rapidly and that it is both the duty and the interest of South Africa's friends in the west (Marxists would say its accomplices in the capitalist conspiracy) to urge the Republic's government to alter its ways before midnight strikes. This difference of perception, if it had continued, could have damaged the Western alliance in the future, particularly if, as then seemed likely, it became impossible for contingency plans to be coordinated at the European level, to deal with a possible interruption in the supply of South African minerals.

Arms Embargo

One of the very few collective actions against South Africa by the United Nations has been an embargo on the export of arms to that country. Initially the decision was advisory rather than mandatory, but a number of powers, including the United States, Britain (since 1974), and Germany, but not France, observed it. However, when the ban became mandatory (the resolution was taken at the United Nations in November 1977 and came into force the following March), France immediately announced that it would be observed. In all four countries there are complicated procedures for establishing what materials fall under the embargo, which naturally give rise to differences of interpretation.

Minerals*

Britain and Germany share very great dependence on South African minerals. German studies show that Germany has been judged most at risk in respect of chrome, vanadium, manganese, and blue asbestos. It was therefore at one point decided to stockpile these four South African minerals as well as cobalt from Zaire, though it appears that the plan has since been shelved. Similar plans, about which virtually no information is available (not even the list of minerals to be accumulated), were made in France, though it is clear that French dependence on South Africa is greatly diminished by the presence of semi-captive mineral supplies in former colonies in West Africa and in the overseas province of New Caledonia. In Britain the whole question of stockpiling is the subject of an Inter-Departmental Committee, whose conclusions, if any, have not been published.

Joint Western European Relations with Southern African States

While Western European states continue to pursue their own individual policies in the international sphere, or group together with other Western states as in the Contact Group on Namibia (see below),

*Also see ch. 2, Table 2.

they maintain their special links through the European Community. The most distinctive characteristic of the Economic Community is its Common Market which chiefly affects agricultural produce. It is increasingly felt, however, that greater coordination of their economic and political international relations would enable them to play a more effective role in international affairs.

The Lomé Convention

The current and most formalized economic relations of the European Community as a whole with other states are through the Lomé Convention. This Convention, which is administered through the European Commission, establishes a special relation between the member states of the European Community and some sixty African, Caribbean, and Pacific (ACP) states. The nine African-controlled states in Southern Africa, which have recently associated themselves as a group in the Southern African Development Coordination Conference in an effort to reduce their dependence upon South Africa, especially in transport and food (see chs. 7 and 8), fall into the category of developing states for which the Lomé Convention was designed, but they became eligible when each achieved independence, and in each case special negotiations had been necessary. Angola and Mozambique have not yet become members, although both are now independent states.

The Lomé Convention was first signed in 1976 (Lomé I), and renegotiated in 1979 to run for a further four years from 1980 (Lomé II). The substance of the Convention concerns economic relationships, notably privileges given to the European market, and stabilization of ACP export prices and development projects undertaken through the European Development Fund. This aspect of the Lomé relation is often emphasized, indeed, perhaps, rather excessively, by officials in Brussels. In fact, however, the relationship is intensely political, as are the European bureaucracy and the emerging ACP secretariat themselves. The political meaning of this institutional link may be interpreted in different ways by commentators of various ideological bents, but, however interpreted, it must surely be seen as a potent factor in the competition between East and West in the Third World.

This aspect of Lomé is well illustrated by the case of Mozambique.

So, too, is the competition between members of the Community itself, which is only superficially disguised by their unity of interest, at another level, in maintaining and extending the Lomé relationship.

Mozambique, which is perceived as an important crossroads of East-West competition for influence, has been energetically wooed by the Community to accede to Lomé and there may even have been some hopes that the suitor's chances would be improved by the relatively trouble-free accession of Zimbabwe, which occurred in 1980. Mozambique, however, has been slow to decide because of the "Berlin clause" of the Convention (Annex 35 to Lomé II, following Annex 24 to Lomé I), which requires partner states to recognize the rights and responsibilities of the Western powers (the United States, Britain, and France) in West Berlin.

The "Berlin clause" has naturally been of concern to both East and West Germany: the former is already well established in Maputo, the latter is said to have been rather heavy-handed in its persuasions, no doubt because its policy toward Mozambique, as so often in its Third World connections, can only fully be understood in the context of its competition with East Germany.

In particular, the Federal Republic has argued that, although Community aid may legally be given on a regional basis to a group of countries, even if not all members of the group are Lomé partners, the case of Mozambique falls outside the spirit of the law. In the West German contention, regional aid can be extended to non-members only if they are prevented by circumstances beyond their control from acceding to the Convention. This is plainly not the case with Mozambique, which has been offered membership. It is apparent, however, that Mozambique would prefer membership in the Soviet bloc's Organisation of Economic Co-operation (which would be inconsistent with accession to Lomé, though not with membership in the World Bank), but its application met with difficulties on the grounds that Mozambique is not an industrialized country (see also ch. 8).

By contrast, Zimbabwe's accession to Lomé went smoothly on the Zimbabwean side, though there were some difficulties relating to tobacco, an Italian concern, and sugar, on which the French were reluctant. Unexpectedly, the special tariff agreement which already existed with South Africa presented no problem, but in any case, has since been abrogated by South Africa.

It is inconceivable that the present South African regime could join

Lomé, since the development by the European Commission of a South Africa policy acceptable to the African, Caribbean, and Pacific states is essential to the Convention's success in Southern Africa. Not only has this a bearing on Mozambique's possible future membership, and for Angola, and eventually Namibia, but it relates to the question of human rights, which was discussed extensively preceding the last renegotiation of the Convention.

Dr. David Owen and others argued (with the specific case of Uganda under Idi Amin in mind) that Community aid should not be given to countries where human rights were grossly violated. The ACP states argued, on the other side, that human rights, though desirable in themselves, were not a proper part of an avowedly economic relationship and should be discussed in other bodies. Although this view won the day, it is possible that the question will again be raised by the Community at the next Lomé renegotiation and in that case the European hand will be greatly strengthened if there is an acceptable and plausible South Africa policy, centering on the Republic's denial of rights to most of its citizens.

European Political Cooperation

Consideration of political matters relevant to Southern Africa takes place from time to time in the supranational commission itself, but more directly through what is termed European Political Cooperation (EPC). This term designates the process, as already mentioned, by which the member states coordinate their foreign policies, and sometimes even take steps toward the formulation of a single joint foreign policy. The process takes place under the umbrella of the Council of Ministers, and therefore outside the European Commission, and in a sense provides not only a different, but a rival, source of foreign policy, though at high level EPC meetings in Brussels it is usual for a representative of the Commission's secretariat to be present.

EPC meetings, however, are by no means confined to that city. At Foreign Minister level they take place in the capital of the country holding the presidency of the European Community for the current six months, but as the scope and practice of EPC has grown, the range of subjects with which it is concerned and the variety of levels at which officials may meet in the various European capitals have been greatly extended. Furthermore, such meetings may take place at very short notice (as they did during the Iranian crisis), and may even be arranged directly between officials in different Foreign Ministries, rather than through their local embassies.

EPC meetings also take place on a regular basis in capitals outside Europe to which ambassadors of the ten member states are accredited. In South Africa, for example, diplomats of the six member states that are represented there at ambassadorial level meet monthly. There, however, unlike, for example, Zimbabwe, their deliberations concerning negotiations with South Africa over Namibia are somewhat overshadowed by those of the Contact Group of five, Britain, France, Germany, the United States, and Canada, which were the Western members of the Security Council when the negotiations started.

In relation to Southern Africa, EPC has a relatively short history. It can be traced to the meeting of the nine Foreign Ministers at Luxembourg on 23 February, 1976. Under the Presidency of Gaston Thorn, then Luxembourg's Minister of Foreign Affairs, they adopted a declaration which called for the cessation of all external military intervention in Angola;* congratulated the Organization of African Unity (OAU) on its efforts to find an African solution there; asserted the Nine's readiness to develop cooperative relations to the extent desired by the African states; supported the right to self-determination of the Rhodesian and Namibian peoples; and condemned South Africa's policy of apartheid. The statement went on to say that although each state would recognize Angola individually, this would be done in a concerted manner, in order to demonstrate that it proceeded from a genuinely common will.

On April 2, 1976, there followed a further declaration on Rhodesia and on September 28, 1976, the Dutch Foreign Minister, speaking as President of the Council of Ministers and of EPC, made a major speech at the United Nations on behalf of the Nine, which stated joint positions on Rhodesia, South Africa (including the "purported independence" of the Transkei), and Namibia.

CODE OF CONDUCT FOR EUROPEAN FIRMS

In more recent times a major example of joint action toward South Africa has been the Code of Conduct for European firms with inter-

*See John Marcum, "Angola: Perilous Transition to Independence," in *Southern Africa: The Continuing Crisis,* 2nd ed., Gwendolen M. Carter and Patrick O'Meara, eds. (Bloomington: Indiana University Press, 1982).

ests there. The Code was mooted on 12 July 1977 by Dr. David Owen and Herr Hans-Dietrich Genscher, who had been Foreign Minister of Germany since 1974, at a meeting of Foreign Ministers of the Nine, in order that the West should have something positive to say at the anti-apartheid conference held in Lagos the following August. It built upon the Code of Practice already in operation in Britain. This code resulted from revelations made in *The Guardian* of the substandard wages paid by British companies in South Africa, which were followed by a visit to South Africa by trade union leaders and a Parliamentary Committee of Enquiry.

The European Code enjoins employers to allow employees "to choose freely and without any hindrance the type of organization to represent them" and, if they choose a trade union, to recognize it. Employers, moreover, should do what they can to counter the bad effects of the migrant labor system; pay initially at least 50% above the minimum subsistence level; give equal pay for equal work; introduce training schools to promote African advancement; set aside funds for such purposes as black hiring and education and other fringe benefits; desegregate places of work; and, finally, publish a detailed annual report on the progress made in applying the Code. The Code is not unlike the American Sullivan principles, with the important emphasis that the latter include no specific reference to migrant labor and trade unions.

The Code was adopted by the Nine in EPC and has since been regularly debated in that forum. The varying British, French, and German attitudes to it well illustrate the diversity which can exist behind the joint declarations issuing from EPC. The British believe that, since the Code is one of the few constructive joint measures to have been agreed upon by the Nine in relation to South Africa (Greece only joined the community in 1981), the most should be made of it. In particular, they urged that publicity should be given to companies' reports, and that some sort of joint assessment should be made by the Nine of the Code's operation and effectiveness, though this would not necessarily be made public (apart from Britain, reports have been produced by the governments of Germany, Belgium, Denmark, Italy, and the Netherlands).

Prior to the election of Socialist President François Mitterrand, the French were firmly opposed to the proposal that a joint assessment should be made, since, although they insist that the practice of French firms has long equalled, or indeed surpassed, the standards enjoined by the Code, they believed that the use of the Code itself was little short of a waste of time. They maintained that while it might well be suitable for British businessmen, who are accustomed to filling in forms, it was of little relevance to France, where only about twenty-five companies would be affected (a reflection no doubt of the French emphasis on local manufacture under license, and other forms of association with South Africa-based firms) and that some of these had few, if any, black employees. Furthermore, since there is no obligation upon companies to report and the Code itself is voluntary, it was very difficult to persuade French companies to take any interest in it, particularly in the absence of any significant interested public pressure. If, however, enough companies do report (which seems unlikely, since no effort is even being made to encourage them to do so), the individual reports will remain unpublished.

The German government has experienced difficulties over the Code because of the robust individuality of German businesses. All companies whose exports to South Africa receive Hermes financing (a form of insurance against nonpayment for exports, administered by the government) must, if they have subsidiaries there, sign a declaration that they have seen and approved a statement that was signed by the German business organizations after a meeting on 27 September 1977 with the State Secretary of the Ministry of Foreign Affairs. The statement says that the parties approve of the principal aims of the Code and are willing to see that its general principles are translated into practice.

The agreement was reached after a long tussle over Article 7 of the Code, which concerns reporting. The initial proposal made by the business organizations was that companies would each write a report for the Bundesverband der Deutschen Industrie (BDI) and the Deutsche Industrie und Handelsbank (two of the signatory bodies) which in turn would write and submit a general report to the government. This was not acceptable to the government, which feared the possible adverse effect on public opinion of such an indirect and private method of reporting. Long negotiations ensued, lasting from August 1978 until February 1979. The government finally decided that individual companies would report directly to the Ministry of Economics, which would then produce a general report for publication. The report was long delayed and eventually appeared in January 1980. By then, there was a growing belief in the BDI (as indeed among South African businessmen) that the reformist nature of the Code fitted in with what appeared to be the reformist intentions of the South African government itself with respect to wages, training, common facilities, and trade union rights.

Response to the Namibian Issue

The protracted negotiations about Namibia between the Contact Group of five and South Africa have been a splendid device for harmonizing the pursuit of the major powers' interests in Southern Africa with the more general concern constantly expressed at the United Nations ever since that body inherited a legal responsibility for that territory from the old League of Nations.* They have made some members of the Contact Group even more aware than before of the extent of their common interests with South Africa, and therefore of their interest in encouraging change in the Republic. Furthermore, some of the excesses of the United Nations (notably the General Assembly resolution that SWAPO is the sole authentic representative of the Namibian people, and more recently the refusal to allow South Africa to take its seat for a debate on Namibia) have had the unfortunate effect of pushing the five and South Africa closer together than is wise.

The Contact Group negotiations with South Africa have never gone smoothly, but an agreement on a conference to be held in Geneva in January 1981 offered hope of an acceptable settlement. In the months preceding the Geneva Conference, great efforts were made to persuade South Africa that the moment of decision could no longer be postponed. That decision was between an internationally acceptable arrangement for a transition to independence, and an internal settlement on the Muzorewa model, by transferring administration in the territory to the Democratic Turnhalle Alliance (DTA) led by Dirk Mudge which associates moderate whites with ethnic homeland leaders. The Geneva Conference proved a failure, and thereafter South Africa veered toward the latter option, transferring administration in the territory to the DTA in September 1981.

The Reagan administration had naturally needed time to formulate

*See ch. 2 above and chs. 5 and 12 of Carter and O'Meara, eds., *Southern Africa: The Continuing Crisis.*

its Southern Africa policy, but, even so, proceeded with disconcerting slowness. Dr. Chester Crocker's appointment as Assistant Secretary of State was long delayed by Senator Helms, and the new administration was slow to appoint an ambassador to Pretoria. Right-wing pressure from home probably led Crocker to take a line more acceptable to South Africa than to Dirk Mudge's DTA, so that if eventually SWAPO comes to power in Namibia, the claim can be made in South Africa that the fault is not that government's, but the DTA's. On the other hand, by delaying a settlement, South Africa was allowing time for the Reagan administration to formulate a Southern Africa policy sympathetic to the Republic, and for the effective South African lobby in the United States to ensure that its voices are heard. Finally, it must be clear to South Africa that, once Namibia is settled, the spotlight will be even more harshly on South Africa than at present. This only reinforces the Republic's interest in delay.

The way forward for the Contact Group has been far from clear. Until lately they have been united with the Republic in the view that sanctions, or the threat of them, would be inappropriate and ineffectual, as well as damaging to other states in Southern Africa. But the accession to power in France of President Mitterrand, and continued international pressure, led them to continue their efforts to secure an acceptable settlement. This task has involved persuading influential African states to accept that the Namibian question should be pursued by diplomatic means rather than through recourse to sanctions. Meanwhile (and once again, South Africa gains from the passage of time) the Contact Group has been obliged to consider what concessions can be made to the Republic, if only to accommodate changed American perceptions.

The West and South Africa: Policy Options

The questions of Namibia and South Africa are inextricably entangled, but the West has no choice but to take them in turn. The United States shares the general Western interest in the preservation of peace in Southern Africa and, therefore, in the promotion of change. It does not, of course, have a direct interest in the Lomé Convention, or share the historical and emotional links which Britain uniquely suffers, or have the same investment, trade, and mineral dependence, and so in the past has been more free to criticize South Africa. Under the Reagan administration, however, with its greater emphasis on world strategy, than former President Jimmy Carter's, and its lesser emphasis on human rights, that inclination toward hostile criticism has been removed; instead, the United States has joined Britain and, until recently, France in being prepared to adopt a relatively soft line towards the Republic.

The Western veto of a sanctions proposal, followed very shortly by meetings between South African Foreign Minister R. F. Botha, Alexander Haig, the American Secretary of State, and even President Reagan himself (in contrast with Prime Minister P. W. Botha's refusal to receive Dr. Crocker) has encouraged the Republic to hope that it may eventually be welcomed back into the Western fold with America taking a correspondingly firmer line in its dealings with black states. Indeed, Mr. Botha's treatment in Washington seemed the beginning of such a welcome.

This is not to say that there is no disillusionment with the West in South Africa. On the contrary, there is a great deal. Some influential opinion there is in favor of reducing reliance on traditional allies in the West who they feel have proved broken reeds, and concentrating instead on winning new friends in Africa. It can, however, be argued that that line of policy, if adopted, would itself be a roundabout way of promoting the overall objective of winning South Africa's way back into the good graces of the West.

Any Western policies must be constrained by the need to guard against the possibility of a number of unwelcome developments. These include: temporary withholding of supplies by the South African government, as a kind of reverse sanction intended to preempt sanctions by the West; similar withholding (perhaps in revenge for insufficient support now) by a future government, which will have sprung from one of the present liberation movements; the interruption of railway traffic from mines to ports; the possibility of a period of chaos attending the transfer of power from white to black; and/or full-scale civil war of unforecastable duration.

There can be no doubt that denial of access to South African minerals would be a severe inconvenience to Britain (as, in the view of the Reagan administration, it would be for the United States). But since the West is their chief and often only customer, it would seem likely that there would be continued access with a multiracial or even a black government in that country. There are also alternative sources of minerals in Southern Africa, notably in Zimbabwe, which already produces chromium and cobalt—two of the scarcer metals—as well as nickel, gold, and silver, in considerable quantities although not on a scale to rival South Africa. Zimbabwean mining production, already well established, seems likely to avoid the difficulties that Botswana and Zambia have encountered with their copper production. Nonetheless, in the short run, access to South African minerals remains essential, although not to the same extent for each of the Western powers.

For Europe and the United States the moment of decision is approaching, though the urgency of the impending policy choice is to an extent obscured by the political complexion of the British and American governments. The choice lies between even closer political and diplomatic ties with South Africa than at present exist, combined with tactful criticism and quiet encouragement of reformist forces, primarily within Afrikanerdom (this is the "establishment" already referred to) or a policy of disengagement. The latter should not be confused with disinvestment, though it might include discouragement of new investment.

The policy of disengagement would follow from an unfavorable assessment of the pace and extent of internal change in South Africa, which would in turn suggest an eventual violent outcome. That judgment would combine with a further and much broader judgment that internationally Europe could not indefinitely continue on close terms with both South Africa and Black Africa, nor play its full part in the North/South dialogue and Third World affairs generally, if relations with South Africa remain close.

The process of disengagement could take various forms and in any case would have to be consistent with the continuing maintenance of vital interests in the Republic, and bear in mind the constraints on policy already indicated. It might, however, include some diversion of political energy to support the SADCC states and encouragement of investment in them, with corresponding moves by European governments to distance themselves from South Africa. At the same time Europe might bring itself to do what it has always avoided, namely, to present the South African government with a detailed agenda for change. The latter course is fraught with hazard and would probably not be pursued in public, but if Europe and the United States persist in pressing for change in South Africa, it is reasonable for the Republic to expect eventually to receive a more precise answer to the question "What change?" than it has received hitherto.

Clearly, there will be no dramatic shift in policy; the choice is between emphases, and any shift that occurs will emerge gradually from a growing climate or consensus of expert opinion, rather than as a dramatically sharp decision. The assessment of internal reform in South Africa, which is naturally made much of by the Republic's information machinery, will be crucial. But if reforms are judged unlikely to be sufficient to neutralize the likelihood of change of a more radical, and probably violent, nature, then it would be wise for European governments to establish close and sympathetic links with the liberation movements, even if the links remained clandestine, or at the very least to encourage nongovernmental organizations to deepen their connections with the movements.

Much was expected (by many academic and other commentators) from the *verligte* movement in 1980, and on the whole the results have been disappointing. Everything now depends on Prime Minister P. W. Botha's own assessment of his election results. If he can shrug off the disaffection shown by the high HNP vote, then the prime minister may be willing to proceed with a determined program of internal reform. But if he fails to do so, whether because the balance of power in the party is unfavorable or because he loses, for some other reason, whatever momentum and conviction he now has, then there can equally be no reason for Europe to go on pinning its faith on reform from within. By the end of 1982 sufficient evidence will be available for a choice to be made between the trends or emphases suggested earlier, and the beginning of any process of reassessment should not be longer delayed.

It is easier for Britain than for other European countries to manage a shift of emphasis because of the wealth of available expert opinion and the multiplicity of active bodies associated with South Africa. Thus, without any clear-cut statements being made, it is possible for indications of governmental thinking to be given in a variety of ways, ranging from private discussions with experts to open encouragement such as was given by former Foreign Secretary David Owen to the Anti-Apartheid Movement.

On the other hand, the overwhelming British interest must be to get away from the "image" of having a special responsibility for South Africa. The long years of frustration in Rhodesia since UDI in 1965, not to mention the ups and downs of Federation from 1953–63, have in part brought about this mood of "never gain." The obvious way for Britain to "shed the load" of special responsibility is to act in concert with other powers whenever possible, whether it be with the Contact Group of five or as a member of the ten-nation European Community.

The overriding trend, therefore, should be toward a growth of European Political Cooperation among the ten member states of the Community in relation to South Africa and to Southern Africa as a whole, a growth led by Britain and actively supported by West Germany and France. That growth, despite the preferences of some Western governments, will (if the *verligte* movement is judged to have failed) be accompanied by a movement toward disengagement from close relations with South Africa.

4.

The Middle East Dimension

Colin Legum

It would be easy to dismiss the role of the Middle East powers in Southern Africa as being insignificant, except in the case of Israel; but this view is incorrect. The policies of the Arab nations do, in fact, constitute an important element in the international involvement in the region, while Iran in the days of the Shah made a decisively important contribution in assisting the South African regime to reduce substantially its heavy dependence on oil imports.

South Africa's foreign policy toward the Middle East has been shaped by four major interests: to keep open the flow of oil from the Gulf states; to obtain arms and defense technology from Israel; to expand its trade; and to promote its conceived security interests in the Indian Ocean.

The other countries in the region—notably Botswana, Lesotho, Swaziland, Malawi, and, more tangentially, Mauritius—all share a common interest in attracting Israeli economic and technical aid as well as Arab financial support. It is a striking fact that the only four member states of the Organization of African Unity (OAU) which refused in 1973 to sever their diplomatic links with Israel were Swaziland, Malawi, Lesotho, and Mauritius. Although the latter two subsequently informally dropped their open diplomatic relations with Israel (without actually severing relations), they have continued to maintain their economic links—much in the same way as do Botswana, Zaire, Kenya, Ivory Coast, Ghana, and Nigeria. Despite the threat by the League of Arab States to impose an oil embargo on all Third World countries which refuse to end their ties with Israel, no punitive action has been taken against Swaziland and Malawi for their open flouting of the League's policy. However, direct Arab economic

115

aid in the region has been given only in Lesotho, to help build an international airport at Maseru.[1]

The Iran Connection

Notwithstanding its sharp break with the policies of the Shah, the Khomeini regime has, as yet, not taken any formal steps to liquidate Iran's important interest in the South African National Petroleum Refinery (NATREF), in which the now nationalized Royal Iranian Company has a 17.5% interest. NATREF was responsible for developing the oil-from-coal industry, which is crucial to South Africa's lessened dependence on oil imports. In exchange for a substantial minority interest in NATREF, the Shah agreed to supply oil to South Africa. He also sent several hundred Iranian workers on contract to the refinery at Sasolburg; these workers have since left. The Khomeini regime has prohibited the export of Iranian oil to the Republic.

The Shah's alliance with South Africa was dictated by his concern to "stop the spread of Soviet influence" in Africa and especially along the oil sea lanes of the Indian Ocean. He saw the Iranian navy as having a role to play in that area, and regarded the Pretoria regime as a buttress against the USSR. (At the same time, he defended his other flank by channelling funds to the OAU Liberation Committee.) South Africa's great interest in Iran was that, as a non-Arab country, it was not under the same pressures to engage in an oil embargo against the Republic.

The Role of the Arab Countries

Until the October 1973 war with Israel, the Arab countries took no active interest in the affairs of Southern Africa; they had even ignored the OAU's earlier call for an oil embargo on South Africa. The only interest of the League of Arab States up to that time was to seek to win over OAU support for the Palestinians' cause by assiduously promoting a propaganda campaign designed to draw a parallel between the "white settlers" of South Africa and the "Zionist settlers" of Israel. But this campaign had one practical result: the Palestine Liberation Organization (PLO) began to establish direct links with the

Southern African liberation movements, with both sides pledged to support each other's struggles.

The role of the Arab states changed after October 1973 when the OAU reversed itself completely to adopt a pro-Arab position in the conflict with Israel. Under the new compulsion of the Arabs' use of the oil weapon, and with the onset of the era of escalating oil prices, the OAU moved toward institutionalizing its relations with the League of Arab States. This development had two important consequences for Arab policies toward Southern Africa. The first was to produce greater support for the liberation struggles in South Africa, Namibia, and Rhodesia; and the second was a more positive response to the OAU demand for an oil embargo against South Africa, notably by Arab oil producers writing into their contracts with transnational companies an "end-user" clause forbidding onward shipping of oil to South Africa. These sanctions have never been fully implemented because of the difficulties of monitoring the international oil trade. According to a Dutch monitoring group, fifty oil tankers sailed from Saudi Arabia to South African ports during 1979 and the first quarter of 1980. The Saudi authorities admitted that only fifteen of these cases had proper "end-user" certificates returned by the oil companies. Despite these evasions, the greater readiness of the Arab oil producers to join in an embargo against South Africa has made it harder, and more expensive, for the Pretoria regime to get its oil supplies. This development made the Iranian connection even more important than ever; hence the serious setback for South Africa when the Shah's rule was swept away.

The Israeli Connection

Two important considerations have determined Israel's relations with South Africa and Rhodesia (Zimbabwe) since the birth of the Jewish state in 1948: a trade interest and, more crucially, the position of the sizable Jewish communities in both those countries—over 110,000. These communities have been notably pro-Zionist, and many Jews from the area have emigrated to Israel (especially after the advent of the apartheid regime), thus drawing closer the bonds between the *Yishuv* and the *galut* Jews in Southern Africa. The earlier Israeli governments were concerned about not seriously upsetting the

South African government for fear of harming the Jewish community interest, and also from a wish not to make it harder for them to continue their generous financial support to Israel.

However, the Israeli leadership was at the same time concerned to expand its diplomatic and trade interests with the rest of the Third World and particularly with the Black African countries. Policy, particularly under Ben Gurion and Levi Eshkol, was therefore ambiguous. While taking a strong moral position against the racism of apartheid, they maintained their diplomatic ties with Pretoria, sought to avoid giving offense by Israel's votes at the United Nations and, without publicity, worked to expand their trade with South Africa. As Israel's connections with Black Africa became more important after the late 1950s (beginning with particularly warm relations with Nkrumah's Ghana), the government found it increasingly more difficult to maintain a low-profile policy toward Pretoria—especially in facing issues at the United Nations. When Golda Meir became Foreign Minister and, later, Prime Minister, she took a much more committed position against Pretoria, which greatly upset the South African and Rhodesian Jewish communities. She was also strongly criticized by her right-wing opponents, led by Menachem Begin's Likud party. But she gamely stuck to her guns.

Three events radically changed Israel's relations with South Africa: the virtually total break of African diplomatic relations with Jerusalem after October 1973; the controversial U.N. General Assembly vote in November 1975 which equated Zionism with apartheid; and the election of Menachem Begin's Likud government in 1977. Israel's sharp diplomatic setback in Africa surprised and shocked Israelis, many of whom felt they had been "betrayed" by Africans after their country had devoted substantial resources to providing economic and technical aid. (Most Israelis seem to have simply ignored the corresponding economic advantages in trade which had accrued to their country.) While Meir refused to soften her stand against the regimes in Pretoria and Salisbury, her successor, General Itzhak Rabin, did not share her strong feelings about South Africa. He was also more attentive to the pressures of his military-industrial complex, which saw ways of lessening Israel's heavy military development costs by exporting weapons. However, it was the United Nations' vote equating Zionism with apartheid that dramatically changed the climate of

Israeli opinion toward having close dealings with South Africa. Israelis saw this comparison as a cruel and undeserved slur against themselves, and were outraged that 28 African countries should have voted for such a resolution, with only 5 voting against and 12 abstaining.

By putting Israel into the same "pariah" category as South Africa and Taiwan, African support for the Arab-initiated resolution contributed substantially toward producing a political climate in Israel which favored Begin's own long-established policy of widening Israel's links with South Africa. He consequently met with little serious opposition when, in 1977, he virtually declared an open season for retired Israeli generals to offer weapons for sale in Southern Africa and for businessmen to engage in multifarious trading deals, which they were no longer expected to conduct discreetly. Begin's first Finance Minister, Simcha Ehrlich, himself went to South Africa where he defiantly flouted African opinion by proclaiming the value of a South African-Israeli connection.

From Israel's point of view that connection was especially valuable at a time when the Arab boycott was having more serious effects and when the opportunities for expanding trade with the Third World were contracting. (This was not true, though, of Black Africa where, despite the severing of diplomatic links, Israeli trade has continued to increase annually—especially with important markets like Nigeria, Ivory Coast, and Kenya, as well as with countries like Zaire.)

South African exports to Israel rose by 95% in 1978, and by 85% in the first five months of 1979. The total value of exports to Israel in 1978 were about $51 million, making it the Republic's fastest growing market. Boosted by a long-term coal contract, exports for 1979 were estimated at $60 million. Imports from Israel rose from $9.4 million in 1971 to $37.7 million in 1979. This figure does not include arms shipments. South Africa and the United States are the only two countries which have increased their investment in Israel in recent years.[2] In 1978/9 South African investment (mostly Jewish) amounted to over $12 million, while projected investment for 1979/80 stood at just under $8 million. In 1978, 400,000 tons of South African cargo were shipped to Israel, of which over half was iron and steel, and 80,000 tons paper. Timber exports reached 100,000 cubic meters. Other exports included asbestos, canned fruit, sugar, ferro-manganese, and pesticides. About $50 million of diamonds went to Israel's diamond-cutting industry, but these do not appear in official figures. The chairman of the South African–Israeli Chamber of Economic Relations estimated that total exports to Israel would top $75 million a year by 1982. The chamber now has a membership of 250 firms. Israeli exports to South Africa grew by 57.5% to over £9 million in 1978. The largest single Israeli export is potash from the Dead Sea. Other export items include scientific-based and high-technology products, paper products, and base metals.

The growth of the Israeli connection has been of particular importance for South Africa because the United Nations' partial arms embargo of 1963 was making it harder to obtain reliable supplies of sophisticated weapons. While France has been of much greater importance as a supplier of arms, Israel was able to offer a small range of extremely useful weapons as well as the military expertise which has enabled South Africa to develop its own modern arms industry.

Because of the secrecy which surrounds arms deals with South Africa, it is impossible to obtain accurate information about the extent of Israeli shipments. However, it is possible to detail a number of the arms deals that have been made.[3] They include:

- 6 *Reshef* missile-armed fast attack craft (FACM), with another 6 on order but not yet supplied. (These are designated "Minister" in South Africa.)
- 6 *Dvora* missile-armed fast attack craft.
- At least 1 missile-armed *Corvette*.
- The *Gabriel-2* ship-to-ship missiles (SSM), designated "Scorpion" in South Africa.

It seems unlikely that Israel has supplied any fighter or bomber-aircraft since these do not show up in any of the authoritative records about the composition of the South African Air Force, whose frontline planes came mainly from France. There have also undoubtedly been large orders for small Israeli weapons, especially the *Uzzi*.

Israel has been mentioned, along with France and West Germany, as being among the countries which have contributed to the development of South Africa's nuclear development program. The Israelis firmly deny any such involvement. It is frankly impossible to come to any positive conclusion either way. What seems fairly clear, though, is that the Israelis were not involved in the nuclear explosion test which was said to have occurred in the Atlantic on 23 September 1979.

The Israeli government announced in 1977 that it would faithfully observe the United Nations mandatory arms embargo; but because of the difficulties in effectively monitoring clandestine arms sales it is not possible to determine whether all military relations between South Africa and Israel have, in fact, ended since General Moshe Dayan made his pledge four years ago.

5.

The African Dimension

Colin Legum

Just ten years after the apartheid regime came to power in South Africa in 1948, President Kwame Nkrumah made his famous utterance on the eve of the decade of Africa's decolonization in the 1960s: "The freedom and independence of Ghana is meaningless unless it is linked up with the total liberation of Africa." That commitment was inscribed five years later in the Charter of the Organization of African Unity (OAU), Article II of which declared one of its purposes to be to "eradicate all forms of colonialism from Africa." At the foundation meeting of the OAU in 1963, President Ben Bella of Algeria, in a short but rousing speech, pledged 10,000 Algerian volunteers to help free African nations still under white minority rule. "We must all agree to die a little . . . so that African Unity may not be an empty word," he said to rapturous applause. Taking up his theme, Tanzanian President Julius Nyerere declared: "The time for allowing our brethren to struggle unaided is gone . . . from now on our brethren in nonindependent Africa should be helped by independent Africa."

Independent Africa's role in the affairs of Southern Africa has been by far the most crucial element in the international involvement in that region since 1963. Not only did the OAU member states contribute directly through their active support to the liberation movements and by their efforts to isolate the regimes of South Africa, Rhodesia, and the former Portuguese colonies; they also strongly influenced the role and policies of the extracontinental powers.

It was, of course, much easier for the anticolonial powers, like the Soviet bloc and China, to align themselves behind the OAU's policies than it was for the major Western powers, whose interests in Southern Africa conflicted at important points with their interests in the rest of the continent—especially during the 1960s and early 1970s, when the white-dominated regimes were still predominantly strong and seemed to be capable of weathering the onslaughts made against them. Only when their challengers began to emerge as serious threats to the *status quo* regimes, thanks largely to the support they received from independent Africa, did the Western powers begin to trim their policies and seek to harmonize their conflicting interests between the two political systems in the continent—majority-ruled and minority-ruled. This exercise became much more difficult for them after the collapse of the Portuguese empire in 1973. It is hard to argue against the proposition that, but for the existence of the OAU and its success in maintaining a broad consensus for its policies in Southern Africa, the political contours of the region and the international involvement in its affairs would have been remarkably different from the present picture.

A "strategy for liberation" for completing the "unfinished African revolution" was formulated in rather general terms by the OAU at its inauguration. There were three elements in the strategy. The first was a policy for isolating the Portuguese, South African, and Rhodesian regimes within the continent itself by such means as proscribing diplomatic ties between OAU member states and the white minority regimes; by maintaining an economic boycott of South Africa; and by restricting other forms of contact.

Malawi was the only OAU member which did not heed the ban on formal diplomatic ties with Pretoria. And while the trade boycott was never made fully effective, it was nevertheless largely successful in limiting South Africa's export market to its natural economic hinterland.

The second element of the liberation strategy was to involve the international community in backing the policy of isolating Lisbon, Pretoria, and Salisbury. This aim was pursued through direct appeals to the major trading partners of the white-ruled regimes, and by using international forums to keep up the pressures for this demand. The United Nations General Assembly proved to be a particularly receptive arena for the OAU's campaign—so much so that the major Western powers found themselves, by the late 1960s, in a minority in that world forum, and forced to fall back on their entrenched position in the Security Council to defend themselves from the international pressures built up by the OAU. The sharp cutting edge of its campaign at the U.N. was the demand for a program of international sanctions against South Africa and Portugal and, after the Unilateral Declaration of Independence (UDI) by the Smith regime, also against Rhodesia. The adoption of mandatory sanctions against Rhodesia in 1966 marked the high point of this campaign; it was also the first occasion when Article 41 of the U.N. Charter (which provides for mandatory sanctions) was successfully invoked. Pressures for sanctions were also successful in getting a mandatory arms embargo declared against South Africa.

The Commonwealth of Nations provided a second international forum for the promotion of the OAU's objectives. Among the significant victories won by the African Commonwealth members of the OAU were the exclusion of South Africa from the Commonwealth in 1961; Britain's agreement not to negotiate a settlement with the Smith regime that did not have the approval of "all the peoples of Rhodesia"; and the Lusaka agreement of 1979, which produced the Lancaster House talks and the subsequent victory of the Patriotic Front in Zimbabwe.

The third element of the OAU strategy was support for the armed struggle of the liberation movements in the Portuguese territories, Rhodesia, Namibia, and South Africa. At its inception, the OAU established a standing multinational Liberation Committee through which to channel African economic and military support to the guerrilla movements recognized by the organization. The Liberation Committee also became the channel through which foreign military assistance was to flow to the liberation movements. Although the Soviet bloc, especially, did not always respect the OAU's directive on this point, nevertheless a substantial part of the military aid from outside the continent, and virtually all that originated within it, was channeled through the Committee. The OAU's insistence on this point stemmed from its desire to prevent the liberation movements from being exploited by foreign interests; it also enabled the organization to establish its own priorities for the development of the armed struggle in the different parts of Southern Africa, with the first priority going to the anti-Portuguese struggle and the second to the Rhodesian front.

The OAU "strategy of liberation" can thus be seen to have been important not only for the way in which it had shaped the form of independent Africa's involvement in Southern Africa, but also for the contribution it made to raising the level of international involvement in the region and in determining the nature of that involvement.

Apart from the "strategy of liberation," the other key document in the OAU's approach toward the problems of Southern Africa was the Lusaka Manifesto of 1969. It was originally signed by thirteen governments, but was later endorsed by the OAU, which then lodged it as a formal declaration of its policy with the U.N. The Manifesto opened with the statement that:

> When the purpose and the basis of states' international policies are misunderstood, there is introduced into the world a new and unnecessary disharmony. Disagreements, conflicts of interest, or different assessment of human priorities, already provoke an excess of tension in the world and disastrously divide Mankind at a time when united action is necessary to control modern technology and put it to the service of man. It is for this reason that, discovering widespread misapprehension of our attitudes and purposes in relation to Southern Africa we, the leaders of East and Central African States, meeting at Lusaka on April 16, 1969, have agreed to issue this Manifesto.

The Manifesto set out the collective African view toward the nature and problems of the societies in Southern Africa:

> We wish to make it clear, beyond all shadow of doubt, our acceptance of the belief that all men are equal, and have equal rights to human dignity and respect, regardless of colour, race and religion, or sex. . . . On the basis of these beliefs, we do not accept that any one group within a society has the right to rule any society without the continuing consent of all the citizens.

After admitting shortcomings in their own states, the signatories went on to state that if it were simply a question of imperfections in the societies of Southern Africa, there would be no justification for the active hostility toward the regimes of the region as such. But, they argued, the position is that these regimes are "deliberately organizing these societies" in a way that denies the principles of human justice. "It is for this reason that we believe that the rest of the world must be interested. For the principle of human equality, and all that flows from it, is either universal or it does not exist." The Manifesto emphatically declared:

> Our stand towards Southern Africa thus involves a rejection of racialism, not a reversal of the existing racial domination. We believe that all the peoples who have made their homes in the countries of Southern Africa

are Africans, regardless of the colour of their skins; and we would oppose a racialist majority government which adopted a philosophy of de-
liberate and permanent discrimination between its citizens on grounds of
racial origin.

Having stated this philosophic approach to society, the Manifesto
came out firmly in favor of a peaceful solution to the problems of the
region:

> We would prefer to negotiate rather than to destroy, to talk rather than
> to kill. We do not advocate violence; we advocate an end to the violence
> which is now being perpetrated by the oppressors of Africa. If peaceful
> progress to emancipation were possible, if changed circumstances were
> to make it possible in the future, we would urge our brothers in the
> resistance movements to use peaceful methods of struggle, even at the
> cost of some compromise on the timing of change.

The Manifesto made a clear distinction between the colonial situations in Angola, Mozambique, Rhodesia, and Namibia and the different status of South Africa. "The Republic of South Africa is itself an
independent sovereign state and a member of the United Nations."
The case for international intervention in the affairs of such a sovereign state was stated to be that

> the whole system of government and society in South Africa is based on
> the denial of human equality; and the system is maintained by a ruthless
> denial of the human rights of the majority of the population and thus,
> inevitably, of all. For this reason Africa cannot acquiesce in the mainte-
> nance of the present policies against the peoples of African descent.

The Lusaka Manifesto became the cornerstone of the OAU's approach to the role which the continental governments and the rest of
the international community were expected to play in removing the
last remnants of the racially discriminatory societies in Africa. The
preference of the OAU has remained for peaceful rather than violent
solutions—as was demonstrated on each occasion when the opportunity for peaceful negotiations presented itself. Thus, after the collapse of Portuguese colonialism, the OAU played an active role in
helping to arrange the last stages of decolonization by successfully
encouraging collaboration between the guerrilla leaders and the new
regime in Lisbon. The Organization strove to ensure a peaceful transition in Angola by insisting on the right of all three of its liberation

movements to be included in a coalition government of independence—an effort ultimately frustrated by foreign intervention.

The so-called Front Line States (Tanzania, Zambia, Botswana, Angola, and Mozambique) eagerly took up the offer of then-U.S. Secretary of State Kissinger to participate in an Anglo-American initiative to end the fighting in Rhodesia. They played a key role in ensuring the success of the Lancaster House talks and in helping to prevent the breakdown of the final transition process that led to the birth of Zimbabwe. (In this latter effort, Marxist Mozambique played a particularly significant part.) When the Western members of the Security Council—the so-called Contact Group—launched their initiative to achieve a peaceful settlement within the U.N. framework in Namibia, the Front Line Presidents, once again, showed their eagerness to cooperate in bringing about a negotiated settlement; in this particular case, Marxist Angola showed itself to be as keen as anybody else to defuse the fighting in Namibia and to encourage all the parties to the conflict to sit around a table to discuss a peaceful way out of the violent struggle.

Thus, while the OAU has not shirked from supporting the armed struggle where no alternative seemed possible, it has at the same time shown itself ready at all times to cooperate with the rest of the international community in seeking peaceful negotiations for the conflicts of the region wherever the opportunities presented themselves.

In the various conflict situations in Southern Africa, the African leaders have been the principal actors, pursuing their own independent policies and interests, and without showing subservience to any of the extracontinental powers, whether Western or Communist.

Even though the Western powers failed to provide military and economic support for the liberation movements, leaving the Soviet bloc and China as their principal armorers, the OAU has nevertheless always been ready to respond to opportunities to cooperate with the Western powers whenever the latter have chosen to align their policies with those of the OAU. The OAU has never submitted to the views of the Soviet bloc when its own approach to particular situations differed sharply from that of Moscow—as over the settlement of the Rhodesian crisis or the Western initiative in seeking to negotiate an internationally accepted settlement in Namibia.

6.

Nigeria and Southern Africa

Olajide Aluko

The Organization of African Unity (OAU) has played a major role in the effort to complete the unfinished task of the total decolonization and eradication of apartheid and racism in Southern Africa. Nigeria, the most populous and potentially the most powerful Black African state, has been the moving spirit behind most of the policies and postures of the OAU and elsewhere that have related to Southern Africa.

Nigeria's Significant Achievements in Southern Africa

Nigeria spearheaded the move that led to the withdrawal of South Africa from the Commonwealth at the Prime Ministers' meeting in London in March 1961. A decade later, General Gowon's Nigeria blocked the proposal for dialogue with South Africa at the June 1971 OAU Summit meeting in Addis Ababa, Ethiopia.

Still more striking was Nigeria's open opposition in 1975 to U.S. policies in Angola, which it interpreted as support for the South African invasion of that country. The American Embassy in Lagos was bombed in January 1976, and over the following seven months, requests by the American Secretary of State, Henry Kissinger, to visit Lagos were refused three times, partly also because of Kissinger's efforts to secure a Rhodesian settlement. The Nigerian decision to recognize the MPLA, led by Agostinho Neto, as the legitimate government of Angola turned the scales against its America-supported opponents, Jonas Savimbi's UNITA (National Union for the Total Independence of Angola) and Holden Roberto's FNLA (National Front for the Liberation of Angola). Nigerian recognition of the MPLA

128

government was soon followed by most of the other African states, and eventually by all Western countries except the United States.

Nigeria's consistent opposition to the Ian Smith regime in Rhodesia, and to that of its Muzorewa-Smith successor, became an important factor in preventing the latter's recognition by the Conservative government that took office in May 1979. The year before, Nigeria had begun to take an active role in negotiations to secure a more acceptable black-white settlement in Rhodesia than the Muzorewa-Smith constitution of 3 March, 1978. Shortly after President Jimmy Carter was welcomed to Lagos in March 1978—a reflection of a new closeness between the two countries arising from Carter's policy on human rights, his concern for Africa, and American awareness that its trade with Nigeria had already outstripped that with South Africa—Joseph Garba, former Commissioner for External Affairs, participated in a number of meetings in London to discuss such possibilities. He was present in August 1978 when ZAPU's Joshua Nkomo met with Ian Smith at President Kenneth Kaunda's State House Lodge outside Lusaka. When it proved impossible to arrange a second meeting in which ZAPU's Robert Mugabe would be included, he was flown to Lagos to be briefed by Garba. Any chance of continuing negotiations disappeared, however, when ZAPU forces shot down an Air Rhodesia Viscount near Kariba with numerous civilian casualties.

Prime Minister James Callaghan had refused to monitor the controversial Zimbabwe-Rhodesia election in mid-April 1979, won by Bishop Abel Muzorewa, but Margaret Thatcher, whose Conservative government came into office two weeks later, sent a team of observers to determine whether his victory had been in a "fair and free" contest. The impliction was that if the answer was affirmative the Muzorewa-Smith administration would be recognized, Rhodesia returned to legality, and U.N. sanctions lifted. But on 24 May, 1979, the same day that Mrs. Thatcher received a positive report on the election, Nigeria rejected all British tenders for a mammoth port project, asserting that until the Conservative government clarified its attitude toward Rhodesia, no proposals from British companies would be considered.[1] In July, Nigeria nationalized the British Petroleum share of Shell BP in which the British government had an interest. Nigeria's actions led the Front Line States to invite it to participate in their planning to prevent the threatened recognition, if necessary by joining the guerrilla struggle, and shook the new British government.

Lord Carrington, the new Foreign Secretary, realized the need for caution. Despite a majority vote in the American Senate in favor of lifting sanctions, President Carter had refused to do so. Prime Minister Malcolm Fraser of Australia rallied Commonwealth Prime Ministers against recognition; Mrs. Thatcher gave in to their persuasion at the Commonwealth Prime Ministers Conference in Lusaka; the Lancaster House conference between the rival Rhodesian parties took place; and Robert Mugabe became Prime Minister of independent Zimbabwe in April 1980. While there had been many actors in bringing about this resolution of one of Africa's toughest problems, the Nigerian role had been among the more decisive ones.

Nigeria's Policy toward South Africa's Control of Namibia

Nigeria's consistent opposition to white minority regimes in Southern Africa has led it to focus its attention recently on South Africa's continued control of Namibia. Early in 1980, President Shehu Shagari declared at Niamey in the Niger Republic that his government would take all measures necessary to ensure the speedy independence of Namibia. At the OAU Summit meeting in July 1980, he asserted that "Namibia must be independent next year"[2] (1981) and added that its "independence without Walvis Bay is a sham."[3] He also reaffirmed Nigeria's support for Namibia's and South Africa's liberation movements. In his address to the U.N. General Assembly on 6 October 1980, President Shagari again condemned the continued illegal occupation of Namibia by South Africa, and pledged that Nigeria would "continue to assist, encourage and support that struggle for independence in Namibia, and the elimination of apartheid in South Africa, with all our might and resources."[4] He called the termination of apartheid and racism in South Africa "the challenge of our decade. . . ."[5] In November 1980 President Shagari said that Nigeria was prepared to start an arms race with South Africa if Pretoria continues its arms buildup.[6]

What is the cause of this new urgency in Nigeria's policy toward South Africa? In the first place, the Nigerian government does not want the enthusiasm for decolonization and the elimination of white minority rule to be lost after the independence of Zimbabwe in April 1980. Secondly, the policy has been designed to galvanize public opinion behind the federal government at home.

More specific questions must also be asked about Nigeria's policies toward the white supremacist regimes in Southern Africa. What is the nature of Nigeria's interest in Southern Africa? What are its objectives? What is its capacity for attaining these objectives? What have been the past and present strategies for Nigeria toward South Africa, and with what results? What policy options does Nigeria have in the eighties in relation to the white supremacist-controlled areas of Southern Africa, Namibia, and South Africa itself?

It is easier to ascertain Nigeria's objectives in Namibia and in South Africa than the nature of its interests there. Its objectives are broadly similar to those of the OAU, the eradication of apartheid and racism in South Africa, and the attainment of majority rule and independence in Namibia.[7] Broadly speaking, Nigeria's interests in white-controlled Southern Africa can be grouped into three categories: racial, security, and economic.

Racial Concerns

Nigeria shares with most of mankind its abhorence of institutionalized racism. Its moral indignation against apartheid and the mass violation of fundamental human rights in South Africa and Namibia is fueled by Pretoria's continuing defiant attitude. Moreover, Nigeria, like most other Black African countries, finds it hard to understand why discrimination should be based on color and race. Colonialism involved some elements of racial discrimination experienced by many Nigerians and other Africans, and apartheid represents the worst form of colonialism, enslavement, and oppression. Much more than European colonialism, it rules out racial equality and the principle of self-determination.

Thus while apartheid has raised moral questions and anger, it has been compounded by the racist basis of the system. The moral issues have been exacerbated by the racial factor, and apartheid has become the greatest single rallying point for opposition, not only in Nigeria, but also among other black peoples both within and outside the OAU. The identification which Nigerians feel with the black majority being oppressed in South Africa and Namibia has been an important element in shaping Nigeria's attitudes and policies toward what remains of the white redoubt.

Security Considerations

While the Balewa government's opposition to South Africa during the 1961 Prime Ministers' Conference was based principally on moral grounds, the participation of the white supremacist regimes on the side of Biafra during the 1967–70 civil war convinced Nigerian leaders that these white minority governments posed a dangerous threat to the security and the survival of Nigeria as a united country. Dr. Okoi Arikpo, the Commissioner for External Affairs, said early in 1970 that the first bomb dropped on Lagos was manufactured in Rhodesia (now Zimbabwe) under Ian Smith's regime.[8] The South African government also provided moral, material, and military support to the Biafrans. After the civil war, Nigerian leaders remained convinced that the white supremacist regimes would continue to pose threats to the independence, sovereignty, and territorial integrity of the country as long as they existed. As General Gowon put it at the OAU summit in September 1970 at Addis Ababa: "We know from experience that in opposing colonialism and racialism in Angola, Mozambique, Guinea-Bissau, Zimbabwe, Namibia and South Africa, we are serving the cause of our own freedom and independence."[9]

In addressing the Assembly of Heads of State and Government in June 1971, General Gowon reemphasized the link between Nigeria's own security and independence and freedom in Southern Africa by declaring that:

> The forces which impede the freedom and independence of Africa and which at the same time seek to undermine our achievements remain very formidable. . . . They will never leave us alone to develop our natural and human resources to our advantage. They will forever want us to waste our time and energy in negative pursuits.[10]

All subsequent Nigerian leaders have shared this view. General Murtala Muhammed described the South African invasion of Angola as "a conspiracy against our continent."[11] Indeed, the 1976 Adedeji Report on foreign policy maintained that the expansion of South African military capabilities and its extension "into African countries and oceans" must be seen as "a threat to Nigeria's security. . . ."[12] While the danger and threats posed to Nigeria by South Africa may have been exaggerated by various Nigerian leaders, there is no doubt that the authorities in Pretoria will exploit any opportunity to weaken and destabilize the most populous, and potentially powerful, black country in the world. This is understandable given Nigeria's posture on the question of apartheid, separate development, and racism in Southern Africa, and the fact that the greatest potential threat to

South Africa's white regime is black nationalism rather than international communism.

Black Solidarity

The issue of race in shaping Nigeria's attitude to the white supremacist regimes has been relatively new. Under the Balewa government in the early sixties the country took a moral attitude to the apartheid system and racism in Southern Africa. However, the experience during the civil war when the majority of black people inside and outside Africa supported the federal government while the majority of the white population in North America and Western Europe were either indifferent or hostile to Lagos brought an element of black solidarity to the planning, policies, and pronouncements of Nigerian leaders.

Under General Gowon this element was hardly visible. It was not that the Gowon government did not promote the concept of black solidarity. It was that it went about it in a more discreet manner. Under the regime of Muhammed-Obasanjo it was raised to an important aspect of public policy. Indeed, the Adedeji Report on foreign policy in 1976 declared that one of the objectives of the country's external policy should be the defense and the promotion of the rights and interests of all black people within and outside Africa.

The Shagari government has given greater emphasis to this concept of black solidarity than ever before. In his first address to the National Assembly on 16 October 1979, President Shagari declared that one of his foreign policy objectives would be to promote the interests of "all black people throughout the world."[13] He has since repeated this commitment elsewhere. Stressing the importance of the black man everywhere, President Shagari declared, at the U.N. General Assembly on 6 October 1980, that ". . . the destiny of Nigeria is inextricably linked with the fortunes of all the countries of Africa and all the peoples of African descent abroad."[14]

Given the fact that Nigeria is the largest black country in the world, with a population of nearly 80 million, and given its relative wealth, it is understandable that it should be championing the cause of black people in Africa, especially in Namibia and South Africa. But to attempt to pursue the interests of *all* black people throughout the world is impractical. The interests of black peoples are too diverse, even in

Africa, to say nothing of those outside the continent. Nigeria does not possess the capacity to pursue that type of nebulous policy.

The pursuit of a dynamic and vigorous foreign policy requires ideals such as black solidarity, the Pan-Negro movement, or universalist ideologies such as capitalism or communism. But a country that seeks to pursue such objectives in its foreign policy must have the appropriate muscle to move them forward.

Furthermore, charity begins at home. The Nigerian government is primarily supported and financed by the taxpayers of the country to serve the interests of the country and its people. All other interests are secondary. Moreover, such ideals or philosophy must first take root firmly in the country that wants to propagate it to the rest of the world. In the case of Nigeria, questions of ethnic rivalry, jealousies, and hatred are far from being resolved. So this must necessarily weaken the ability of the Nigerian government to advance the cause of black solidarity abroad.

Nonetheless, by dramatizing the exploitation and oppression of black people in Southern Africa, the federal government succeeded in whipping up greater support for black solidarity among the Nigerian intelligentsia. With the encouragement of the Gowon government, a liberation fund was set up early in the seventies by the Afro-Asian Solidarity Organization. Later in the seventies, the Southern African Relief Fund was established. But both happened during the military regime when the country was under emergency laws and regulations. The civilian government is unlikely to be able to elicit such support from the public.

Economic Interests

Economic interests have hardly featured in the speeches of Nigerian leaders on South Africa and Namibia. While Nigeria has banned all economic and commercial ties with South Africa, business and government leaders are anxious to promote economic and trade ties with these territories once they come under black majority governments. For instance, while in the future Nigeria could sell oil to these territories, it could in return obtain the right to fish off the coast of Namibia and get access to the industrial goods and minerals of South Africa and Namibia.

All this remains for the indeterminate future. In the meantime, Nigerian government leaders have been silent about economic inter-

ests of their country in those territories. In 1978, when Chief Ade-
yemi Lawson, President of the Nigerian Chamber of Commerce,
Industry, Mines, and Agriculture, after visiting the Front Line States,
recommended establishing economic and commercial ties with South
Africa, the weight of public opinion was critical of his stand.[15] The
federal military government denied that its policies worked against
the country's economic well-being abroad, and maintained the official
ban on economic, commercial, and technical ties. Whatever goods
come to Nigeria from South Africa and whatever Nigerian crude oil
gets to South Africa through third parties has been shipped illegally.

Nonetheless, there have been some unofficial moves toward developing economic and commercial ties. Once their sharp divisions on
the political, diplomatic, and security levels are resolved, substantial
economic links can be expected.

Nigeria's Capability to Fulfil its Objectives

The capability of Nigeria to make South Africa comply with its
objectives and interests is very limited. The concept of capability is
difficult to define precisely because it involves both tangible and in-
tangible elements.[16] The three main elements are economic, military,
and political capabilities.

Economic Capability

Nigeria has great economic potential. It has a population of some
80 million people, an area of 356,669 square miles, and is rich in
agricultural and mineral resources. Its agricultural products include
cocoa, palm oil, ground nuts, logs, cotton, rubber, and coffee. Its
mineral resources include tin, columbite, tantalite, wolfram, gold,
lead, zinc, limestone, clay, kaolin, marble, coal, uranium, lignite, natural gas, and crude oil. Apart from the latter industry, few of these
resources have been mobilized, let alone developed.

Since the mid-seventies the country has been producing an average
of 2 million barrels of crude oil a day, but other sectors of the economy have declined. Indeed, agricultural production has so sharply
declined since the late seventies that about 13 percent[17] of its total
imports are for food. In the early seventies, even during the civil war,
agricultural output was so good that Nigeria was able not only to feed
its own population, but also to export to other African countries and

even overseas, but the situation has now been reversed. Apart from heavy dependence on food imports, there have even been occasional food shortages.

Manufacturing industry is in its infancy, contributing less than 6.5 percent of the Gross Domestic Product in 1979. The level of technological development is very low. In 1980, crude oil contributed about 80 percent of the federal government revenue and over 92 percent of its foreign exchange earnings.[18] Although increases in the price of oil enabled the country to build up its 1980 reserves, its overall economic position is not strong. A glut in the oil market and price decreases, as during 1977/78, would bring about a severe balance of payments crisis. In fact, the 1980 balance of payments surplus of 1.53 billion[19] was largely due to the high prices of oil following the crisis in Iran, and the subsequent Gulf war between Iran and Iraq.

Despite the oil boom, the country has been borrowing money from abroad since 1977. In the 1981 budget proposals presented to the National Assembly by President Shagari on 24 November 1980, there was provision for a substantial external loan.[20] The need for external loans is likely to be higher during the coming years with the launching of the Fourth National Plan 1981–86.[21]

Per capita income has been about $400 a year; and the 1978 GDP was estimated at $35 billion. The economy remains predominantly a colonial one, depending on the export of primary products and the import of finished goods. In almost every sense, it is still underdeveloped. Thus the capacity of the economy to support an active policy in Southern Africa would seem slim. But, as demonstrated in regard to Zimbabwe-Rhodesia, there is another aspect of the economy that gives the country some leverage over Western powers. Apart from crude oil, Nigerian economy seems to be the fastest growing market on the continent.

Trade between Nigeria and most of the major industrial Western countries has increased considerably, surpassing that of their trade with South Africa. In 1980, Britain exported over £2 billion in goods to Nigeria, and Nigerian exports to the United Kingdom during the period were valued at about £238 million, thus giving a trade balance of over £1.7 billion in favor of the United Kingdom. The same is largely true of Nigerian trade with France, and with West Germany. The United States for some time has run large deficits with Nigeria.

One of the significant points that can readily be seen from Tables 1

Table 1
Nigeria's Exports to Some Western Countries

Country	Total Value & Percentage of Oil Exports						Total Value & Percentage of Non-Oil Exports					
	1977		*1978*		*1979*		*1977*		*1978*		*1979*	
	₦ Mill.	%	₦ Mill.	%	₦ Mill.	%	₦ Mill.	%	₦ Mill.	%	₦ Mill.	%
U.S.A.	2,995.3	41.8	2,382.1	44.1	4,758.0	46.8	60.7	10.9	79.1	11.9	81.6	12.2
U.K.	446.2	6.3	141.2	2.6	213.5	2.1	171.3	30.7	185.5	28.0	181.3	27.8
France	549.3	7.8	610.4	11.3	1,026.1	10.1	16.4	2.9	61.1	9.3	64.3	9.6
Netherlands	720.6	10.2	713.0	13.2	1,291.2	12.7	134.2	24.1	99.6	15.0	91.8	13.7
West Germany	367.8	5.2	405.1	7.5	691.3	6.8	89.1	16.0	115.9	17.4	117.9	17.6

and 2 is that, while over half of Nigeria's total exports went to the United States, only about 10 percent of its imports came from there. In 1979, oil accounted for over 46.8 percent of its exports to the United States. But in 1980, the percentage of Nigerian crude that went to the United States was just over 30 percent, while the corresponding percentages to the Netherlands and France during the same year rose to 13.56 and 13.50 respectively.[22]

Table 2*

Nigeria's Imports from Some Western Countries

Country	Total Value of Imports in ₦ Million and Percentage of Total					
	1977		*1978*		*1979*	
	(₦ Million)	*%*	*(₦ Million)*	*%*	*(₦ Million)*	*%*
U.S.A.	776.0	11.1	885.7	10.9	789.4	10.9
U.K.	1,153.7	21.9	1,780.5	22.0	1,596.8	22.1
France	485.1	6.9	585.0	7.2	528.7	7.3
Netherlands	292.0	4.2	334.1	4.1	289.7	4.0
West Germany	1,094.6	15.7	1,279.5	15.8	1,144.3	15.8

*1. *Annual Report and Statement of Accounts of the Central Bank of Nigeria* December 1979 (Lagos, Government Printer), pp. 74–76.

The value of investments in Nigeria, especially from Western countries, has been considerable. The heaviest investments are in the oil industry, liquefied natural gas, agriculture, construction, banking and insurance, and manufacturing industries. While it has been difficult to establish the precise value of these foreign investments, it is estimated that in 1980 American investments in Nigeria amounted to over $3.5 billion,[23] a result in part of the nationalization of the assets of British Petroleum in July 1979 for shipping Nigerian oil to South Africa. The bulk of American investments is in the oil industry, followed by investments in agriculture, which are closely supervised by the U.S.-Nigerian Joint Agricultural Consultative Committee.

British investments amounted to about $1,500 million in 1980 and those of the Netherlands, West Germany, and France were also about $1,500 million each. Like their American counterparts, most of the Western European firms have been doing a lucrative business in contract jobs such as planning and building the new capital in Abuja, constructing roads and bridges, and developing pharmaceuticals, banking, and insurance companies. The implication of all this is that Nigeria can exert considerable political leverage on these countries if it should so decide.

Military Capability

In sharp contrast to Nigeria's economic potential, the military capability of the country is very low, compared to that of South Africa. The size of the Nigerian armed forces, put at 146,000, is more than adequate for the needs of the country, but they are ill-equipped. Although the army has recently acquired some light tanks, it does not have a single destroyer, submarine, or minesweeper. The air force, with 6,000 men and women, has only 21 combat aircraft and 6 medium range c-130h transport planes. It has no modern bombers or fighter squadron.

Although the country spent about 8 percent of its GDP on defense (i.e., about $2.67 billion)[24] during the 1977/78 fiscal year, about 90 percent of this amount, according to Lt. General T. Y. Danjuma, the former Chief of Defense Staff, was spent on salaries and personal emoluments. Even though defense expenditures have been rising under the civilian administration, only a small fraction has been used for acquisition of modern weapons.

The level of military technology in the armed forces is very low. Most of its weapons are imported from the developed countries. Although there is a defense factory in Kaduna for the production of light arms, its production is limited, even though in April 1980 the Defense Minister, Professor Iya Abubakar, told the press that arrangements to manufacture some arms locally had reached an advanced stage.[25]

Morale, leadership, and training within the armed forces are clothed in secrecy, and it is difficult to say how important the leadership of the armed forces considers advanced training. Of the 10 army officers originally nominated for training in the Department of International Relations, University of Ife, during the 1980/81 session about half were not released for the program.

Given its poor, outdated equipment, the Nigerian military is not a mobile force. It cannot seriously support or engage in any active operation outside Nigeria's borders which would involve supplying the army by land, sea, and air, as the 1979 Chad debacle proved. Hence, in relation to Namibia and South Africa, Nigeria's military capability is extremely limited, if not nonexistent. Despite the increased expenditure on defense since the 1970s, the military capability of the country is now lower than in the mid-seventies.

Political Capability

The country now seems more united than during the First Republic. But although the constitution vests in the federal government the conduct and control of external relations and defense, the Shagari government's control of these responsibilities is not nearly as absolute as was that of its military predecessors. Under the 1979 constitution, which was patterned on that of the United States, the president cannot declare war without the approval of both houses of the National Assembly meeting in joint session. He cannot legally send any member of the armed forces into combat duty outside Nigeria without the approval of the Senate. The Senate must also ratify the appointments of heads of diplomatic missions before they become valid. Moreover, no treaty can come into force until the National Assembly has enacted it into law.

A further restraint on executive power is that no money can be spent by the president from the consolidated revenue fund without the authorization of the National Assembly. It was under this provision that the National Assembly queried the president's $10 million grant to Zimbabwe at its independence.

Apart from these constitutional restrictions, the Federal cabinet is formed from a coalition of two different parties, the National Party of Nigeria (NPN) and the Nigerian People's Party (NPP). While the president is from the NPN, his Minister for External Affairs, Professor Iya Abubakar, is an NPP man. This fact sometimes creates difficulties in the formulation of foreign policy, and especially in regard to Southern Africa. The most notable example was the Minister's statement in Lagos in December 1980 opposing the use of force to change the "status quo" in South Africa as possibly "counter-productive."[26] This position is diametrically opposed to that of President Shagari, thereby giving the public the impression of a division over policy toward South Africa within the federal government.

Reflecting the diversity in culture, history, tradition, and religion within the country, the Nigerian Federation consists of nineteen states of which the governing coalition controls nine, with the other three parties governing the rest. Even under the military, the vast diversity in the country had dictated caution and moderation in the country's foreign policy postures,[27] and the present internal balance of power provides an additional reason why the government must tread cautiously abroad.

In any case, South Africa and Namibia are far distant from Nigeria. The nearest point to Nigeria of either of these territories must be between 4,000 and 5,000 miles. This physical distance would create enormous logistical problems for Nigeria, especially if its troops were to engage the South African forces in combat. At present, the Nigerian armed forces lack the capacity to operate in such a distant region, especially since South Africa is an industrial giant with enormous military and economic capability.

While South Africa has only 86,050 men and women[28] in its armed forces, it can quickly mobilize about half a million people by using the Citizen Force and reservists. Moreover, the army is mobile and well equipped with modern weapons.[29] Its navy is also well equipped, while it is said that the South African air force has the capability to strike targets as far away as Zaire and perhaps beyond.

Very little has been published about South Africa's nuclear capability, but it is widely believed to have it. In September 1979, a flash in the Atlantic Ocean was said by some experts to have been a nuclear test carried out by South Africa, possibly jointly with Israel. Although South Africa denied this, political analysts such as Robert Jaster believed that South Africa was responsible for the test.[30] Dr. Jaster also believes that the South African authorities would not hesitate to use tactical nuclear weapons against an invasion of Namibia by conventional troops operating from the southern part of Angola.[31]

The level of military technology in the Republic is very high. While South Africa still obtains some equipment from abroad, it is almost self-sufficient in the production of arms, ammunition, and other types of equipment including missiles, electronic equipment, and even maritime assault vessels.[32] Different kinds of aircraft, including fighters, helicopters, and light-strike aircraft, are being produced under French and Italian licenses.[33]

The economic capability of South Africa is also high. Its GDP in 1979 was estimated at $54.3 billion. Although its population of about 28 million in 1980 is only about a third that of Nigeria, the country is rich in strategic, mineral, and industrial resources. The South African government has been producing oil from coal in order to reduce its dependence on the outside world for its oil requirements. The output of its gold mines has kept its balance of payments in surplus since the seventies. Furthermore, the agricultural capacity of the country is great, and it has been exporting food to neighboring African states such as Botswana, Lesotho, Swaziland, Mozambique, Zambia, Zaire, and Kenya.

Western capital has long been involved on a massive scale in the exploitation of the mineral, industrial, and agricultural resources of South Africa. Partly as a result of the low cost of unskilled labor in the Republic, almost all the companies, including subsidiaries of Western multinational corporations, have succeeded in maximizing their profit beyond what obtains in other parts of the world. Because of the combination of all these factors, South Africa has recorded the highest rate of growth in the world since 1945.[34]

Despite United Nations protests, in which Nigeria plays an important role, South Africa continues to control Namibia and is said to have nearly 50,000 of its own and locally organized troops there. Namibia is rich in agricultural and mineral resources, being the world's largest supplier of karakul, and the second largest supplier (after South Africa) of gem diamonds.[35] Other mineral resources include phosphate, zinc, tin, vanadium, petroleum, and uranium. The territory also has a thriving fishing industry. Most of the firms operating in Namibia are either South African-owned or Western-owned. Major mining companies in the territory include the Consolidated Diamond Mines, a subsidiary of De Beers Consolidated Mines Ltd., and the Tsumeb Corporation, jointly owned by Newmont Mines and American Metal Climax Corporation.

It is clear that Nigeria's ability to take any direct measures against South Africa in order to attain its objectives is minimal. Some Nigerian leaders have urged that its oil should be used as a weapon against South Africa, but since Nigeria's oil does not go there it could only be used to pressure Western powers to act against South Africa.

Nigeria does attempt to apply pressure on South Africa by assisting its immediate neighbors and the liberation movement. It also uses propaganda and conference diplomacy.

Aid to Liberation Movements

Since its establishment, in 1963, Nigeria has been contributing generously to the oau Liberation Committee Special Fund. Moreover, since the end of the civil war in 1970, Nigeria has not only increased its contributions to the Liberation Committee Fund but has also been providing direct material, military, financial, and moral aid to the three leading liberation movements: the African National Congress (ANC), the Pan-African Congress (PAC), and the South-West African People's Organization (SWAPO).

Since the mid-seventies, Nigeria has been providing them with an annual financial subsidy amounting to about ₦5 million.[36] Since the second half of the seventies, they have been allowed to open offices in Lagos. In addition, scholarships are provided for study at various Nigerian institutions. Some members of these liberation movements are given military training in Nigeria.[37]

Nigeria has not been impressed with the performance of either the ANC or PAC, so it decided in 1977 to recognize a "third force"[38] called the South African Youth Revolutionary Council (SAYRCO), led by Khotso Seathlolo. The Nigerian government believes that young people such as this shook South Africa with the Soweto uprising of 1976 and that they could threaten and even undermine the existence of the apartheid system in South Africa. It has thus been providing military aid, including military training, to the members of SAYRCO, and coordinating their training with that of the Palestinian Liberation Organization (PLO). SAYRCO has its headquarters in Lagos, and its members enjoy diplomatic immunity as do the representatives of other liberation movements. Members of SAYRCO are also given scholarships by Nigeria for futher studies in that country.

Nigeria has also been providing material, military, and moral aid to SWAPO.[39] Since the independence of Zimbabwe, Nigeria has sent arms, watches, clothing, relief supplies, drugs, and food weekly from Lagos through Rwanda to SWAPO by Nigerian military transport planes.[40]

Propaganda Efforts

On the propaganda level, the Nigerian government has been trying to publicize the evils of apartheid. The external service of the Federal Radio Corporation beams regularly to Southern Africa. Unfortunately, the Nigerian transmitter is of poor quality, so its broadcast is rarely audible in Maputo or Salisbury. Moreover, South Africa's superior technological devices block the Nigerian broadcasts, and prevent them from reaching local audiences.[41]

At home, the Nigerian government encourages anti-apartheid publications and the formation of anti-apartheid organizations. The most
notable of these is the National Committee on the Dissemination of
Information on the Evils of Apartheid. The hosting in August 1977
in Lagos of the U.N. Action Conference on apartheid was part of the
propaganda warfare against South Africa. The South African Relief
Fund, set up by the government in 1977, was to raise money for the
liberation movements, but also to mobilize public opinion for their
cause within Nigeria.

Nigeria has been active in using international conferences to mobilize international opinion against South Africa. As noted above, Sir
Abubakar Tafawa Balewa, the Nigerian prime minister, was the most
vocal critic of South Africa at the Commonwealth Prime Ministers'
meeting of March 1961. All subsequent Nigerian leaders have followed this trend, some with increased vigor. General Gowon spearheaded the opposition to dialogue with South Africa in 1970/71, and
at the OAU Summit meeting in June 1971 he gained the support of
over two-thirds of the heads of state and government against any
dialogue with Pretoria. Nigeria has continued to champion the anti-
apartheid crusade at the U.N. General Assembly and at Security
Council meetings. The major reason why Nigeria successfully sought
the nonpermanent seat on the Security Council in October 1977 (in
opposition to the Republic of Niger whose nomination had earlier
had the support of the OAU Summit) was to have an important voice
in shaping developments in Southern Africa, especially in Zimbabwe,
Namibia, and South Africa.

One of the immediate objectives of Nigeria's campaign against
South Africa is to isolate it diplomatically, economically, militarily, and
culturally. While some success has been recorded in areas such as
sports and U.N. conferences, it has not proved possible to isolate
South Africa in military, economic, financial, technological, and even
cultural fields.

The Obasanjo government tried to isolate South Africa economically by making it impossible for any firm operating in South Africa
to get new contracts or even to do business in Nigeria. The government promised to set up an economic intelligence unit to monitor the
activities of all multinationals operating both in Nigeria and in South
Africa with a view to taking appropriate steps against them. But because of the heavy involvement of multinational corporations in the

Nigerian economy, there was very little the government could do. Apart from nationalizing British Petroleum and, in 1978, the assets of Barclays Bank, no other important foreign firms have been taken over.

For economic reasons the Nigerian government has been unable to stop multinationals such as the Standard Bank, the ICI, Shell, Texaco, and Gulf that operate in Nigeria from continuing or expanding their business interests in South Africa. Political factors such as domestic pressures as well as the lack of regard by the Reagan administration for Nigerian and African views on apartheid and the Namibian question might lead the Shagari government to take reprisals against some Western interests. Both President Shagari and his ministers have made this clear on several occasions. With the present over-supply of oil to the world market, Nigeria may not be able to threaten to cut off oil supply to the United States. If the market position were to change, however, Nigeria might use oil as a political weapon against the United States.

Western firms which deal with South Africa might be denied contracts in Nigeria. Moreover, Nigeria might take political, diplomatic, and cultural measures against Western powers that work against the implementation of Resolution 435 of the Security Council on Namibia, or that support South Africa. Indeed, unless the Reagan administration changes its policies toward Southern Africa, such as the attempt to repeal the Clark Amendment and back the Savimbi dissidents in Angola, the Nigerian government may be forced to take measures against the United States.

Despite Nigeria's efforts, the armor of apartheid has remained undented. Whatever changes have been made by South Africa have been in response to its own economic needs and to critical opinions in Western capitals, especially the insistence on human rights by the Carter administration during its first two years. Pretoria continues with its apartheid policy, and new Bantustans such as Ciskei are being prepared for pseudo-independence. Political and economic rights are still denied to the black majority population. In military terms, South Africa has become a more formidable power now than it was in the sixties. As Peter Calvocoressi stated recently, "In the sixties South Africa was nervous about her position in Southern Africa, but by the end of the seventies much had changed. South Africa sustained Smith's rebellion almost single-handed. It ended its acute dependence on foreign oil. . . . It is getting its way in Namibia where, only a few years ago, it feared the establishment of a hostile state."[42]

Policy Options in the 1980s

Any writing about the future is a risky venture. But in some real sense the future is a function of the past and the present. So Nigerian policies toward South Africa and Namibia during the rest of this decade will resemble its past and present policies.

Given the size, population, and economic and military potential of Nigeria, it cannot easily retreat from the struggle against apartheid. Therefore, in the 1980s it must continue to intensify its material, military, moral, and diplomatic support for the liberation movements in South Africa and Namibia.

However, Nigeria has to supplement its past policies with new ones if a significant impact is to be made. It must be fully recognized in Lagos that South Africa can only be toppled by military force, as the Adedeji Committee maintained as far back as 1976. A similar view was expressed recently by *West Africa,* 3 November 1980. If Nigeria cannot send troops directly to Namibia, it must be ready to assist Angola with men and materials to defend its southern border with Namibia. This will help the Angolan government to flush out the remnants of UNITA rebels, and will also strengthen SWAPO's base of operation. But this cannot be done until the capability of Nigerian armed forces has been improved.

Since South Africa has nuclear capability, there is no reason except expense why Nigeria cannot develop its own bomb. *New Nigeria,* 7 November 1980, describes the controversy over the costs of a nuclear device. In 1976, Nigeria signed an agreement with West Germany for a nuclear reactor and work has started on this project. The acquisition of a nuclear device could give a signal to Pretoria that Nigeria cannot be subjected to political blackmail by apartheid bombs.

At the U.N. General Assembly Nigeria should try to work with Third World members for a new strategy for passing a Uniting for Peace Resolution over Namibia. The passing of such a resolution should be accompanied by military preparedness by a number of countries including Nigeria. With proper planning and coordination, South Africa's position in Namibia could become threatened and untenable.

Furthermore, the Nigerian government must be prepared to take tougher measures against any of the Western powers that are insensitive to Nigerian opinion on apartheid and the continued illegal occupation of Namibia by South African forces. The Great Powers must learn that Nigeria's opposition to apartheid is not negotiable.

During the last two years of the Obasanjo regime Nigeria came to be too much identified with American interests in Southern Africa. The present Nigerian government does not profess "socialism" and while this position has made some Western powers, such as the United States, take Nigeria's support for granted, it has made Nigeria suspect in the eyes of freedom fighters.[43] Should the Shagari government take tough measures against the United States, that would make his government more popular at home.

Finally, in the eighties, Nigeria must work in close concert with the Front Line States and the OAU over what policies are to be adopted. For instance, for nearly two years, until July 1980, Nigeria was the only OAU member state to recognize the PAC faction led by Leballo. Up until now only Nigeria has been supporting SAYRCO. Nigeria should now try to make SAYRCO acceptable to the Front Line States, not as rivals to the ANC and the PAC, but as their partners in the common struggle.

If Nigeria is able to adopt the policy options suggested above, it will have done much toward achieving its objectives in Namibia and South Africa. Its ability to follow any of these options will, however, depend on the capacity of the federal government to ensure political stability, economic prosperity, and social progress at home.

7.

South Africa in the Political Economy of Southern Africa

Kenneth W. Grundy

In the 1980s, no longer buoyed and buffered by a ring of white-minority colonial and settler territories, shorn of its external defense perimeter, South Africa now faces a new set of pressures and readjustments. While there are elements of continuity from the past, there are also key changes, such as the independence of Zimbabwe, which will inevitably affect the role South Africa will be playing in the political economy of Southern Africa.

Successive accounts of international relations in Southern Africa have usually begun with the generalization that the Republic of South Africa stands as a dominating presence astride the region. So great is the economic might of South Africa and so well positioned is the Republic geographically that it still easily overshadows the combined economic weight of its black-governed neighbors. Thus South Africa attempts to utilize its economic and military power in an effort to maintain its own stability and security, and to achieve its regional political objectives. To displace Pretoria's control and to render its regime vulnerable would appear to necessitate at this point some extraregional forces working together with the forces of liberation in the region. But pressures by South Africa's increasingly militant black trade unions and other signs of growing instability militate against the dominant role it once played.

Nonetheless, South Africa continues to outproduce all its neighbors combined and, indeed, has 77% of the total national production of the ten Southern African states of the region. In 1978, the GNP per capita for the region was $880; for South Africa, it was nearly double, amounting to $1,609. In Mozambique, in contrast, the comparable figure was $153.[1] Thus South Africa's economic influence is very substantial. But times are changing and new political and economic configurations are emerging which may well help to rectify these imbalances.

A Shrinking Hinterland

The Historical Basis

As a mineral, agricultural, and industrial power in a region of otherwise underdeveloped economies, South Africa would naturally be expected to serve as a focus for economic growth and a magnet for capital, skills, labor, and technological leadership. This has traditionally been the situation: South Africans, especially the business community, have long perceived the African countries to the north as South Africa's "hinterland."[2] The Anglo-Boer Wars of 1880–81 and 1899–1902 were appropriately contests over who would dominate that hinterland.

The very founding of Southern Rhodesia in 1890 emanated from South Africa, although the flag that was planted was the Union Jack. Cecil John Rhodes, the founder of the British South Africa Company, had secured the Royal Charter and organized the Pioneer Column to assist in its mineral exploitation. His agency continued to administer Rhodesia until 1923. At that time, after its white settlers had narrowly defeated by referendum a proposal to amalgamate Rhodesia into the Union of South Africa, the British government granted the settlers what was described as "responsible self-government." Thenceforth, British and South African capital competed for economic control of Southern Rhodesia and of Northern Rhodesia (now Zambia). The South African model of racist control could not help but spill over the borders into neighboring territories as settlers and ideas flowed outward.

Yet General Jan C. Smuts for years labored in the belief that Great Britain and South Africa could reach accommodation on regional hegemony. An understanding between the two forces, Smuts thought, would facilitate South Africa's northward expansion. This became virtually impossible as white settler interests assumed command in Rhodesia. After Rhodesia's Unilateral Declaration of Independence (UDI), Great Britain was forced to abandon its contradictory role as both a counterweight to and partner in South African expansion. It became nearly impossible for intrusive Western economic interests to offset South Africa in the region.[3] It is no accident that the "outward policy" and increased South African economic and political activity throughout Southern Africa did not come about until after the British phase-out from the region.

But much of the South African rhetoric of the late 1960s and early 1970s reflected the euphoria carried by a hiatus in the armed struggle for the liberation of the region.[4] It occurred during a period of economic growth in South Africa and frustration for black nationalism regionally. During the decade 1959–1969 the average annual increase in real income in South Africa had been 6%, considerably exceeding population growth. In per capita terms this represented an increase of around 3% per year.[5] The southward thrust of African nationalism had been delayed by the Katanga secession from the Congo. Rhodesian UDI was a more determined counterhistorical effort. Portuguese resistance to change bolstered by Pretoria and Salisbury temporarily obstructed the nationalist movement southward.

The Limits of Hegemony

But there were absolute limits to the hegemonic potentialities of a white-ruled South Africa—ideological barriers and economic limits. Wealth and political power do not always go hand in hand, a fact not always appreciated by Pretoria. And there are other built-in factors that have led to a steady erosion of South Africa's regional power— among them black nationalism in South Africa and in neighboring states, global anti-imperialism, and the provincial perspective (as opposed to the worldwide perception of British imperial interests) that a settler regime brings to its expansionist enterprise.[6] What South Africa's leaders work for is an approval by the capitalist giants of Pretoria's own brand of subimperialism or intermediary capitalism. Global capitalist interests and their imperial governments have learned to adapt to governmental and policy changes in the developing world. Capitalists in settler societies lack that flexibility. They can no longer retreat to another part of the empire and recoup their losses, and they fear that to devolve their authority risks everything.

The capitalist West, though it profits from it, is not openly willing to carry without reservation the burden of complete identity with an overtly racist system.[7] Much of the ongoing foreign policy debate in

Pretoria centers on the issue of how far it must bend to gain that Western endorsement.[8] Periodic murmurs of neutralism between East and West, of threats to go it alone, of hostility to the West cannot mask the essential symbiosis between Pretoria and the West.[9] That linkage is increasingly illustrated by the recent gestures and statements of the Reagan administration. They need one another, but they still do not trust one another, since each can conceive of arrangements that might be more beneficial to itself.[10]

One of the more obvious features of the past decade has been the shrinkage in South Africa's northern hinterland, or at least in South Africa's virtually free access to "its" hinterland, and in its ability to translate continued economic muscle into political leverage. More than any single happening of the 1970s, the Portuguese coup of April 1974 set in motion a string of events that steadily eroded Pretoria's sense of security and space. Pretoria's diverse responses seem to indicate indecision as much as they do flexibility. Within the ruling elements of the National Party a foreign policy debate periodically surfaces—how best to conserve a fundamentally unstable regional order.[11] In the National Party, in the South African foreign service, and in the intellectual community are reflected reputedly deep cleavages between *verligte* (enlightened) and *verkrampte* (narrow-minded) nationalists. There is little disagreement over ultimate ends: to save the Afrikaner nation and its social structure, and, to the greatest extent possible, to preserve white political and economic dominance. The *verligtes* tend to be flexible, pragmatic, and willing to accommodate in order to defuse growing tensions. The *verkramptes* place much stock in displaying firmness. Each policy challenge is to them an opportunity to demonstrate determination and commitment to the status quo—an object lesson in strength. Both groups are conservatives—they differ as to acceptance and interpretation of change and, to a society unsure of itself, it becomes a deep cleavage fraught with hidden meaning.

South Africa's economic relationships with Angola were never considerable, though at one time they were potentially important. Its economic links with Mozambique and Zimbabwe have not been reduced significantly since the Portuguese coup. But the underlying mood among white South Africans is increasingly of constraint and constriction—of lost opportunities and regional isolation. The options and alternatives narrow.[12] Ten years ago South Africa could openly count upon Rhodesia, Portugal in Angola and Mozambique, and its own direct control of Namibia, as well as reluctant interaction with Botswana, Lesotho, and Swaziland. The outward policy and detente were aimed at diplomatic and economic breakthrough farther afield. Talk was of winning over black governments that possessed bona fide nationalist credentials—perhaps Kenya, Zaire, Zambia, as well as Malawi, Ivory Coast, Gabon, or Liberia. The breakthroughs never came.

Today, when Pretoria enthuses over a constellation of like-minded Southern African states, which do they mention? Venda, Bophuthatswana, Transkei? South Africa's leaders continue to hope that Botswana, Lesotho, or Swaziland can be persuaded to associate grudgingly with such a combination. Possibly they fantasize that Mozambique and Zimbabwe, out of sheer desperation, may tacitly participate. Much of this South African speculation is wishful thinking. As long as Pretoria insists on including its "homelands," either in the guise of independent states or as locally autonomous subdivisions, independent black states, as members of the OAU, will not join or even silently acquiesce in such an association. Structurally, South Africa would have to shape a "constellation" as a series of bilateral arrangements for even these remote dreams to become reality. Indeed, with the constellation idea now over two years old, we are hearing increasingly of two or more levels of cooperation. There is, so it would seem, an "inner" constellation comprised of South Africa and its "independent homelands" and a desire for a "wider" constellation with prospects for creation markedly more remote. Constellation in this context is reflected in concentric circles with varying degrees of acceptance, collaboration, and, for Pretoria, control.

This has had its domestic South African side effects too. Eleven years ago the South African Minister of Police and Interior could brag that there was not one known "terrorist" at large in his country.[13] South Africa can make no such claim today. If government can hope to dispel a feeling of encroachment on white-ruled South Africa, it has not publicly revealed its formula.

The internal-external linkages in foreign policy may also be reflected by the fact that it is precisely the domestic apartheid order that the foreign policy seeks to assure that makes foreign policy overtures to Black Africa non-starters. The internal system itself explains the failure of cooperative ideas from being successfully launched. No popular black government would openly identify with South Africa and thereby imply acceptance of a racist social structure. Pretoria almost inexplicably seems to think that "practical" economic considerations can outweigh emotional and realistic political factors. Its efforts are destined to failure until a genuine internal shift of power takes place. Pretoria still assumes that foreign policy changes will preclude the need for serious political rearrangements that give black South Africans real power.

The Mugabe electoral victory, preceded by the political-military success of the Patriotic Front, provided an unexpected blow to a Pretoria convinced that it "understood" Zimbabwean politics. Where were our intelligence people, they ask. How could they have failed to assess the popularity of Mugabe? This, coming on the heels of their military retreat in Angola, surely provided introspective moments for the more thoughtful of Pretoria's foreign policy and defense analysts. The implantation of avowedly revolutionary governments, hostile to apartheid, in Luanda, Maputo, and Salisbury stripped South Africa of neighboring governments where it had had a fairly free run militarily, politically, and economically. The Limpopo, not the Zambezi, is the new defense perimeter, the new salient, the new "border area."

A Constellation of Southern African States

An Old Idea Resurrected

Because of this situation, we have seen over the past three years the attempted resurrection of an old idea, that South Africa can serve as the focal point for the creation of a combination of regional states based principally upon economic considerations. Diverse structural models have been advanced in the past, from "co-prosperity sphere" and "common market" to the most recent amorphous scheme, the "constellation" of states.[14] Seldom are these newer ideas completely fleshed out. Politically, the more specificity brought to proposals at an early exploratory stage, the more likely opposition can coalesce, organize, and zero in on individual aspects of the proposals. In South Africa the language of power can be imprecise, especially when sketching directions of constitutional and structural change. This leaves politicians greater freedom to dissemble, retreat, and even to disown their own ill-defined positions. There is some measure of this strategem in South Africa's position. But part of the imprecision is because many of these specific ideas have been advanced before, in one form or another, and rejected. They are, simply put, impractical, politically unacceptable, and unrealistic.

This has not prevented Pretoria from advancing such ideas and from devoting considerable energy to their propagation. The government's elaborate pavilion at the Rand Easter Show in 1980 was given over to this theme. Throughout his tenure as prime minister, P. W. Botha has made repeated reference to the need for cooperation among the states of Southern Africa. Through 1979 his ideas about regional affairs began to take shape around the theme of a constellation of states. An interdepartmental committee chaired by the secretary for foreign affairs was established, known as the Committee for Economic and Development Cooperation in Southern Africa. Later a committee of experts headed by the government's chief economic advisor was appointed.[15] Each successive speech on the topic seemed to be more complete, more specific. As for function, the Prime Minister has proposed that particular attention be paid to:

- Monetary arrangements such as those involved in the rand monetary area agreement;
- The establishment of a multilateral development bank for Southern Africa, the rationalization of the existing development corporations, and special arrangements to encourage all business enterprise;
- The fiscal and other financial relations between the government and South Africa and the various categories of other states;
- Regional development, industrial decentralization, and customs union matters; and
- Agricultural development and food production.[16]

Yet Botha consistently refused to name the countries he proposed to include or to define the structure of the envisioned "constellation." In the No Confidence debate in February 1979, after briefly outlining various cooperative schemes in the region, he made offers of "cooperation" and "an agreement which will comprise a non-aggression treaty," all predicated on a desire "to keep communism out of Southern Africa."[17] He elaborated on these views later in the debate on the Prime Minister's Vote.[18] Again vigorous diplomatic and propaganda activity began to elicit black curiosity and even some mild interest. The ministers of foreign affairs and economic affairs met their counterparts from Botswana, Lesotho, and Swaziland in Mbabane in April 1979 in an attempt to get talks off the ground on the "Southern African alliance" that Pretoria favored.

Botswana, in particular, would not be inveigled into the process. Little progress was achieved.[19] That apparently did not discourage the government of South Africa from continuing to push the issue.

The Constellation and Domestic South African Concerns

Part of South Africa's persistence is because the constellation concept is bound up in a central issue in domestic South African politics—the constitutional configuration of relations with those homelands presumably seeking or achieving "independence" from the Republic. Diverse plans have been put forth by various commissions and study groups, public and private, partisan and nonpartisan, official and unofficial. Most prominent among the recent schemes have been the Schlebusch Commission, the Quail Report, the Buthelezi Commission, and the Lombard Plan. These plans have stimulated renewed debate on the territorial configuration and political redistribution of power within South Africa (South Africans seem to prefer the term dispensation).

The recommendations of the Schlebusch Commission of inquiry into the constitution on the matter of relations between the central government and the homelands called for Coloureds and Indians to participate in a limited fashion in a new nominated President's Council with advisory powers. Although blacks were excluded from this Council, they were to be able to have some policy input by means of a projected Consultative Council of their own. The present homelands program was to be retained. These recommendations were roundly rejected by most Coloured and black spokespersons and by the official opposition, the Progressive Federal Party (PFP).[20] Even the homelands leaders criticized the recommendations because blacks were not to be included in the powerless but not insignificant President's Council.

The commission appointed by the Ciskei government and chaired by George P. Quail examined the alternatives open to the Ciskei "homeland," and particularly the feasibility and practicality of "independence."[21] The various options—the status quo, full internal autonomy, federalism, confederalism, the constellation idea, a unitary state, amalgamation with the Transkei, independence, and a "multiracial condominium"—were discussed in some detail, especially the ramifications of independence. The Commission concluded that "independence" without significant concessions from Pretoria was an unattractive option. It preferred a negotiated political arrangement involving the whole region either along federal or confederal lines or in the form of a multiracial entity or condominium that would remain a part of South Africa. Despite these findings, the Ciskeian government decided later in 1980 to accept "independence" in December 1981 along the lines taken by the Transkei, Bophuthatswana, and Venda, even though the difficult issue of South African citizenship for Ciskeians residing outside the homeland was not resolved any more favorably than was the case for those other three homelands.

The 42-member multiracial Buthelezi Commission established by the KwaZulu government was asked to consider the political future of KwaZulu and Natal "within the context of South Africa and Southern Africa and to relate these conclusions to the issue of the constitutional future of South Africa as a whole."[22] The Lombard plan is among the several schema submitted to the Buthelezi Commission. It was financed by the South African Sugar Association, an industry deeply involved in the Natal economy. In that plan Professor Jan Lombard proposes a new constitution for Natal in which all apartheid laws are abolished and in which local authorities gain greater autonomy. Three main regional bodies, a homeland authority, a metropolitan authority, and a rural authority, would come together in a Natal/KwaZulu "overbody." Similarly, already "independent" former homelands would be included in other regions in the country. Each of eight proposed, largely self-governing regions would have similar structures which would join together in some as yet undefined confederal central government for all of South Africa. In the words of the Johannesburg *Star,* "The people of each region should seek prior consensus among themselves about the specific form of political participation within the region."[23]

One can see how broad ranging are some of the ideas being advanced. Some involve radical territorial and political changes. Others talk of partition along racial, ethnic, or modern/traditional lines. The government and the National Party and its various think tanks are also giving vent to their imaginations. Most seem to appreciate that the current arrangements will not suffice. But most nongovernment schemes seem unable to reconcile the dilemma of the need for radical change and the Nationalists' determination not to lose their grip on state power.

Hence, these constellation proposals ostensibly addressed to foreign affairs are to some degree a form of thinking aloud about what in reality is also a domestic issue. Blueprints for future territorial arrangements, including plans for mixed, dual, or irregular citizenship, and convoluted redefinitions of sovereignty, are drawn up in white South Africa with amazing energy. Moreover, rumors of which grand design is allegedly preferred by Prime Minister P. W. Botha (it would be impossible to infer that the National Party, in all its diverse aspects, has such a single preference) spin out of Pretoria regularly.[24] What most of these plans have in common is that black spokespersons have had little to do with their conceptualization. Those few blacks that have been involved in the government's planning hardly qualify as authentic voices of black nationalism. The very act of participating would in itself strip an aspiring black leader of any claims to legitimacy in the community. White nationalist leaders currently are not really interested in genuine "power sharing," as such proposals for the dilution of majority power are called. What seems to have emerged is, in the words of the PFP's Horace van Rensburg, a constellation with a "shortage of stars."[25]

Rooted in Capitalist Development

Repeated appeals to and repeated rebuffs by black leaders outside South Africa seem not to have altered Pretoria's stance, except perhaps to lengthen Pretoria's time frame and to sober the regime into reducing its geographic horizons. In his most complete exposition of the constellation idea, the prime minister addressed a specially arranged meeting with cabinet and business leaders.[26] It is significant that he chose this audience to announce this policy, for it served to highlight the underlying reasons for the constellation. In his words, they are "to promote free enterprise" and to resist "the Marxist onslaught," *and* to point up the essential collaboration between business and government. To this end the private sector is to be enlisted to march shoulder to shoulder with government against "foreign elements" (the Soviet bloc) that have come "to enslave and destroy." While rejecting the model of the European Economic Community, the Prime Minister nonetheless called for the creation of "machinery" to handle more efficiently the already high level of economic "interdependence." The objective ultimately is stability through regional economic development. Although it is not phrased in so many words, the economic might of South Africa, therefore, can be used to assure the necessary gradual or evolutionary quality to a managed change, and to defer and dissipate revolutionary verve by a modulated distribution of the rewards of economic growth. And because of South Africa's central role in the process, trickle-down enriches South Africa, stabilizes the region, and rewards black neighbors who play ball. The business leaders liked what they heard.

Appreciating the sensibilities of independent black states, Mr. Botha indicated that the "constellation of states" concept does not primarily denote a formal organization but rather a grouping of states with common interests and developing mutual relationships. Nonetheless, he invoked the already existing examples of the Rand Monetary Area and the Customs Union (involving Botswana, Lesotho, South Africa, and Swaziland and providing for, originally, a common currency, a central reserve bank, tariffs and customs regulations and restrictions, including duties collection and redistribution to member states), and SARCCUS (Southern African Regional Council for the Conservation and Utilization of the Soil). But these are hardly inspirational institutions these days. In October 1980, Zimbabwe left SARCCUS, apparently because South Africa is a member.[27] Yet Pretoria continues to invoke these names as if they can magically persuade independent black states to cooperate with them. Add the prospect for joint planning and action, topped off by an "effective institutional framework," which might presumably include a regional development bank and greater liaison with business, and Pretoria is prepared for another effort at streamlining its economic domination of the region. Public relations activities were redoubled to sell their endeavors.

Running throughout government thinking on regional constellations is an uncharacteristic affinity for a version of economic determinism. The primacy of economic forces somehow, it is believed, will bring rational actors (as if states would behave like classic "economic men") to the realization that too much will be lost by not continuing and expanding what are thought to be essentially technical/economic ties. It stems from a philosophy of the free market as the invisible guiding hand, ultimately rational, directing eventually all forms of social behavior. It also parallels quite closely the ideas of classic functionalist integration theory. As formulated by David Mitrany, functionalists preferred to conceive of international or supranational functions, services, and interactions as technical matters, nonpolitical in nature, and well removed from the pressures of ideology, political interests, and "irrational" concerns such as nation, status, or personality.[28]

Economic agreements and customs unions of various kinds may indeed stimulate trade and transactions. They may also lead to an awareness that individual states' machinery cannot alone solve evolving problems. With time, as organizations are established and grow, "spillover" ostensibly occurs and peoples increasingly come to develop shared values. It is expected that a community of interests will emerge that contributes to and facilitates a deeper integrative effort. But these assumptions, though presumably logical, are nonetheless faulty. Loyalties, in reality, do not always follow economic interests. Time, it is contended, is on the side of integration. Rather, in the case of an ill-formed or nonexistent community of interests, time merely provides an opportunity for deeper political conflict. Paying primary attention to economic interests when making difficult decisions makes sense only when the ideological and political framework within which interests interact can be taken for granted. When the framework is, instead, one of conflict and mutual rejection, politics becomes more than an important consideration, it becomes absolutely indispensable. In Southern Africa, the structure of relationships, internationally and within individual states, is still very much subject to revolutionary change. The states and the peoples today lack a shared value system.

The loose economic subsystem presently dominated by South Africa has been constructed, enlarged, and now tenaciously defended because it enables the Republic to enrich itself at the expense of its regional neighbors. The economy is a major instrument of South African foreign policy. It is used to provide stability for the region, a stability which protects the domestic and international order that works to the advantage of the white dominant order. The other states, sensitive to the South African posture, wisely and naturally resist being drawn in. The proponents of a South African–based constellation are realists when it comes to wanting to extend and entrench the regime's politico-economic power. They are naive in thinking that black-governed states would accept such arrangements.

As would be expected, within days the scheme was denounced in Black Africa.[29] It is seen for what it is, a plan to enable South Africa to sustain itself under a minority government subject only to nominal change. The idea, first launched to involve the Zimbabwe-Rhodesia of Bishop Muzorewa and Ian Smith, found itself stillborn. The internal settlement's failure to stabilize Zimbabwe and the popularity and electoral victory of Robert Mugabe's wing of the Patriotic Front provided the potential members with an altogether alternative vision.

SADCC

The 1980 Lusaka Summit

On the crest of the Zimbabwe victory, a one-day summit met in Lusaka in April 1980 to coordinate regional development and to take steps to lessen the black states' dependence on South Africa. Nine states were represented, including the five Front Line States (Angola, Botswana, Mozambique, Tanzania, and Zambia), Zimbabwe (though not yet formally independent), and Lesotho, Swaziland, and Malawi. The summit approved a declaration drawn up at a Southern Africa Development Coordination Conference (SADCC) held nine months earlier in Arusha, Tanzania.[30] The Lusaka joint declaration called for better integration of the black states' economies, and the leaders approved a seven-point plan to reduce economic dependence on South Africa. Additional steps to coordinate activities were announced and a division of labor was agreed upon for carrying through on the proposals.

The Front Line States

Promise and hopes were high after this meeting. The states of Southern Africa had had considerable experience at high-level diplomatic coordination. The Front Line States, in particular, had since 1974 been meeting, planning, taking joint stances, and being deeply involved in the political and military efforts to liberate minority-ruled Southern Africa. In the process they honed their diplomatic skills and emerged as a surprisingly cohesive and influential new factor in regional affairs.[31] Their experience, leading up to the Mugabe victory in Zimbabwe, gave reason for optimism that the same principles of patient consensus and resolve might lead to success on the regional economic front.

The Lusaka meeting approved the creation of a Southern African Transport and Communications Committee based in Maputo, and measures to control foot and mouth disease led by Botswana in cooperation with the EEC. Botswana was also to ask the International

Crops Research Institute for the Semi-Arid Tropics (ICRISAT) to establish a regional agricultural research center. In addition, arrangements were included for the creation of a regional development fund, permanent administrative machinery, harmonization of industrialization and energy policies, and other joint economic concerns.[32]

This summit marked an important turning point in the political-economic struggles in Southern Africa. It symbolized a realistic black awareness of the need to strengthen their own cooperative institutions in order to reduce their growing reliance on economic contacts with South Africa. In short, if the struggle for the eventual achievement of majority rule in South Africa and Namibia is to be successful, regional states must get their own economic houses in order. Zambia and Mozambique, for example, have suffered directly from the Zimbabwean conflict. Zimbabwe itself is rebuilding its public sector. Angola likewise has borne an inordinate share of the costs of the struggle over Namibia.

Domestic Political and Economic Challenges to SADCC Success

The domestic political economies of these states pose problems that prevent governments from concentrating their full efforts on regional economic issues. They deflect attention from the larger economic picture. In Zambia, the number of persons in wage-paid employment has been falling steadily since 1975, this during a period of population growth. Few new employment opportunities are created. The gap between urban and rural incomes widens as those who are employed agitate for more pay. A series of strikes through 1979 and 1980 severely weakened the economy, especially the copper industry.[33] Then, in October 1980, there was an attempted coup in Lusaka and a number of top Zambian officials were apprehended in the aftermath.[34] Small wonder that in this state of internal disturbance, the economy falters. Indeed, economic dislocation, mismanagement, and corruption account in large measure for the dissatisfaction on which the unrest feeds.[35] With such pressing domestic concerns, there is little opportunity to devote time to one of the root causes for economic decay, the regional nexus.

Zimbabwe also confronts problems. Emerging from wartime conditions, the new government was immediately faced with resettling refugees, reactivating many of the public services that were cut back and even abandoned in some areas (schools, clinics, cattle dips, and so forth), and retraining and demobilizing upwards of 30,000 fighting men from diverse and at times competing guerrilla, private, and regular military formations.[36] The sheer costs of supporting a large military establishment are staggering. Present army strength is around 50,000 (45,000 of which have been integrated from the ZANLA and ZIPRA liberation forces of Robert Mugabe and Joshua Nkomo). In February 1981, a beer brawl developed into violent ethnic fighting outside Bulawayo, and had to be quelled by the regular Zimbabwe security forces. It resulted in some 200 dead.[37] Subsequently all the guerrillas were disarmed. The costs of these responsibilities have only partially been offset by the termination of sanctions and renewed injections of foreign investment and economic assistance. The positive economic performance of Zimbabwe in its first years of legitimate independence is encouraging.

While there have been substantial social and economic changes in Angola and Mozambique, economic failures are compounded by organized and externally aided internal resistance. The Mozambique Resistance Movement (MRM) operates chiefly in northwestern areas of the country, selectively intimidating supporters of the central government and striking at economic installations and political and governmental institutions. Its diffuse campaign against the FRELIMO government has destroyed rail and power lines and launched a terror campaign even in some urban areas. Since MRM seems to operate most effectively on the route from Umtali (Zimbabwe) to the port of Beira, the economic consequences of MRM are potentially extensive. At present MRM seems to get almost all of its assistance from South Africa. It operates a radio transmitter in the northern Transvaal, and it is alleged that South African military aircraft supply the rebels. Pretoria, as usual, denies complicity.[38] There is, of course, no denying the late January 1981 South African military strike at ANC offices and houses in the suburbs of Maputo.[39] The South Africans regularly intervene, in one form or another, in Mozambique's affairs, and this reality is an insult to Mozambique's sovereignty.

The links between South Africa and UNITA in Angola are even closer and broader than the South African ties to MRM. Thanks to South African assistance, UNITA continues to operate in southeastern Angola and to tie down government and Cuban troops. UNITA operations coupled with frequent South African cross-border incursions make difficult the diversion of sufficient resources for regional economic enterprise and planning. In fact, South African military incursions into Zambia, Mozambique, and Angola have been a regular feature of regional affairs since the Portuguese coup. There is no way these facts can be ignored when looking at the larger economic picture. Yet in this unsettled environment, the governments must rebuild their shattered political institutions and deteriorating economic structures. They do this for their own internal purposes, as well as to enable them to try to force change on South Africa. The Lusaka summit did not mean an abandonment of the fight against apartheid—rather, it is a consolidation of the gains thus far, and a preparation for confrontations anticipated with South Africa.

While the South African government apparently operates with the notion that its own economic strength will eventually win for it acceptance and survival, that country was conspicuously excluded from the Lusaka and subsequent SADCC proceedings.[40] Despite close economic links with South Africa, or rather because of them, black states seek to reduce their economic vulnerability. They seem to be saying, in a most pragmatic way, "Seek ye first the economic kingdom, and all things shall be rendered unto you." They also realize that this will be a long haul, and that short-term solutions, scapegoating, and other forms of excuse-making will not really carry the day. A sober Robert Mugabe put a diplomatic gloss on the Lusaka conference. When asked how long it would take to lessen Southern Africa's dependence on South Africa, he said: "I don't think one can really say. But all countries recognize the reality of the present economic links with South Africa, and it was emphasized that the conference was not really against South Africa, but rather directed towards the attainment of economic independence."[41] Other leaders likewise stressed the need to build first "the foundation and not the roof."[42] Nonetheless, powerful South Africans like Harry Oppenheimer smugly insist that "no economic grouping of southern African States could afford to exclude the most powerful and most highly developed country in the area. . . . The facts of geography and economics will win over even the minds of obstinate men."[43]

The Follow-Up to Lusaka

Although the Lusaka conference may have been a promising beginning, it was no more than an early step. Joint planning preceded the Lusaka conference and followed in its wake. Related but not formally affiliated countries assembled in Botswana in January 1980 to discuss the formation of a preferential trade area that would exclude South Africa. Also attending were representatives from the United Nations and the Organization of African Unity as well as from various Southern African liberation movements.[44] Regularly, ministers from Botswana, Lesotho, and Swaziland meet to discuss common problems (labor, commerce, finance, development, among others) independent of Pretoria's input.

Later seven regional states formed a Labor Ministers' Commission to explore the possibility of ending labor migration to South Africa by African workers from independent states.[45] Yet they admit that unless new jobs can be created in these states—and the record has not been promising—it will be difficult to stem the flow of work seekers.

The direct follow-up to the Lusaka summit was a ministerial meeting of SADCC held in Salisbury in September 1980.[46] Its activities indicate that SADCC is gradually evolving its reportorial and organizational structures. Ministers resolved to appoint a council of ministers to supervise the activities of the organization, and to form a permanent secretariat to service and coordinate SADCC activities. Botswana was asked to form a committee of experts to recommend secretariat details of service, structure, and budget and, at a later summit, in July 1981, was requested to provide the permanent secretariat.

In the field of transport cooperation, delegations from five states— Zaire, Zambia, Zimbabwe, Malawi, and Mozambique—met in Maputo, in July 1980, following a meeting of their chief executives (except for Malawi) in June at which they discussed ways of reducing their dependence on South Africa's railways and ports, principally by expanding use of those of Mozambique. The increased reliance on Mozambique's facilities was reflected in two agreements between Mozambique and Zambia (to provide for the use by Zambia of the ports of Maputo, Beira, and Nacala) and Zimbabwe (to resume transport and communication links between the two countries).[47] Further exploration of alternatives took place in August when railway officials of five states met in Bulawayo and Malawi-Zambia and Zambia-Tanzania-China negotiations took place to expedite improvement of their common rail routes.[48]

The Southern African Transport and Communications Commission, which had set up three permanent organs, continued the momentum in January 1981 by establishing working groups for specific projects. They divided responsibilities still further, allocating to Mozambique ports, Zimbabwe civil aviation, Botswana telecommunications, Zambia railways, and Angola road transport.[49] To match up projects with offers of assistance, to coordinate transnational projects, to follow through on the enthusiasm of the current enterprises takes energy, concern for detail, experience, and commitment. Many aid donors and possible investors are standing on the sidelines waiting for evidence of these qualities. So far, at least, energies have not flagged.

The Maputo Fund Raiser (1980)

The SADCC summit meeting in Maputo in November 1980 planned to launch more positive and substantive programs to aid economic independence from South Africa.[50] The two major aims of the conference were to explain their development plans and to secure financial pledges for regional projects from governments and intergovernmental funding agencies. Representatives of around thirty industrialized states and members of OPEC were invited to Maputo. In addition, the EEC, the African Development Bank, the IMF, the Arab Bank for Economic Development, COMECON, Scandinavian agencies, and OPEC's Special Fund attended. The first projects to be ready for assistance were included in a 300-page survey of regional transport. It was a vast fund raiser, with the nine Southern African states trying to secure $2 billion worth of aid.

At the conference's end, pledges were said to amount to $650 million over the next five years, including $380 million from the ADB, $100 million from the EEC, which had already committed a further $800 million through its Lomé Convention (the agreement between EEC members and almost 60 African, Caribbean, and Pacific states involving trade and aid provisions), $50 million from Italy, and $25 million from the United States. Other countries made indeterminant pledges. Though it appeared that one-third of the necessary $2 billion had been pledged, in fact little more than $50 million represented new money. Complications threaten the EEC's role, since West Germany has blocked EEC aid to Angola and Mozambique since 1979 because neither has signed the Berlin clause recognizing the rights and responsibilities of the Western powers—the United States, Britain, and France—in West Berlin, which East Germany finds unacceptable. This recognition is a fundamental point in the West German Basic Law.[51] Should Mozambique sign the Lomé Convention (it has been invited to but so far has chosen to withhold agreement), then a resolution is possible, since the Berlin clause is an annex to the EEC/ ACP (African, Carribbean, and Pacific) states agreement. But other- wise, since Mozambique (with its ports and transport facilities) is ex- pected to absorb 40% of the total aid (some $833 million), regional transportation projects may be in jeopardy.

The Machel government has not been a favorite of Western capi- talist governments and interests, especially those in the United States. Mozambique has not joined the World Bank or the International Monetary Fund and refuses to facilitate business with some major Western financial institutions according to terms they favor. In effect, Machel has currently chosen to associate only on a limited and selec- tive scale with potential sources of Western investment and assistance; instead, for various reasons, he has sought out the socialist alternative, talking of joining COMECON, the Soviet–East European economic com- bination. COMECON, however, has shown little interest in Mozambican membership, and overall the socialist bloc is not in a position or in- clined to provide more than minor economic/technical assistance. With Mozambique showing this ideological preference at the same time that it is targeted to be the infrastructural keystone of the SADCC program, Western donors are wary of greater financial involvement. Yet Western business firms want to expand their activities in Mozam- bique and Angola. Their chief frustration is the United States govern- ment, not the African authorities.

ZIMCORD *(1981)*

The SADCC regional plan must also be viewed in concert with an- other large-scale financial fund raiser hosted by Zimbabwe in March 1981. Although it was designed to provide funding for the economic and social recovery of a single country, many donors saw it as an opportunity to concentrate their aid packages and thereby to aid the region when they could not bring themselves to commit extensive funding to a broad and somewhat undefined regional plan, or else, because of the Berlin clause, to a legally awkward one to aid Mozam- bique or Angola.

ZIMCORD, an acronym for the Zimbabwe Conference on Recon- struction and Development, attracted more than 200 delegates representing 44 countries, 11 international agencies, and 16 U.N. bodies. The Mugabe government placed before them a new three-year development plan to rebuild the economy. The results were as gratifying as they were somewhat unexpected. In addition to pledges of some $500 million made before the gathering, a further $1.4 billion was promised during the conference. The largely Western international community that attended seemed to express their sense of obligation to help Zimbabwe. By and large, the socialist countries have not tendered much assistance. Zimbabwean officials labeled ZIMCORD a "resounding success."[52]

"Chained to the Dungeons of Apartheid"

South Africa's economic advantage in the region is still considerable. Except for the significant example of Angola, all regional states have for years had major infrastructural, financial, and commercial links with the Republic of South Africa. Samora Machel, president of Mozambique, describing these ties recently, said that the black states of Southern Africa were "chained to the dungeons of apartheid" because of the colonial links forged in the last century.[53] The herculean tasks facing Black Southern Africa and increasingly being dealt with in a cooperative fashion, most notably by SADCC, will not easily be completed. Sights are set very high, no less than a revolutionary alteration of patterns ingrained deeply in the regional template. And they seek to make these changes in the teeth of determined and well-financed South African resistance to change as described and analyzed below.

Mozambique

There may be no love lost between Maputo and Pretoria, but the two economies are in many ways symbiotic. Because of Mozambique's deep economic trouble, the proximity of South Africa, and the existence of long-standing and intimate economic linkages, South Africa continues to play its economic role. There are profits to be made, products and services needed from Mozambique, and a mutually reinforcing relationship of sorts.[54] But Mozambique, at present, must perceive the South African link as more vital to it than South Africa perceives its Mozambique ties.

Mozambique's principal foreign exchange earnings still grow out of relations with South Africa. The foremost source of foreign exchange in this service-oriented economy has been charges on transit trade and port fees. With the border with Rhodesia closed from 1976 to 1980 in order to adhere to sanctions, the relative importance of South African business had increased. After an initial post-independence decline in productivity of the ports and railways, South African Railways mounted a program to revitalize the system by loaning staff and equipment. Cooperation reached a peak in February 1979, when executives of the railways, harbors, and airlines of the two countries met in Johannesburg to sign an agreement updating the 1970 document. Rail traffic from the Transvaal to Maputo rose from 15,000 tons a day to 30,000 by 1981, an overall jump from 6 million to 12 million tons in 1980–81. Improvements to the port have moved along apace, as have general railway improvements.[55]

It is symbolic that when the SADCC conference was held in Maputo in November 1980 the authorities had to requisition the hotel rooms occupied by the South African Railways functionaries working with the Mozambique authorities. But these are the sorts of incongruities one comes to expect in Southern Africa.

But the undeniable leverage possessed by South Africa is periodically exercised, perhaps merely to demonstrate to neighboring governments what could be done. One not unusual example occurred in March 1981, when South African Railways put an embargo on South African exports through Maputo.[56] On the surface it was an operational problem, for SAR freight cars were backing up in Mozambique and not being returned quickly enough. Delays at the port were ostensibly responsible, so the SAR refused to permit more SAR freight cars to enter Mozambique. But the act must be seen as part of the larger South African policy of pressuring the Mozambican government. The 1981 military attack on the ANC houses outside of Maputo is a more graphic illustration of a different but related tactic.

"Railway diplomacy" has been used at other times, effectively, for limited political ends. This particular instance, which lasted only three days, could herald a conscious reduction in the use of Maputo by South African firms. In the long run, however, the South African ports are congested and, moreover, Maputo is more direct for users in the Transvaal and expecially Johannesburg. Clearly, pressure is intended, but is two-sided.

On another occasion, Prime Minister P. W. Botha warned neighboring governments that they risked having their grain supplies from South Africa cut off if they continued to support the call for mandatory sanctions against South Africa in the U.N. General Assembly. Later still, similar threats might have been in response to an electoral campaign complaint from the right-wing Afrikaner party, the Herstigte Nasionale Party, that the government had "sold mealies to terrorists."[57] In dozens of small ways, Pretoria puts black governments on notice that South Africa has the capacity to make economic life difficult for them unless they cooperate or at least tone down their hostility.

After independence the flow of Mozambican laborers (mostly recruits for South Africa's gold mines) declined from 127,198 in 1975 (November) to around 30,000 in 1979. By mid-1980 this had crept back to 56,424 registered workers (46,700 in mining).[58] There are also large numbers of unregistered laborers. Estimates range above 100,000 in most cases. In 1979 the FRELIMO government began pressing for a new labor agreement with the gold mines to guarantee employment for more Mozambicans.

The third major source of foreign exchange for Mozambique has been from the sale of electricity from the Cabora Bassa hydroelectric generators to ESCOM, South Africa's parastatal Electricity Supply Commission.[59] South Africa is Cabora Bassa's principal customer, as it was the major contractor and source of funding, and all power passes through the Apollo substation near Pretoria, even that destined for Maputo and other points in southern Mozambique. In December 1980 the MRM, opposed to the FRELIMO government and reportedly aided with South African arms, claimed responsibility for dynamiting power pylons in the Limpopo Valley, temporarily disrupting electricity supplies.[60] By mid-1979 the final stage of the power station was completed, enabling South Africa to increase purchases. Periodic sabotage hurts both countries, occasionally plunging parts of Johannesburg into darkness, but also robbing the Maputo government of the expected revenue from the dam.

Other elements of South African economic leverage on Maputo include the fact that South Africa currently supplies about 40% of Mozambique's imports, mostly food. This is an increase from 1979, when South Africa supplied 14.4% of Mozambique's imports, and can vary with the quality of the two countries' respective growing seasons.[61] Even so, this trade constitutes considerably less than 1% of

South Africa's total exports. Put simply, South Africa depends far less on commercial links with Mozambique than Mozambique does on South Africa; and were it not for the port of Maputo and the electricity purchases South Africa could easily get on without Mozambique. Mozambique would be hard pressed to contemplate that possibility without massive foreign assistance.

Botswana, Lesotho, and Swaziland

There is little need here to detail the economic encapsulization of Botswana, Lesotho, and Swaziland.[62] Although Botswana and Swaziland are now able to take advantage of borders shared with independent black states, the fundamental economic designs of the past fifty years are still important. Transport lines, electricity grids, trading relationships, the Common Customs Union, labor flows, investment patterns are woven into a single fabric. The bias may be twisted, but the texture and durability have only begun to fade.

The former British High Commission territories have made determined efforts to reduce their vulnerabilities. Lesotho is widely regarded as the most defenseless and economically encapsulated of these three countries. For that reason, its efforts are particularly illustrative, since for it to take steps to escape, greater costs and risks are involved. Although Lesotho may have done the least to alter existing patterns, it deserves special notice.

With the aid of the Ford Foundation, Lesotho's Ministry of Finance has undertaken a study of Lesotho's international economic relations. Their findings included the view that Lesotho's withdrawal from the Southern African Customs Union may not be as costly as had generally been supposed. Although Lesotho received $89.25 million from the Customs Union pool of commonly collected customs, excise, and sales tax revenues in 1979, up from $70.125 million in 1978, the importance of this source of funds is declining. As a proportion of government revenue, the 1979 figure was 65.2%, down from 74.5% in 1978.[63] Despite the decline these are not insignificant contributions. Few governments would risk the economic dislocation a cutoff of such revenues would entail. South Africa in January 1981 signed a cooperative water agreement with Swaziland and made available a $2 million loan to assist Lesotho's farmers.[64] Despite a commitment to change, geopolitical and economic factors continue to weigh heavily. The heart may favor disengagement but the realities make it difficult.

Factoring in the other elements of dependence, trade, transport routes, migrant laborers, investment patterns, although ties are being reduced in proportionate terms, the overall scarcity of choice makes major shifts unlikely. Try as they will, and often efforts have been genuine, the sheer size of the Republic's economy exerts its gravitational pull. Botswana, Lesotho, and Swaziland are the moons to the Republic's earth—their orbits may be altered by dint of prodigious sacrifice and effort, but they still remain in the economic force field of their stronger neighbor.

Zimbabwe

Zimbabwe provides another example of a country that had expanded economic links with South Africa during the last fifteen years. UDI and sanctions provided the Republic and its business community with enhanced opportunities to displace Great Britain as Rhodesia's chief partner and protector.[65] In 1965, Britain was by far the most important buyer of Rhodesian tobacco, and the main Rhodesian foreign exchange earner. Britain was the chief external source of capital for Rhodesia. At UDI British investment in Rhodesia totaled around $600 million. Finally, 21.9% of Rhodesia's total exports prior to UDI were purchased in Britain, and 30.3% of Rhodesia's total imports came from Britain. In contrast, Great Britain, Zimbabwe's second largest supplier, provided just 10% of its imports in 1980 and purchased 7.7% of Zimbabwe's exports.[66]

UDI, followed by U.N. sanctions, which South Africa ignored, and Portugal's expulsion from Africa in 1976, reinforced South Africa's already strong competitive position in Rhodesia's economy. South Africa soon became Rhodesia's principal link with the outside world. The Rhodesian dollar was directly convertible only with the South African rand. Trade between the two countries was expanded. Before UDI in 1964 only 7% of Rhodesia's exports went to South Africa and 24% of its imports came from South Africa. By 1968 these figures were 29% and 54% respectively. These percentages hovered between 30% and 40% of Zimbabwe's imports and about 25% of its exports.[67]

With the end of sanctions trade began to shift. For September 1980, the first time since 1964, official country-by-country data was reported by the Zimbabwe government; almost 25% of Zimbabwe's imports came from South Africa and 18% of its exports went to South Africa.[68] As the year went on these proportions crept higher. South

Africa's share of Zimbabwe's external trade for August–November 1980 was 35% of the imports and 19% of the exports. These figures should decline in the future since, in March 1981, South Africa cancelled its preferential trade agreement with Zimbabwe and Zimbabwe retaliated in kind. For South Africa, total trade with African countries amounted to around $1.29 billion in 1979, and this increased by 36% in 1980, to $1.74 billion.

South Africa has wisely exploited an accessible market. South Africa's proximity gave it advantages. Its willingness to ignore, indeed to undermine, sanctions helped. South African products slotted neatly into Zimbabwe's import needs without endangering Zimbabwe's own industries, themselves creatures of a post-UDI import substitution policy. There is little reason to expect this dominance to dissipate in the short run, although Prime Minister Mugabe is already making efforts to reduce it. British, European, and American products may have difficulty breaking back into the Zimbabwean market because many of their products would run into a tariff system designed to protect infant Zimbabwean industry.[69]

South African financial aid and investment have grown too, although they were long dominant in Rhodesia. Despite sanctions and its global illegality, Rhodesia managed to attract considerable amounts of new capital and reinvested profits during the nearly fifteen years of UDI. Perhaps as much as one billion Rhodesian dollars in foreign investments entered it, increasing foreign investment by over 300%, despite official sanctions![70] According to one estimate, South African firms own at least one-third of Zimbabwe's capital stock.[71] Foreign capital remains crucial to the Zimbabwean economy; about 70% of the country's capital stock is controlled abroad. Major shares of mining (accounting for 90% of mine production), manufacturing, and bank-controlled agriculture and ranching reside in foreign hands. One of Zimbabwe's top three banks (Rhobank) had been 60% owned by Nedbank of South Africa until Nedbank's shares were bought out by the Zimbabwean government early in 1981.[72] South Africa's Anglo-American Corporation, Messina Transvaal, and Johnnies, and Britain's Lonrho and Rio Tinto vie for dominance in the mining sector.

Along with enlarged trade and investment, transport links with South Africa were expanded, just at a time when Rhodesia saw its alternative routes being closed. At UDI Rhodesia had four major railway routes—the Beira line, the line to Lourenço Marques (Maputo), the railway through Botswana to the Cape, and the route to Lobito via Zambia and the Congo. The oil pipeline from Beira to Umtali was closed by sanctions in 1966. (It was supposed to be reopened in early 1981, but technical problems and damage delayed the flow of oil products until late in the year.)[73] There were, of course, road connections to each of these territories and to South Africa. Ian Smith's closure of the border with Zambia in 1973 and the FRELIMO government's decision to close their border with Rhodesia in March 1976 reduced Rhodesia to just two southerly routes, including the newly constructed route directly to South Africa. Its opening in October 1974, however, faced Smith with additional problems, technical and operational bottlenecks at South Africa's crowded ports, and total dependency on routes through a single state. Again South African leverage over the Rhodesian economy had been amplified by the press of events, including sanctions designed to humble a racist state. Without Pretoria, sanctions would have taken a deeper bite than they did; without South Africa, Ian Smith's regime would have been scuppered long before it was.

Today roughly 90% of Zimbabwe's overseas exports move through South Africa's rail and port systems. Zimbabwe's rail system is dependent on SAR freight cars, locomotives, and other equipment. Its telecommunications network is linked into switching and relay centers in Johannesburg. This was the legacy inherited by Prime Minister Mugabe. The present Zimbabwean government is out to correct these vulnerabilities. Zimbabwe has managed a trade surplus. The 1981 grain crop not only satisfied domestic needs but enabled the country to export grain. A great deal of political and economic reorganization has taken place, in farming, land settlement and ownership, the legal system, the civil service, the political parties, industry, finance, the armed forces; in short, in practically every facet of civilian affairs. They are extensive changes, although not adequate to satisfy the Mugabe government's radical critics. But they prepare the ground for further material progress, provided stability and capital requirements can be secured.

Zambia

The past few years have seen South Africa enhance its economic position in relation to Zambia. Each successive escalation of the Rhodesian conflict had provided South Africa with additional points of entry into both sides. As Zambian trade with Rhodesia was practically terminated after UDI, South Africa was able to pick up much of the slack with both partners. The final phases of the Zimbabwean independence struggle prompted Dr. Kaunda to rely more heavily on South Africa than he would otherwise have wished, all in the hope that a return to normalcy would follow a satisfactory Zimbabwean resolution.

The Benguela rail route to Lobito was closed to Zambian traffic in August 1975. It is still not fully operative. The Tazara line had been sabotaged by Rhodesian operatives as had the Great North Road. Inefficiencies on the Tazara and at the port of Dar es Salaam compounded Zambia's difficulties, and led to a decision in October 1978 to reopen the southern railway through Rhodesia, which had been closed since January 1973. Although much of the right of way damage has been repaired on Tazara and Benguela, port problems continue in Dar and political differences with Angola and Zaire still prevent full usage of those routes. Other transport difficulties cropped up. In April 1979 Rhodesian forces destroyed the ferry at Kazangula linking Zambia and Botswana. Not until the Mugabe government took office was the ferry reopened. Zambia also tried to open a new road route to the west, through Namibia and Botswana. But objections by the SADF, which feared SWAPO infiltrations encouraged by Zambia, led the South African government to scotch these plans. Since it has problems shipping copper, Zambia found itself facing severe foreign exchange shortages. Transport bottlenecks limited vital imports and led to agricultural setbacks. Zambia felt desperate, and South Africa, which had been pressing for enlarged ties, happily picked up the slack.

Since the reopening of the bridge at Victoria Falls in autumn 1978 (it never had been entirely closed to rail traffic despite claims to the contrary), South Africa has made available 1,500–2,000 freight cars to carry Zambian traffic, which amounted to between 240,000 and 305,000 tons of copper (around 40–45% of the copper output) being exported annually, through South African ports. According to one estimate this represents around 46% of all the external trade of Zambia and of Zaire's Shaba Province and a two-way traffic totaling 109,000 tons a month.[74] Whereas in 1977 nothing at all transited the southern rail route from Zambia to South Africa, in 1978 that was raised to 9% (by weight) of all Zambian foreign trade and to 41% in 1979. Dar es Salaam and the Tazara Railway slipped from 83% in 1977 to 74% in 1978 to 49% in 1979.[75]

In trade, as well, South Africa has again taken a strong place in Zambia's import picture. South African transporters estimate that Zambia imports between 50% and 60% of all its supplies from South Africa. Regular air freight service operates daily from Johannesburg to Lusaka.[76]

Zaire

Even Zaire is very much a part of South Africa's economic hinterland, in terms of trade and rail links, and to some extent politically, in their common opposition to the MPLA government in Luanda. South Africa has been underwriting this growing trade relationship, developing credit ties through the semi-official Credit Guarantee Corporation and the South African Industrial Development Corporation. By 1979, 9.2% of Zaire's imports came from South Africa, representing around 21% of South Africa's exports to Africa.[77]

Aid and Assistance

In order to reinforce commercial and financial ties with the region, the South African government has for years engaged in a foreign aid and technical assistance program.[78] Individual projects have tended to be limited and highly specific; for example, food deliveries in an emergency, specialized teams to control mine fires, assistance to refugees from Angola, medical assistance, and the secondment of public officials on specialized assignment. Other assistance for infrastructural projects and technical/scientific research cooperation is common. But assistance tends to be concentrated on a few countries, and nowadays longer-term commitments have been reduced.

The Basis of Economic Domination

Overall, South Africa's economic tentacles reach afar, and are prehensile. Part of this stems from Pretoria's conscious intention to use economic contacts for political ends. Part is a product of the asymmetric strengths and weaknesses of respective area economies. Part grows out of the fact that South Africa long had the only industrialized economy in Southern Africa, except for some industry in Rhodesia. Its products enjoyed the competitive advantages of place utility, that is, reduced transport costs and shorter waiting periods. And part has grown out of the failure of many black states to satisfy their own economic needs. They cooperate with South Africa purely out of desperate necessity.

The alternative of not dealing with South Africa is less acceptable. With slovenly economic and administrative performance, some black states have contributed to the very conditions they least desire. The harsh realities of economic life in the region have brought many politicians to realize that if they are eventually to reduce dependence on South Africa, they had better get their own economic houses in order. Dangerous shortages of maize, for example, partly due to drought, have existed at times in Mozambique, Zambia, and Zimbabwe, and possibly in Botswana, as well as inside South Africa's own "homelands." The South African government agreed to sell sizable amounts outside its boundaries to carry these countries through the emergency. Not until 1981 did Zimbabwean production enable that country to supply its own needs and to sell its surplus in the region. Other key products, fertilizers, mining equipment, parts for factories, and other foods are needed. In these circumstances, Pretoria tends to have a magnified sense of economic self-importance.

Conclusion

In Southern Africa, both groupings of contestants call for regional unity. The issue turns on who is to be included and who is to lead. It was Zimbabwe's presence at Lusaka and Maputo that supplied the grounds for hope that the black states may succeed. Eventually, Zimbabwe will play a pivotal role in any South Africa-less community, and that is precisely what Mr. Mugabe himself envisions. "I think Zimbabwe," he said back in March 1980, "will be the pivot in such an economic arrangement because in all of the free countries of southern and even central Africa we probably have the most highly developed economy and infrastructure. . . . [I]t is necessary that we play quite a leading part in any economic constellation. . . ."[79]

We have also seen how South Africa's economic muscles are still taut. Its contacts with regional neighbors are extensive and in some cases intensive. It would appear to the uninitiated that by all the classical economic indicators South Africa can live secure in its economic future.

The ZIMCORD outcome provides Mr. Mugabe with greater encouragement and with the stimulus to battle on. There is a great deal of interdependence in Southern Africa, but there is little symmetry to these relationships. It constitutes what Keohane and Nye call asymmetrical interdependence.[80] The two sides do need one another, but it is a matter of degree. South Africa is sensitive to changes in Black Africa. Black Africa is also sensitive to events in the white-dominated South. But when it comes to vulnerability, the black states are less able to weather difficult circumstances. They have fewer choices and fewer opportunities. This is, after all, what underdevelopment is all about— fewer chances to control one's own destiny. Black Southern Africa must take solace in knowing that conditions are indeed changing, and what is asymmetrical interdependence today is considerably less loaded against them than it had been years ago.

South Africa's call for a constellation of states seems, like earlier proposals, to be unrewarding. It is shapeless, formless window dressing, useful for external consumption, to paint a picture of reasonableness and cooperation. Because of South Africa's domestic race politics, it will lead nowhere outside its boundaries.

Despite an increase in black awareness of the realities of economic life, the political factors are clear. Economic power is today, in Southern Africa, just economic power. To parlay economic power into political and military power there are costs. Just how to make the transition from one to the other mode of power is not altogether clear.

The leaders of Black Africa, having seen the success of the liberation movements in Angola, Mozambique, and Zimbabwe in the past half-dozen years, enjoy the psychological euphoria that accomplishment provides. They live with the sense that the struggle is not complete and, despite the economic penalties, that movement is in the right direction. Pretoria takes heart from the economic situation. Black Africans find their hopes fueled by the political changes they have seen brought about.

Alchemists spent centuries trying to transform all manner of substance into gold. In reversing the process, the alchemists of Pretoria today seek to turn gold into acceptance and security. But they too, have been, thus far, frustrated, and they will continue to be frustrated. Though the South African economy ranges over the region, there is less geographic scope for political influence. Politicians may reason that reduced access necessitates incursion. South Africa is forced to rely increasingly on its military might and uses it in punitive and preemptive strikes. South Africa may continue to enjoy economic cooperation, but it will not lead to security or political acceptance. It is a simple political aphorism that those with economic wealth and power prefer that issues be decided by market considerations where their economic weight takes precedence. Those without wealth rely on their political strengths to offset economic weakness. South Africa, finding that its neighbors have been taking measures to discount South African economic clout, has fallen back on its most desperate line of defense, an aggressive regional military policy. It is a stopgap strategy that is bound to fail in the longer run.

8.

The Role of Donor Agencies in Southern Africa

Richard A. Horovitz

South Africa must play a particular role in the positive realisation of development in southern Africa. . . . South Africa is on a different level from its neighbors in terms of the scope of its economy and the extent of its development. Obviously, therefore, we can make a notable contribution to the region. . . . with multilateral cooperation the states of southern Africa can achieve far more through joint planning and action, as well as the pooling of resources than through individual action.   (*Johannesburg, 22 November, 1979*)[1]

We the undersigned, as Heads of Government of majority-ruled States in southern Africa, offer this declaration to our own peoples, to the peoples and Governments of the many countries who are interested in promoting popular welfare, justice and peace in southern Africa and to the international agencies who share this interest. In it we state our commitment to pursue policies aimed at the economic liberation and integrated development of our national economies and we call on all concerned to assist us in this high endeavor.   (*Lusaka, 1 April, 1980*)[2]

These two statements posit two very different models for regional cooperation in Southern Africa. Prime Minister P. W. Botha outlined the first concept at a gathering of South African businessmen in a speech entitled "Towards a Constellation of States in Southern Africa."That "constellation" approach, articulated as early as 1964 by South Africa's then Prime Minister Hendrik Verwoerd, initially called for a "southern African common market" tightly under Pretoria's

The author wishes to acknowledge the assistance of Craig Howard in researching this chapter.

179

control. In the ensuing years, an increasingly prosperous South Africa reached out to its natural hinterland in search of "satellites" for markets for its products and for sources of cheap labor. Over time the majority-ruled black states in Southern Africa became increasingly dependent upon South Africa.

The second statement came less than a month after Robert Mugabe's electoral victory in Zimbabwe, when leaders of nine independent black-ruled Southern African nations met in Lusaka to issue a declaration of regional cooperation and determination to achieve economic liberation from South Africa. African representatives at that seminal meeting of the Southern African Development Coordination Conference (SADCC)[3] assessed the needs of the region and the roles that international actors could play in fulfilling them. Their list of five priority areas forms the basis for examining donor activity in Southern Africa.

The intent of SADCC members is to form a cooperative and interdependent grouping of countries which will reduce South Africa's economic stranglehold on the region. Aware of the fragility of African political unions, their leaders, gathered in Lusaka, patterned their cooperative vision along economic lines, using the Economic Community of West African States (ECOWAS) as a model rather than the more tightly integrated former East African Community. They stressed the need to establish and strengthen regional transport and communication systems, emphasizing that improved rail, road, and river transport could help their countries share agricultural and manufactured goods and thus reduce their dependence on South Africa. They also urged sharing energy and industrial bases, and manpower training, with the clear implication that independent Zimbabwe would play a central role. SADCC members called upon "governments, international institutions and voluntary agencies" for financial support to achieve their goals.

Shortly after the Lusaka meeting, Matthew Rothchild, assistant editor of the *Multinational Monitor,* a monthly published by the Corporate Accountability Research Group in Washington, D.C., raised questions about the utility of Western assistance and the attitudes of Western donors.[4] A growing literature suggests in fact that almost all foreign assistance keeps recipient countries in the status of neocolonial appendages by obliging them to acquire goods, equipment, and personnel from the donors.[5] The Lusaka nine hope this to be untrue, but feel that economic dependence on the West is preferable to an exclusive dependence on South Africa (which simultaneously strengthens the apartheid regime).

The Genesis and Evolution of Development Assistance

Until the beginning of the twentieth century the concept of development assistance was largely unknown. Prior to 1900, religious orders had engaged in both charity and missionary work, and private citizens of one country often responded with aid to natural disasters in another. Organizations like the Red Cross grew up to coordinate the collection and distribution of relief assistance, which usually took the form of emergency food, clothing, and housing materials. That pattern of ad hoc responses continues to the present day in response to famine or earthquakes that disrupt local life and evoke sympathy and concern elsewhere. More fundamentally, private foundations, like those endowed by the Rockefellers and the Carnegies, and church-related groups like the American Friends Service Committee, began between 1900 and 1945 to research the root causes of ongoing suffering and to seek innovative solutions. Concern for assisting "development" by public as well as private agencies did not develop, however, until after the Second World War.

The period from 1945 to the present has seen the creation of a myriad of bilateral and multilateral public agencies including USAID, the World Bank Group, and various U.N. organizations. Religious denominations have grouped together to provide aid through umbrella organizations like the Church World Service and Catholic Relief, and private foundations have become increasingly concerned with international issues. Some postwar aid to Western Europe has still followed the "relief" model, the CARE package being the classic symbol of such an approach. More constructively, the Marshall Plan and the World Bank assisted war-decimated but technically skilled Western Europe by providing it with the capital investment necessary to rebuild industrial structures and to regain or surpass previous economic levels. As sub-Saharan African countries began to achieve independence from 1957 on, it became apparent how inadequately prepared the colonial period had left them. Donors continued to assume, however, that supplying the missing human and capital infrastructures of the modern industrial state would stimulate economic growth and thereby ensure development.

The precursors of official British aid were the budgetary subventions which the U.K. had started offering its more impoverished colonies and territories (including Botswana, Lesotho, and Swaziland) in the 1930s. Later in that same decade, the first "Colonial Development and Welfare" grants were made, mainly for capital expenditures. They continued up to the 1960s. At independence the British concept of aid widened to include providing technical assistance to new governments, usually in the form of "supplementations" to the salaries of former colonial civil servants.

In the post-independence early years, it was private American foundations rather than the U.S. government that took the lead in supporting "nation building." The foundations, especially Carnegie, laid great emphasis on strengthening educational systems. Rockefeller also concentrated on strengthening local universities and on the extension of agricultural and medical services, while the Ford Foundation supported university training and the development of national planners and public administrators, on the theory that government services could be markedly improved by skilled direction and rational planning methods.

By heavily funding international agricultural research centers, the Ford and Rockefeller Foundations also continued to support research intended to create new technologies where existing ones were insufficient. The most widely acclaimed breakthrough was the "Green Revolution": the development of high-yield food crops through a combination of improved seed varieties and technical innovations like irrigation and chemical-based fertilizers. At the same time, the World Bank concentrated on providing loans for constructing (or reconstructing) physical infrastructures—roads, ports, hydroelectric dams, and communications networks—which would accelerate overall economic growth and development.

The standard rationale for such undertakings was that "the developed nations possessed technology and wealth which they had the opportunity and obligation to share with the developing countries."[6] An alternative, if less benevolent, interpretation put forth in some quarters was that the developed nations wanted to ensure that Third World political independence did not lead to economic emancipation because they still needed the mineral and agricultural resources of the developing world, and to maintain outlets for their surplus capital and technology as well.

Rethinking Aid Effectiveness in the 1970s

By the early 1970s, a number of doubts were being raised, not only about the motives of the aid purveyors but, perhaps more importantly, about the efficacy of a "trickle-down" approach aimed at raising living standards for all people by maximizing economic growth through the training of elites in management and national planning. The growing pessimism about the ability of technology to solve the problems of poor people was epitomized by the publication in 1973 of E.F. Schumacher's *Small Is Beautiful: Economics as if People Mattered.*[7] That same year the World Bank's president, Robert McNamara, told its governors at a meeting in Nairobi that the previous phases of "reconstruction" and "development" had indeed bypassed poor farmers, who could not, for example, afford the expensive seeds, fertilizers, and equipment which the new miracle strains required.

In his five-year plan, McNamara outlined a strategy for "integrated rural development" by increasing credit and assistance to small farmers to enable them to produce food for local consumption. Also in 1973 the U.S. Congress enacted its New Directions legislation which mandated attention to the basic human needs of the "poorest of the poor" and made funds available to some private voluntary organizations engaged in grass-roots development activity. The energy-based Green Revolution had in large measure bypassed Africa because the rapid rise in petroleum prices in the 1970s made its methods more costly than its benefits. Moreover, critics today argue that the lot of the poor has not improved appreciably because advances in agricultural technology have not been accompanied by any significant parallel agrarian reform, and that until there is substantial structural redistribution of wealth and income *within* most developing countries (not to mention between the developed and the developing), it is the narrow, landed, power-controlling local elites rather than the landless or near-landless poor who will continue to benefit from foreign assistance.

While sensitive observers like Uma Lele, a distinguished agricultural economist concerned with Third World rural development who is currently in the World Bank office which deals with East and Southern Africa, do not dispute the need to alter the internal distribution

of assets and political power so that the poor of any given country do
not remain systematically excluded, they argue that such changes will
not occur, despite even the best-intentioned projects of external donors, if there is no internal commitment. Although many African
governments rhetorically acknowledge the importance of agriculture
and the rural sector, they continue in practice to tax that sector heavily in order to support urban modernization. Until African policy
makers accept the fact that "the smallholder agricultural sector can
become the engine for broad-based economic development,"[8] Lele
contends, donor activity is likely to have little effect on improving
food supplies or general living conditions for the rural poor.

Dr. Lele acknowledges that the perceived indifference of some of
the educated urban elite to the largely rural needs of their own countries has led to general disenchantment in the international community for providing higher education. One of the reasons for the lack
of a "proagriculture lobby," she argues, is the shortage of educated
and technically trained African cadres. She is not alone, however, in
urging that training efforts not be overly specialized, but rather that
they include opportunities for the kind of broad education which will
prepare nationals for the tasks of conceiving and determining long-
term development policies.

This renewed emphasis on the importance of broad training for
strategy-makers is a shift from the project-specific training many donors now favor. It does correspond, however, to the SADCC requests
for high-level training. Assistance with infrastructural improvements
is another area which, while currently in less favor with some donors
than grass-roots support, is particularly appropriate in the Southern
African context. Although a Marshall Plan approach was not suitable
for the postindependent African nations of the 1960s, Zimbabwe today, with its highly developed but still war-ravaged economy, resem-
bles postwar Europe in certain respects. Thus SADCC's priorities,
which emphasize massive infrastructural aid that requires heavy cap-
italization, indicate that a Marshall Plan model might be appropriate.

SADCC Priorities

The document that emerged from the 1980 SADCC Lusaka summit
meeting, entitled "Southern Africa: Toward Economic Liberation,"

sets forth very clearly the philosophical rationale and the concrete goals and strategies of the leaders of the nine states in attendance. Five critical areas were identified, and further planning and research were undertaken to prepare requests to donors in time for SADCC II, held in Maputo in November 1980.

SADCC accords preeminence to strengthening regional transport and telecommunication facilities, especially for the landlocked states, on the grounds that without adequate regional links all other forms of cooperation become impractical. The first task is to determine which facilities needed rehabilitation and upgrading; the second one to prepare feasibility studies on the creation of new ones. The list of projects in this category prepared for the Maputo meeting would cost U.S. $1.946 million.

A crucial proposal is to deepen and increase the capacities of Mozambique's ports at Beira and Maputo (at U.S. $158 million and $132 million respectively) because they have the potential of servicing at least six states in the region, including land-locked Swaziland, Botswana, Zimbabwe, Malawi, and Zambia. Nacala, Mozambique's third-biggest port, is the deepest on the eastern seaboard and has the greatest potential for expansion. Only about 40% of Malawi's imports and exports go through Nacala because of its congestion and the inadequacy of existing railway links. Strengthening the Malawi-Nacala railway line (a U.S. $200 million project) and improving the port are likely to increase the flow of goods to and from Malawi as well as ease the congestion of Beira, which would then become more attractive to Zimbabwe as an import-export route (see map). Other proposals to improve regional transport include upgrading three major roads in Lesotho (U.S. $167 million); rehabilitating the entire Zimbabwean-owned railway that traverses Botswana (U.S. $100 million); and building new terminal facilities at the Salisbury airport (U.S. $100 million).[9]

High priority was also accorded to improving telecommunications systems which, for example, still make it easier to call from Maputo to Lisbon than to Salisbury, and to study the feasibility of creating new transportation routes. A new railway from Botswana through an independent Namibia to the Atlantic at Walvis Bay, for instance, would create an alternative link to the sea for Botswana, Zambia, and Zimbabwe. The importance of this approach is underscored when it is realized that almost all regional road and rail lines now converge on South Africa, which openly engages in "railway diplomacy" as a means of maintaining its dominance in the area.

The second principal SADCC concern is to improve agriculture and food security, since the majority of the people of Southern Africa are dependent on farming and animal husbandry. Attention was focused on environmental degradation, particularly that caused by desert encroachment and recurrent droughts, as in Botswana, and on the incidence of foot and mouth disease in the region, partly caused by discontinuation of cattle dipping during the Zimbabwe struggle and partly spread by refugees. The latter problem elicited a call for improvement of existing facilities in Botswana for vaccine production. To help increase self-sufficiency in staple foods a specific request was made that ICRISAT (International Crops Research Institute for the Semi-Arid Tropics), which is based in Hyderabad, India, establish a regional center in Botswana.

Manpower training is the third vital area. Inventories were drawn up of training needs and facilities in the region. Existing national institutions of member states are to be used whenever possible to provide accelerated training, especially in functional priority areas such as transport and communications.

As a basis for industrial cooperation, the fourth SADCC priority is a study of the industrial capacities of all member states and their import requirements for foreign goods. The first efforts will be to encourage exports within the region from countries where surplus manufacturing capacity already exists, presumably only Zimbabwe for the moment. Similarly, the fifth priority is to study energy needs to determine which countries require petroleum and electricity and which can and do produce them. The emphasis remains on regional coordination of national efforts rather than on joint undertakings.

Problems SADCC Confronts

A major assumption underlying the organization of SADCC is that its proposed regional cooperation model is sound and can be achieved in the long run. There should be no illusions that this will come about easily, however. Many countries of the region possess only limited economic complementarity at present, and there is some legitimate fear that a relatively strong industrialized Zimbabwe may be viewed by its neighbors as dominant and intimidating, not unlike Nigeria in the West African context, or Kenya within the former East African Community. More importantly, the Republic of South Africa, by combining its advanced industrial capacity with its exploitation of black labor, is able to produce the cheapest commodities in the region, and, even with an improved communications infrastructure, it may be a long time before trade among the SADCC members reaches a level which will be economically justifiable. At present, for instance, it is still four times more expensive to ship Botswana coal to the sea through Zimbabwe to Mozambique than via South Africa. A further concern is that a country like Zambia may have to opt for quick domestic gains rather than long-term regional benefits. Although it is true that Zambia paid a high price for enforcing sanctions against Rhodesia, it also suffers from internal policy mismanagement which its leaders are now no longer able to blame on the struggle against minority rule.

The Role of Donors in Assisting SADCC

The main purpose of this chapter is to examine the commitment of certain public and private Western donors that are assisting the countries of majority-ruled Southern Africa in their effort to redirect the regional poles of attraction away from apartheid South Africa. The two multilateral organizations examined in detail are the World Bank and the UNDP, or United Nations Development Program. USAID is the illustrative bilateral funding agency, and private support is represented by U.S. foundations, church groups, and voluntary organizations. This selection of illustrative donors is based chiefly on the major audience for the work and on easy access to the relevant information.

The United States has been chosen as an illustrative bilateral donor primarily for those reasons. "U.S. contribution to development assistance is disgracefully low," however, as Robert McNamara proclaimed just weeks before his retirement as director of the World Bank. "No other large industrial nation provides as low a proportion of its national income assistance to development assistance," he concluded.[10] The current tendency for the United States (or any other nation) to withdraw from multilateral aid and concentrate on bilateral aid over which it has more political control is potentially dangerous. Enhanced trade and regional stability in Southern Africa, goals toward which the SADCC members aspire, are aims which any U.S. administration should see as consistent with national interests as well.

A strong case could be made for the inclusion of Great Britain, the oldest and still largest single bilateral donor for almost all the countries of the region (see chapter 3). David Jones has demonstrated that, at least for the period 1962/3–1972/3, British aid to the BLS countries (Botswana, Lesotho, and Swaziland) was less bureaucratic, less procurement-tied, and speedier than USAID.[11] A fair portion of the aid from Britain, however, went to supplement the salaries of its former colonial civil servants who had become "technical assistants" after independence.

Other omissions caused by lack of time or space are a discussion of food aid, of U.N. volunteers as well as those from the United States and Canada, and of the important work of organizations like CARE. Also neglected are West Germany and the European Economic Community, whose recent commitments to Southern Africa have made it the largest single new force on the horizon, despite certain hurdles still to be overcome regarding Mozambique.

Multinational or bilateral aid to Mozambique is crucial to SADCC given the central role the rehabilitation of its roads and ports plays in the regional strategy. The EEC is willing to commit funds for projects in Mozambique, and has encouraged it to apply for association, but the Mozambican government has so far been unwilling to sign any agreement with the EEC that contains the so-called Berlin clause, which acknowledges British, French, and American continuing rights and responsibilities in Berlin. The West Germans will not remove what to them is a standard phrase that appears in dozens of international agreements and over which no other signatory has ever balked. Observers of Mozambique, however, feel that its reliance on East German assistance, especially in the area of security, makes it unwilling to jeopardize that relationship by signing an agreement that violates the terms of its bilateral accords with the DDR prohibiting an endorsement of the Berlin clause.

Individual member states of both the EEC and the World Bank, which also provides no aid to Mozambique since it is not a member (see below), can and have entered into bilateral agreements with Mozambique. The Scandinavians, British, and Dutch are already the largest Western donors active in Mozambique, and France and Portugal have offered over $50 million in low-interest loans to strengthen the rail line running from Zambia through Malawi to the port of Nacala in northern Mozambique. The Arab and African development banks also provide it aid. Eastern bloc aid mainly consists of military hardware and security personnel to Mozambique and Angola, since COMECON's constituent countries have not yet accepted Mozambique as a member.[12]

While outside donors can assist regional efforts at economic coordination, each has its own mandate and *raison d'être*. The review of the selected donor agencies that follows includes a brief look at the structure and sources of revenue of each organization, followed by an examination of the activities it supports in majority-ruled Southern Africa, and typical projects, which illustrate its strengths and weaknesses. Lastly, note is taken of the character and size of outside assistance to blacks in the Republic of South Africa in the areas of legal rights and education.

A goal for development aid should be to avoid redundancy and to capitalize on each organization's comparative advantages. The World Bank, for instance, is clearly better placed than church groups to make loans for heavy infrastructural restoration of transport and irrigation facilities, which in turn will be utilized by bilateral agriculture and food production projects. And until enough problem-oriented social scientists and planners indigenous to Southern Africa are available, UNDP-provided technical assistants may be the best interim solution. By harmonizing their strengths with SADCC's priorities, donors should, collectively, be able to assist the peoples of the region achieve their goals.

The World Bank Group

How It Operates

The largest multilateral source of development financing is the World Bank Group, made up of the International Bank for Reconstruction and Development (IBRD, or simply the World Bank), the International Development Association (IDA) and the International Monetary Fund (IMF). All three lend money for development projects, and all three are country membership institutions. The Soviet Union is not among the 138 members of the IMF, which is a prerequisite to membership in the Bank, although Yugoslavia is a long-standing member and the People's Republic of China recently became one.

The Bank and IDA differ in funding sources and rates of interest charged on loans. The World Bank makes long-term loans to the governments of developing countries at rates lower than those of commercial lenders, while the IDA provides development financing for the very poorest countries in the form of "credit" (or "soft" loans) at no interest, a minimal service charge, and a long grace period. Most of the countries in Southern Africa, apart from South Africa, are considered low-income and qualify for IDA credits. The IMF is traditionally the "lender of last resort" to member governments which are deeply in debt and need to reestablish economic equilibrium.

The bulk of the Bank's resources are derived from its borrowings in international capital markets. Those borrowings are guaranteed by the "callable" capital subscribed by participating governments: funds which the governments promise to provide if so required by the Bank's authorities. Development projects are usually designed jointly by World Bank staff and members of the borrowing country's government. Since the Bank is accountable to its subscriber countries, it must determine the creditworthiness of the country that will have to repay the proposed loan, which is usually made to cover the foreign exchange component of a project. The World Bank and IDA collaborate on many projects in Southern Africa with bilateral aid agencies in the United States, the United Kingdom, and elsewhere, as well as the EEC, the African Development Bank and others of its genre, the UNDP and a host of additional U.N. agencies.

The goal of World Bank and IDA activities in the 1960s was to stimulate economic growth mainly by financing the construction of roads, dams, and power plants. By the time of McNamara's celebrated 1973 Nairobi speech, the Bank had come to realize that agricultural growth by itself did not necessarily diminish rural poverty. The Bank stopped providing loans for non-food export crops and focused attention on small farmers and the hungry, having come to view the reduction of poverty as *the* necessary first step toward genuine development.

The "new style" of World Bank projects which emerged in the 1970s was designed to benefit large numbers of rural poor through comprehensive approaches which included:

> area development, settlement, irrigation and land improvement schemes. Most of the projects have an agricultural base and involve tech-

nological change—frequently the introduction of water, credit, improved seed and fertilizer. . . . The area projects often have some social components—health services, basic education, and water supplies.[13]

In education the shift has been away from loans for secondary and higher education toward primary schools and non-formal projects in functional literacy and numeracy. In the foreword to his last *World Development* Report (August 1980) outgoing President McNamara wrote:

> Human development—education and training, better health and nutrition, and fertility reduction—is shown to be important not only in alleviating poverty directly, but also in increasing the incomes of the poor, and GNP growth as well. The vital message is that some steps we all have long known to be morally right—primary education, for example—make good economic sense as well.[14]

Because the Bank is concerned with "making good economic sense," its lending policies have tended to be extremely conservative. This has resulted in an impeccable financial record which permits officials to boast, "the Bank has yet to be faced with a bad loan."[15] It has also led to charges that Bank loans are tied to the acceptance by Third World countries of market-oriented economic doctrines. More recently, however, the Bank has come under criticism by members of the Reagan adminisration for an opposite set of reasons. They see the Bank's dealings with Third World governments for "basic needs" activities as "undermining the free enterprise system" and promoting socialism.[16] If such critics had their way, the United States would have reneged on a replenishment commitment to the IDA, which has been active in parts of Southern Africa. Instead, the replenishment approved in August 1981 was stretched over four years rather than the intended three.

Relevance to SADCC's *Objectives*

SADCC seeks a degree of security and protection for the countries of the region from the economic and political vulnerability to which each is now subject by expanding the economic pluralism of the region so as to create a more diversified and healthier interdependency. How well does the World Bank approach correspond to SADCC's regional needs as well as those of its individual members? The Bank and IDA have been the largest lenders in the region,[17] and agricultural projects have accounted for 31% of all the loans they have made in the region for each year from 1976 to 1979. Transportation projects accounted for 16, 17, and 18 percent of total loans for 1976, 1977, and 1978 respectively, and then shot up dramatically to 41% in 1979.[18] Education varied between 4 and 10% of the totals during those years, while loans for industrial development went from zero in 1976 to 4% in 1977, 8% in 1978, and 9% in 1979.

Most of the Bank's agricultural projects tend to be comprehensive and country-oriented rather than focused solely on increased production. The Shire Valley Agricultural Consolidation Project in Malawi is a good illustration. It received $10.7 million new IDA credits in 1978, building on two prior credits totaling $19.2 million. Its purposes were to "intensify the provision of agricultural extension services; establish an irrigated seed multiplication farm and a forestation program; provide production credit; improve livestock extension services; expand a fisheries development program; improve village health facilities and potable water supply; and extend farm to market road networks."[19]

Such Bank projects rely heavily on expatriate equipment and personnel. It has been estimated by former Secretary of State Cyrus Vance that for every dollar the United States contributes to the Bank two are spent in the United States.[20] Also, being a bank, it is accountable to the international financial community and so tends to make loans to countries like Malawi, where prospects for default on payments are minimal.[21]

An education project in Lesotho which received IDA credits of $7.5 million in 1978 to develop curricula and facilities for pre-vocational teaching in secondary schools offers another illustration of the Bank's cautious approach. Its ostensible objective was to help reduce Lesotho's dependency on South Africa. The anticipated outcome was described as follows: "The pool of skilled workers within Lesotho will be increased, and individual workers seeking employment in South Africa will be able to obtain higher wages because of an improved skill base, thus enabling them to increase their remittances to their families."[22] While it is perhaps a realistic project in light of present economic realities which force so many Basotho to seek employment in the Republic, it hardly seems in line with the larger SADCC goals of attenuating that need. Nor does it take into consideration certain changes occurring within South Africa itself. A combination of increasing internal population pressures and a tendency toward capital-intensive mining technology militate in any case against the likelihood of guaranteed work for Basotho miners in the Republic. A much wiser Bank policy would seem to be to seek ways of generating new employment opportunities within Lesotho itself.

In addition, critics fault the World Bank for no longer providing high level training opportunities more generously than other agencies, not only because of its greater resources but also because of its sophistication in appreciating the need and still refusing to meet it. Moreover, as early as 1975 the Bank recognized, in a statement on its "Policy Framework," that "a strong commitment to rural development at the national policy level is necessary if the impact is to be effective and broad-based." It further noted that "in many countries the commitment is lacking" and that "often macroeconomic policies are inconsistent with agricultural and rural development."[23] A logical corollary might well have been to devise some means of sensitizing formulators of national macroeconomic policy, perhaps through better training opportunities for indigenous researchers who might provide those policy makers with reasoned and documented arguments. Instead, the Bank opted to remain on the project level, justifying it as where most governments are "prepared to experiment . . . and to examine the results."[24] In much of Southern Africa, however, national commitment is already present. Only Zimbabwe in the region today comes close to having a sufficient number of well-trained national cadres, however. The BLS countries, especially Botswana, could benefit from increases in advanced training opportunities for sophisticated planning coupled with efforts to improve primary and secondary education, and thereby expand the pool of candidates for university-level training.

Although the Bank is supposedly apolitical, some see it as subject to the pressures of its subscribers, the biggest of which, at 25%, is the United States. No Bank loans or IDA credits have been extended to either Angola or Mozambique, a serious problem given the central role that rehabilitation of Mozambican ports must play within SADCC in improving transportation links. As already noted, Mozambique has opted not to join the IMF, which is a precondition to Bank membership, and, technically, this is the reason why it has received no World Bank loans to date. Bank officials express their willingness to consider loans to Mozambique once it becomes a member. The reason often given for Mozambique's reluctance to join the Bank and the IMF is its dissatisfaction with the terms which accompanied IMF involvement in neighboring Tanzania, which obliged Tanzania to curtail or defer certain social programs until its overall economy was stronger. Mozambicans are also said to feel that the IMF's role in Jamaica was objectionally prescriptive. The Bank's lack of attractiveness to Mozambique, for whatever reasons, thus lessens its potential effectiveness in the region.

The Bank's diminishing emphasis on investment in major transportation facilities is also surprising, for the Bank's lending capacity could make available the amounts of money needed to rebuild harbors and railways better than can any other source. The 1980 U.S. Foreign Aid Congressional presentation argued for a $3.6 billion U.S. contribution to multilateral development banks partly on the grounds that "the substantial resources of the Banks also allow them to fund necessary infrastructure projects, requiring heavy capital outlay, which complement our bilateral efforts. . . ."[25]

This question concerning the World Bank's ability to respond to regional as well as to national development needs remains troublesome. Except for Dar es Salaam, Angola and Mozambique contain the only outlets on the Atlantic and Indian Oceans, other than through South Africa, for the six landlocked states of the region, and the World Bank remains the best endowed and most logical source of loans for the heavy infrastructural restoration which is needed if SADCC's policies are to succeed.

The United Nations System

UNDP's *Role*

The United Nations development system is made up of numerous agencies, some of which are new and work on very specialized issues, while others are more established and familiar, like UNESCO and UNICEF. For instance, in Southern Africa, UNICEF is providing aid and social services to mothers and children in the care of liberation movements. It also supports food, water, health education, and nutrition programs which benefit children of the independent countries in the region.[26] The United Nations High Commission for Refugees (UNHCR) organized and coordinated the assistance to Zimbabwean refugees in three camps in Botswana prior to Zimbabwe's independence and their repatriation in 1980. The World Health Organization (WHO) and the Food and Agriculture Organization (FAO) are two of the specialized U.N. agencies which also work in Southern Africa. The role of coordinating and providing leadership for some thirty-five U.N. agencies, referred to as "executing and participating agencies" (such as WHO, FAO, UNICEF, and UNHCR), that are at work in each country is undertaken by the United Nations Development Program (UNDP).

The UNDP has been providing financial and technical support in the developing world for more than thirty years, and over the last half decade it has evolved into an organization that not only coordinates the activities of agencies within the U.N. system, but also facilitates collaboration among other public and private sources of development aid. It currently has one hundred and eleven field missions serving one hundred and fifty two territories and developing world countries, including every black-led country in Southern Africa and three national liberation movements recognized by the Organization of African Unity (SWAPO, ANC, and PAC). South Africa has chosen not to participate, either as a donor or recipient, in the United Nations Development Programme. Each UNDP mission is headed by a Resident Representative, and, in keeping with the organization's increasing decentralization, each "res rep" now has the authority to approve grants of up to $400,000.

How the UNDP Functions

The UNDP itself works in four ways: It provides experts, contracts, equipment and/or fellowships for development projects which are administered by the national government of the country involved. Increasingly, contracts are awarded to firms (and fellowships to institutions) in the developing world. In theory the UNDP only provides the resources; the responsibility for determining the UNDP's role and input in a particular project, and of implementing that project, is in the hands of local country officials. Since 1972, governments have been asked to draw up five-year country programs which indicate the priorities and needs each feels the U.N. system is particularly well-placed to meet. The projected budgets for each country are referred to as "indicative planning figures" (IPF's) from which allocations are made based on the comparative merits of various proposed activities instead of on a project-by-project basis as was previously the case. In practice, governments often receive a good deal of assistance from the UNDP "res rep" and officials of other donor agencies in preparing those documents, as they are designed to appeal directly to the capacities of those various agencies rather than being simply a mininational development plan.

The UNDP's largest contribution is in the area of human resources. It provides both high level "experts" and middle-level personnel, many of whom are former recipients of U.N.-sponsored fellowships. For instance, several South African and Zimbabwean graduates sponsored by UNETPSA (the United Nations Education and Training Program for Southern Africans) are currently participating as U.N. volunteers in a United Nations housing project in Mozambique. Three-quarters of such middle-level personnel are from developing countries, and have skills in architecture, agronomy, engineering, health fields, teaching, and certain aspects of industry. Approximately 60% of the financing for UNDP-aided projects is furnished by recipient countries through the provision of national personnel, project buildings and facilities, and locally available supplies and services. The remaining 40% is financed by the UNDP, whose resources come from the voluntary contributions (about $688 million in 1979) of virtually every member of the U.N. and its affiliated agencies.[27]

The U.N. System and Southern Africa

At least two U.N. programs would appear to be particularly appropriate to Southern African needs. One is the Special Fund for Land-Locked Developing Countries. Out of its list of twenty countries, six (Botswana, Lesotho, Malawi, Swaziland, Zambia, and Zimbabwe) are in Southern Africa. The Fund was set up in 1978 with the aim of improving facilities in order to reduce transit and transport costs which affected countries incur. Illustrative UNDP-sponsored activities include a study for the national airline of Botswana on the role air transport can play in that landlocked country, and an effort to strengthen Swaziland's Civil Aviation Branch through the training of its personnel. The other program, the U.N. Decade for Transport and Communication in Africa (1978–1988), was proclaimed by a General Assembly resolution in December 1977. Among its objectives is "the mobilization of technical and financial resources during the Decade with a view to promoting the development and modernization of transport and communications infrastructures in Africa" with priority going first to regional and subregional projects which had "a regional or subregional impact" in the "least developed, land-locked, newly independent, island and frontline states."[28]

Except for the fact that there are no island states in Southern Africa, all of the other terms apply to one or more of the countries of the region. Five hundred and forty-five projects were devised (coming to $8.0 million). A pledging conference was held in New York in November of 1979. Despite prior expressions of interest, actual commitments were disappointingly low ($128,088). One reason, according to U.N. analysts, is that major contributors prefer to follow their own established procedures for identifying and financing projects, and prefer to negotiate directly with recipient governments rather than through intermediaries. The conclusion reached was that, "because of traditional cooperation patterns, national projects may generally be easier to finance than regional and subregional projects, although the latter have been given higher priority."[29]

The implication in that statement is that the UNDP, despite efforts at regional coordination, has ended up—like the World Bank and most other donor organizations—funding projects on a country-by-country basis. UNDP officials, however, have stated their intention of setting aside a substantial amount in their next five-year indicative planning cycle (1982–86) to be able to respond to regional requests from the SADCC as they emerge, especially in the fields of transport and communications, as well as to be able to provide technical assistance personnel for the SADCC permanent secretariat. What already sets the UNDP apart from the World Bank, USAID, and the EEC is that each SADCC country is eligible for—and currently receives—assistance.

In Mozambique, for example, the UNDP presently devotes three-fifths of its contribution to agriculture and rural development. It is collaborating with the FAO and Nordic countries as a group in support of MONAP (the Mozambique-Nordic Agricultural Program) to revitalize the production of food within the country. That project and related activities in livestock, fisheries, and forestry will consume 55.8% of the $21,745 million of UNDP's "indicative planning figure" for Mozambique for 1977–1981. In keeping with Mozambican government priorities, an additional 30.7% has been spent or is committed to projects in health, housing, education, and training, with 5.7% allocated to transport and telecommunications (and 2.1% to natural resources).[30] In the transportation sector, as with much of UNDP involvement, assistance takes the form of consultancies. The UNDP is providing Mozambique with a variety of short and longer term experts to carry out technical and advisory services in those areas where the non-indigenous personnel, which had occupied high- and mid-level managerial positions, had left the country after independence.

That pattern is similar for UNDP activities in much of the region, as an examination of the country program documents for each nation indicates. Malawi's land-locked situation and its consequent dependence on the Mozambican ports of Nacala and Beira is stated explicitly in the section of Malawi's country program called "Development Perspective and Strategy" but most of the projects described in the "Transportation and Communications" rubric of the "Description of UNDP Assistance" section are rather esoteric activities involving expert assistance in radio frequency management, telecommunication traffic accounting, aerodrome engineering, and the like.[31]

Providing technical assistance and training is the favored UNDP mode of action in the BLS countries as well. Like that of Malawi, the country programs of Swaziland and Lesotho specifically emphasize their transportation difficulties, their lack of trained personnel, and the need to reduce their dependence on South Africa. In Lesotho UNDP experts have, over the last decade, served in such key positions as Managing Director of the Lesotho National Development Corporation, the Director of Posts and Telecommunications, the Commissioner of Mines, Vice Chancellor of the University of Botswana, Lesotho, and Swaziland, and Advisor to the Central Planning Office.[32]

The Country Programme of the Zambian government, however, points out that some visits by advisors sent by various U.N. bodies tend to be of very short duration, consume considerable amounts of government time, and invariably result in recommendations for larger scale assistance in the same field. "The benefits to Zambia of this type of advisory services could be questioned in many instances,"[33] points out the anonymous author. Coincidentally, the country plan for Zambia is one of the few which explicitly outlines strategies for integrating its national development activities into larger, mutually beneficial efforts at regional cooperation. One illustration is Zambia's hope "to participate with its neighbors through geographically contiguous national development projects in the control of livestock diseases which are carried between countries by stray animals,"[34] a concern later echoed in SADCC documents.

There is clearly some dissatisfaction with the U.N. system of providing advisory personnel which are not always appropriate, through a process that can be both cumbersome and political, and which on occasion appears overly concerned with highly visible official projects or relatively esoteric fields despite an acknowledged recognition of the type of problems which plague the landlocked states of Southern Africa. On the other hand, an increasing number of UNDP-supplied expatriate personnel come from elsewhere in the Third World, and their presence in a country like Lesotho has not only helped to increase the absorptive capacity of the institutions in which they have worked, but also has helped lessen Lesotho's historical dependence for special skills on Great Britain and South Africa.

Additionally, the UNDP has historically provided assistance to Southern African liberation movements that are recognized by the Organization of African Unity, which few other donors have done ($20.5 million from 1977–81). An economic and social survey of Zimbabwe which the UNDP financed for the Patriotic Front (PF), and was executed by the United Nations Conference on Trade and Development (UNCTAD), made easier the preparation of background documents for the ZIMCORD donors conference which detailed the newly independent country's needs. Assistance to the PF prior to independence included training in aircraft maintenance, and the transport of foodstuffs, goods, and even students (going to Denmark for a vocational course), as well as support for economic activities in exile like poultry farming.

The UNDP currently provides training funds to the Institute for Namibia's courses in post and telecommunications and self-help housing (encompassing physical layout of settlements, squatter upgrading, building techniques, water supply, drainage, and waste disposal). It has also provided modest funds for an assessment of ANC training facilities at Morogoro (Tanzania), and to help the PAC center at Bagamoyo become self-sufficient in food production. Among UNDP's strengths are thus its willingness to work where other donors are constrained, its ability to provide skilled professionals from all over the globe to help fill Southern African human resource needs, and its capacity to help the governments of the region coordinate their diverse sources of assistance.

Bilateral Assistance: USAID

An examination of U.S. foreign assistance to Southern Africa (or to any other region of the world, for that matter) might usefully begin with a clear and realistic understanding that its motives may be self-interested, and with a reminder that an essential premise of this chapter is that aid so proffered need not be inimical to the requirements of the region. The introduction to the fiscal year 1980 presentation to Congress, designed to "sell" foreign assistance, began by listing its humanitarian aims, but then rapidly passed to its economic advantages. It pointed out that aid provides jobs, since 75 cents out of every foreign assistance dollar is spent in the United States on goods and services,[35] and that aid is good for trade, since assistance to "supplier" countries helps to assure the U.S. access to natural resources and to export markets on which "some two million American farmers and workers now depend."[36] Reagan administration spokesmen have also been explicit about its political utility. Agriculture Secretary John Block announced soon after his cabinet appointment that food would be used as a "weapon" of foreign policy,[37] a new and disturbing concept. Administration suspension of the entire U.S. food aid program to Mozambique some two months later, following the expulsion of alleged CIA agents from Maputo, confirmed his point.

U.S. foreign assistance is allocated on a global basis as follows. The largest portion goes to the multilateral development banks, although half is "callable" capital which, as already explained, requires no actual budget outlay unless requested. For the fiscal year 1980, for instance, requests for foreign economic assistance commitments totaled $8.3 billion, of which $3.6 were bank contributions ($2.1 that went to the World Bank Group, constituting, as already noted, one quarter of its total funding). The next largest sum, $3.8 billion, was earmarked for USAID, which is further subdivided into two categories: Functional Development Assistance ($1.8 billion) and Security Supporting Assistance, primarily the Economic Support Fund ($2.0 billion). The rest is divided among U.N. agencies ($277 million), the Peace Corps ($105 million) and PL 480—the Food for Peace Program ($700 million).[38]

Functional Development Assistance, as required by law since 1973, is used to support projects in agriculture and rural development, health, and education aimed primarily at the rural poor. Security Supporting Assistance, however, which is directed toward "countries where U.S. interests can be served by bolstering economies which have been affected by political or economic crises,"[39] is not governed by any similar set of legal constraints. In 1980 86% of Security Supporting Assistance was destined for the Middle East, and over three quarters went to Israel and Egypt alone.[40] More relevant to this study, however, is that 100 million dollars of it in fiscal year 1980 (admittedly only five percent of the total) was earmarked for six countries in Southern Africa to "relieve economic dislocations resulting from the struggle for majority rule"[41] and was thus exempt from the stipulations of the Foreign Assistance Act of 1973. USAID mission directors in Southern Africa thus have, in theory, both more money and greater flexibility in determining the allocation of those funds than many of their counterparts elsewhere on the African continent, and therefore a potentially greater opportunity to respond to region-specific needs.

AID *and* SADCC

SADAP, the Southern Africa Development Analysis Project, was a congressionally mandated USAID study which produced "A Report to the Congress on Development Needs and Opportunities for Cooperution in Southern Africa" in March of 1979. Following a thorough country-by-country and regional analysis by AID staff and consultants, it sensitively outlined the problems requiring development cooperation among the countries of the region and with AID and other donors. In January 1979, several months before the results were presented to Congress, the findings were reviewed at a colloquium in Washington coordinated by the African Bibliographic Center,[42] in which representatives from various government and multilateral donor agencies as well as an international group of technicians and policy specialists participated. The final AID document thus contained a comprehensive description of many of the same constraints which SADCC members were to enunciate shortly thereafter, and a close reading gives some indications of those concerns that AID considers among its highest priorities.

The AID study acknowledges that most of the independent states rely on South Africa for energy, transport, employment, and imports of capital and consumer goods, and it underlines the importance of lessening that dependency. It emphasizes the extreme poverty that dominates the lives of almost all the people in the region. Pointing out that 70% of the labor force (80% in 5 countries) is employed in agriculture, it focuses on the long-term need to increase food production (and the short-term need for imported food). It also discusses the region's critical manpower needs especially for countries like Botswana, where reliance on expatriate skills are costly and sensitive. Areas of AID concern that are not on the SADCC priority lists include health, urban planning, and assistance to refugees and to those limited government services on which refugees create particular pressure. It should be remembered, however, that AID's study was completed prior to Zimbabwe's independence.

The allocation of USAID monies in Southern Africa over the past several years reveals a strong U.S. commitment to each of the various categories identified in that regional needs assessment and also how far it corresponds to African priorities. Of the $100 million projected for fiscal year 1980, for instance, 43% was for agriculture and land conservation, 21% for education and training, and 6% for health delivery, which are all fairly consistent with worldwide AID patterns. The 15% each for refugees and transportation[43] reflected the perceived needs of the region.

Viewed on a country-by-country basis, the largest recipient was Zambia, which received nearly one-third ($31 million) in the form of project assistance, mainly for agriculture, and an agricultural commodity import program. $42 million also primarily earmarked for rural development went to the BLS countries ($9 million for Swaziland; $16 million for Botswana, which included livestock, manpower, and transportation projects; and $17.5 million for Lesotho, $5.5 million of which was for the southern perimeter road, discussed later). Malawi got $5 million for small holder agriculture projects and Mozambique $3 million for food production. $18 million was set aside for regional work, primarily linked to refugees.[44]

Improving agricultural production in Southern Africa is and has clearly been the principal focus of AID. The approach to which it currently subscribes is "integrated" rural development. That is, like the Bank, AID recognizes that providing access to improved seeds, fertilizers, tools, and markets for the owners and tenants of small farms is all-important, as is helping to provide health, education, and family planning facilities as well as new jobs in market towns and villages. AID policy papers also recognize the need for fundamental societal changes such as a more equitable redistribution of land. They also acknowledge the importance of attractive harvest pricing which would provide small farmers with incentives to produce more food.[45] What AID's papers fail to deal with, however, is how its efforts advance—or hinder—these goals.

The reality being ignored is that marketing policies are usually set by government officials in the capital. Ironically, those indigenous policy makers who regulate sensitive pricing mechanisms may themselves have been deprived of access to an appropriately sophisticated education by AID's shift in emphasis away from university-level training and research toward "poorest of the poor" rural projects. As Joyce Moock of the Rockefeller Foundation points out, the irony continues, for, as the Agency finds itself unable to reach the rural poor because of local managerial and institutional weaknesses, it is forced to rely upon expensive expatriate technical assistance and U.S.-university-based researchers, without ever providing any long-term help to those who set policy.[46]

Most of the non-agriculture-related assistance AID offers to the countries of Southern Africa falls into its "regional" category which until 1980 was almost totally devoted to transportation and the education and training of refugees. USAID's Congressional Presentations for the past several years indicate that until Zimbabwe's independence and the formation of SADCC, AID's view of regional activities worthy of support was rather limited. The 1981 Congressional Presentation made it clear that AID wanted to be responsive to SADCC and proposed increased regional funding (it asked for $39 million and got about 20) to complement, not replace, bilateral programs. Those funds were to be used for transport and storage, technical and managerial training, agriculture and livestock development, and transportation.

The 1982 AID presentations reveal an even clearer attempt to be responsive to SADCC categories. Six times as much was requested for transport ($15 million) as for agriculture ($2.5 million). In the area of transport, assistance is being sought for rehabilitation of the Salisbury/Lusaka road which links Zimbabwe with Zambia and is essential for the transport of Zimbabwe's maize to Zambia. Technical assistance training and capital assistance for equipment for port and rail operations for Mozambique is also being proposed. Zimbabwe's access to the Indian Ocean is a very high SADCC priority. So is the upgrading of alternative routes out of Lesotho. AID also hopes to complete the funding of its so-called Southern Perimeter Road project by the end of fiscal 1982.[47]

Lesotho's refusal in 1978 to recognize Transkei's "independence" made many of its southern routes unusable and made necessary the development of an interior perimeter road. In 1978, AID began funding the design and construction of the portion of that road which runs from Quthing to Qacha's Nek in southeastern Lesotho, and includes the critical 100-year-old Seaka bridge over the Sengu (Orange) River. By the time the project is completed in 1983, AID will have contributed an estimated $8 million, much of it for maintenance centers and equipment. The IBRD is also spending a comparable amount on maintenance and equipment.[48] Lesotho is, of course, the most geographically vulnerable of all the independent states in Southern Africa, and much of its outside aid is to help preserve a distinction between it and the so-called independent homelands which are members of the South African "constellation." The announcement by Pretoria of a more than $1 billion cooperative project to provide water and electricity to Lesotho and the Witwatersrand, constructing four large dams at the source of the Orange River in the mountains, is likely to make South African pressure even harder to resist,[49] although an alternative interpretation is that Lesotho's bargaining power vis-à-vis South Africa will be strengthened by gaining control over water, a vital resource which the Republic needs even more than imported oil or labor.

Transportation and food production are, clearly, the two areas in which USAID's Southern African activities demonstrate harmony with SADCC concerns. Unfortunately, much aid is "procurement-tied." More than half of the AID funds allocated for the Southern Perimeter Road project in fiscal 1980, for instance, were for the purchase of U.S. vehicles and equipment or for expatriate personnel (including maintenance engineers and U.S. academics),[50] although Zimbabwean suppliers, now eligible since independence, should become increasingly competitive procurement sources for AID contracts.

The level of competence of AID-hired technical personnel is variable, and they often lack local language ability and may lack cultural sensitivity as well. The time lag between conception, approval, funding, and implementation of AID projects has been notoriously long, although changes since 1978 have cut the time factor almost in half, and allocation of the Economic Support Fund monies is more rapid than the norm. The agency has its share of bureaucrats, especially in Washington; it also has a growing number of field-based professionals who are capably trained and experienced, increasingly drawn from the ranks of former Peace Corps volunteers or staff with graduate degrees in development-related fields.

The two reservations to be noted about AID in Southern Africa are (1) its relative neglect of suitable training experiences for local middle-level implementers and high-level policy makers, and (2) the fact that it is not extensive enough. The $225 million which the Reagan administration offered Zimbabwe at the Zimbabwe Conference on Reconstruction and Development (ZIMCORD) meeting in Salisbury in late March 1981[51] fulfills the Carter administration pledges of $75 million for the coming years, but it still falls far short of Henry Kissinger's pre–Lancaster House predictions of massive outpourings of aid which would follow an acceptable settlement. From AID's own regional figures, one is able to see that, per capita, Southern Africans currently receive less than either Sahel dwellers or Central Americans. The United States also provides less than Britain, either per capita or in total funds. U.S. financial commitments must match its rhetoric if a regional strategy is to succeed.

Private and Giving Institutions

Foundations

The principal U.S. foundations trace their origins to gifts made upon the death of their benefactors. Although they give primary attention to social welfare concerns in the U.S., three of them, Carnegie, Ford, and Rockefeller, have supported international activities for the past several decades. Foundations remain the largest of the nongovernmental donors, but their resources have diminished dramatically over the last decade both in real and comparative terms. Fields like macroeconomic planning, for instance, for which foundations once provided assistance alone, have been later supported by both the UNDP and the World Bank.

Of the five SADCC categories, private foundations have never provided "infrastructure," other than an occasional university building, nor have they worked extensively in the field of energy. As already mentioned, foundations in the 1960s and 1970s felt that their greatest contributions to development in Africa could be made through providing Africans with educational opportunities, both overseas and increasingly at foundation-strengthened institutions in Africa, especially in fields such as agricultural economics and public administration. The guiding belief that transferring Western technological and managerial skills to key African leaders would help ensure smooth functioning economic growth was most certainly elitist and quite possibly naive, but it was not as invidious as some observers, like Edward Berman, have contended. Berman maintains that the Carnegie, Rockefeller, and Ford Foundations consciously sought to create African scholars who would put their knowledge at the service of the American corporate state, of which those foundations were a creature, in order to maintain U.S. influence in the developing world.[52]

Among private foundations, the Ford Foundation is currently making the most substantial commitment of resources to the region, though its contributions are minuscule in comparison with the other donors discussed so far. Its Eastern and Southern African program has three principal objectives: (1) increasing food production and rural income, (2) strengthening the analytic and planning capacities of African governments and institutions in order to promote balanced and equitable socioeconomic development, and (3) enhancing human rights.

Ford's concern with food production and rural poverty clearly corresponds to SADCC's priority area of "food and agriculture" and its approach has been twofold: to work on advancing agricultural technologies appropriate to the region, and to increase indigenous capacity to formulate policies conducive to equitable rural development. Agricultural research has taken place primarily at the various international centers which Rockefeller and Ford have been supporting for several decades. In the late 1970s, Ford instituted a program of visits and training for Southern African scholars and officials at several of these centers. Zambians have been involved in maize research at the IITA (International Institute for Tropical Agriculture) in Ibadan, Nigeria, and several Botswana attended a six-month course in improvement of sorghum, pearl millet, and ground nut production at ICRISAT in Hyderabad, India, in 1978.[53] Out of such experiences has grown the awareness that Southern Africa, whose rich if variable agricultural potential currently has disappointing yields, could benefit from its own regional agricultural research center. Foundation-supported exchanges may thus have helped stimulate the SADCC II request for an ICRISAT station in Botswana where work on new contributions to increasing regional food security can take place.

One national agricultural research station which the Ford Foundation helped initiate at Ilonga in Tanzania in the mid-1970s also illustrates the way in which relations between the donors have evolved over time. USAID now provides Ilonga with over U.S. $1 million annually for research on agricultural technology designed to assist peasant production. Ford still provides small sums of flexible money for certain supplies and training needs which the much larger AID contributions do not cover.

Enhancing local policy-making ability is a second way in which the Ford Foundation seeks to contribute to increasing food production and rural incomes in Southern Africa. In classic foundation modes of operation, postgraduate fellowships or an occasional visiting professorship are provided to coordinate research, and to encourage the working together of professionals in the region. The specific objective is to improve the quality of university teaching in agricultural economics and rural sociology and thereby improve the facilities through which local universities can assist their governments in formulating policies that will stimulate increased food production. An inherited agricultural problem is that colonial policies almost always favored cash crops (and European farmers) rather than food staples. Independent governments short of revenue often continue to overtax the agricultural sector. Moreover, policies that provide protection for domestic manufactures or overvalued exchange rates may also work against rural food producers and in favor of the industrial sector or urban workers and civil servants.

Practical, problem-solving analysis is needed on just such questions, and, from the Ford Foundation's perspective, is best done by Southern Africans, not only because of their deeper understanding of their own societies but also because they alone can make a lasting impact. Some analysis would further argue that USAID's post-1973 romanticism about directly helping the poorest of the poor has drawn it away from continuing to support some of its most beneficial earlier activities in the area of research and training. SADCC's call for assistance in manpower development supports a capacity-building approach, despite its elitist overtones.

Most of the activities in Southern Africa which the Ford Foundation classifies under the heading "enhancing human rights" are, in fact, concrete attempts to further the primary SADCC objective of economic liberation from the Republic of South Africa. Three of those efforts are (1) supporting joint research in Lesotho between the National University and the government's economic planning office on the costs and benefits of the alternatives to close economic links with South Africa; (2) financing training, research, and planning studies at the U.N. Institute for Namibia in Lusaka, in anticipation of Namibian independence; and (3) providing the government of Botswana with high-level advisers.

Lesotho's participation in the Pretoria-dominated South African Customs Union (along with Botswana and Swaziland), its use of the closely linked currency of the Rand Monetary Area and its dependence on miner's remittances all tie Lesotho even more closely to the Republic than are other independent states in Southern Africa. Most of Lesotho's bankholdings are currently invested in South Africa rather than at home or elsewhere in the region. With grants of $112,000 since 1978, the Ford Foundation has enabled the joint research team to weigh options which may help lessen Lesotho's dependence on South Africa. A $164,000 Ford grant to the U.N. Namibia Institute has facilitated research projects since 1977 on manpower needs, constitutional options, land reform and legal restructuring of an independent Namibia, with the hope that the research training as well as the actual findings will serve independent Namibians well.

The largest regional Ford input in dollar terms, however (approximately $2 million since 1970), takes the form of technical assistance, primarily to Botswana. Until very recently, advisors were provided to the Botswana government in the fields of macroeconomic planning, education, agriculture, and mineral resources, in contrast with other parts of the developing world where Ford had phased out almost all expatriate advisory personnel by the mid-seventies.

The decision to continue providing such services to Botswana until 1982 was not made by the Foundation without lively internal debate. Sympathetic critics have argued that the excessive number of expatriates in its civil service is hindering localization efforts, inhibiting Batswana initiative and fostering continued dependency. Since the Ford Foundation had never provided more than four advisors at any one time, that charge was less applicable to Ford than that those advisors concentrated almost exclusively on fulfilling their immediate responsibilities rather than simultaneously trying to pass on their skills to local colleagues.

Counterarguments were that while several external donors now support the training of local cadres, it would be some time before they would gain the experience of the seasoned and carefully selected policy makers whom the Foundation was able to provide in the fields of agriculture, education, and mineral resources. Botswana government officials maintain, for instance, that Foundation-supported advisors were able to secure millions of dollars in revenue for their country by helping to negotiate favorable contracts for the exploitation of its mineral resources. The strongest selling point for continued technical assistance through 1982 was thus that high caliber advisors had been able to offer the government advice which helped it avoid costly mistakes and permitted Botswana negotiators to gain experience while helping to prevent shrewd and aggressive potential business partners (especially South Africans) from taking advantage of them.

While Botswana's lack of trained cadres at independence made such technical assistance necessary, Zimbabwe possessed a large number of highly skilled nationals who were teaching and working in universities and international agencies around the world when independence came. In that case the Ford Foundation made an immediate $75,000 grant to the new government for the repatriation of black Zimbabweans needed to fill senior positions in the white-dominated public service.

Private foundations have thus been attentive to many of the concerns which the region's leaders perceive as central, although foundations also have their own priorities and agendas. As the Ford Foundation has a highly decentralized structure, its regional representatives have much greater autonomy in determining policies than in many comparable organizations. Thus the ideas of individuals, as well as the dictates of time, circumstance, and Foundation resources, are reflected in the changing activities of Ford's eastern and southern Africa program.

In the 1960s and early 1970s, Ford strongly favored technical assistance and institution-building. By the latter 1970s, emphasis had shifted to increasing indigenous skills. Given the lack of success of both the capitalist and socialist states in alleviating some fundamental human problems, Ford's recent activities suggest dissatisfaction with strictly governmental solutions, and a search for fresh approaches by indigeneous nongovernmental organizations, often church-related groups like Zimbabwe's Silveira House. Likewise, growing concern for social equity has led both Ford and Carnegie to give special attention to the needs and rights of women in the region, the latter having supported the Zimbabwe Women's Bureau even prior to independence.

Church Groups and Private Voluntary Organizations (PVO's)

Although many church groups have been in the forefront of the worldwide struggle against apartheid, they do not appear to have explicitly articulated an overall strategy for lessening the region's dependence on South Africa. Rather, the pattern seems to be for national bodies to raise funds and then transfer them either to Geneva-based affiliates or directly to missionaries in Southern Africa. Leaving aside mission work of the "parish construction" type (although it is very necessary in Mozambique where only the government can hold outdoor meetings), most church-assisted development activities either focus on refugee aid, or community projects, and training or extension activities.

The largest of the umbrella agencies which consolidate and coordinate church contributions to Southern Africa are the Lutheran World Federation (LWF), the Church World Service (CWS), and the World Council of Churches (WCC). The many-branched organizational structures of LWF and the CWS are essentially divided into two functional units, one which deals with refugees and the other with community activities. LWF's refugee assistance activities in Southern Africa have ranged from the more classic functions of providing food, clothing, blankets, and medicine, to managing the UNHCR's three camps for Zimbabwean refugees in Botswana. As the major (though not exclusive) internal avenue of refugee support from the Lutheran community, it provided some $13.2 million from 1978 through 1980 to Southern African refugees in Botswana, Tanzania, Swaziland, and Zambia (which included aid to Namibians in Angola).[54]

Like the U.N. agencies, the LWF has been working in Mozambique since its independence. It established a permanent office in Maputo in 1977, but as noted had provided humanitarian assistance to Mozambican refugees in Tanzania and Zambia during their liberation struggle. It continues today to assist refugees and displaced persons with food and by supplying self-help groups with essential commodities which are not available locally. The LWF's Community Development Service also supports projects in most of the countries of the region in the fields of health, education, integrated rural development, communications training, and "diaconic work."[55]

The CWS functions similarly. CWS assistance is divided between direct responses to countries and contributions to umbrella organizations which in turn fund projects in Southern Africa. In 1980, direct responses ranged from $10–20,000 to each of the black-ruled countries of Southern Africa—60% of which was for relief aid and the remainder for education.

CWS lists its relief concerns as the development of agriculture, water resources, health care delivery, and leadership in relief situations. While supplying temporary relief, the intent is to support ongoing projects which are couched in developmental terms in the hopes that no dependency on external or non-local sources will be created. Project selection is done in each country by a committee composed of representatives of the Council of Churches or other local church personnel and expatriate or indigenous field staff. Though selection is usually independent of the local government, all projects are designed to fit into national and regional development programs.

Educational assistance usually involves local upgrading of personnel in apprenticeship situations alongside an expatriate. Formal academic training is also offered through short-term and full courses of study, primarily within Africa, although CWS sponsors some training in the United States and the United Kingdom. In the future, it expects to focus much of the training in Zimbabwe in areas such as agricultural development, construction, hydrology, mineral development, and health.

CWS has made contributions to the WCC for Southern Africa in response to special appeals for such causes as Namibian and Zimbabwean refugees and emergency Mozambican flood relief. In addition, CWS made a $25,000 undesignated block grant to the WCC annually. CWS aid to the Republic of South Africa and to South African refugees averages about $200,000 a year, most of which goes to the South African Council of Churches for legal aid, material assistance, and bursaries for child education. Another $50–70,000 is given for consciousness raising and other types of programs designed to promote interracial contacts within the Republic. Educational assistance is also available to South African residents and exiles/refugees and provides support for all levels of academic training.

Prior to Zimbabwe's independence, the presence of Zimbabwean refugees created such a strain on the services of the host countries that their governments were glad to receive assistance from a variety of church groups. The Lutherans managed refugee camps in remote portions of Botswana while Quaker and Mennonite service groups supplied educational assistance in the form of correspondence course tuition and remedial tutoring for Zimbabweans in the capital, Gaborone, and they continue to do so for young South African and Namibian refugees. Church-affiliated groups also assisted the resettlement and reintegration efforts for the large number of Zimbabweans who returned from exile after independence.

Many local community projects try to raise funds through skills like handicrafts, and are also supported by church groups and private voluntary organizations. The best of these projects integrate literacy training as needed. Some, unfortunately, lack adequate pre-study and end up with make-work rather than work leading to self-sufficiency. One of the better known is Pelegano Village Industries in Botswana, which has helped to raise local incomes through family-centered economic activities, primarily craft production and collecting wildflowers and herbs, etc., and training in skills such as cement block building construction. It is supported by a number of church groups, and its expatriate manager acknowledges that "Christian motivation has been the driving force behind much of the work of PVI."[56] How it fares once that manager departs will indicate how successful it has been in becoming a truly local project.

Church-supported training activities scattered throughout the region vary a good deal. The Presbyterians support a farm institute in Lesotho and an agricultural training center for Namibians in Zambia, while Methodists provide vocational training in Botswana. One of the more unusual training centers is the twenty-year-old Mindolo Ecumenical Foundation, founded in the 1950s and located in Kitwe, Zambia, which offers courses in journalism and photography to over 900 Southern Africans a year. It is described in United Methodist literature as "a meeting place for African humanists" and has branched out into mobile home craft extension projects and the like.

Western church support, whether channeled by denomination or through the worldwide church agencies, has several advantages over bilateral and multilateral donors. It responds to local African initiatives in almost all cases, and goes directly to local parishes and projects, thereby bypassing government bureaucracies. Many church-sponsored activities, however, are underfunded. Another drawback is that most church-sponsored activities include no formal evaluations or rigorous planning activities. Descriptions are sent overseas to elicit further donations, but they are not analytical.

Projects initiated by external agencies, however well intentioned, usually have to be concerned with demonstrable results to show to donors, and therefore put up clinics or schools without providing for the recruiting costs, such as staffing, supplies, and maintenance, which can become a substantial local burden. AID annually spends about $2 million supporting PVO activity in Southern Africa in the belief that in so doing it can significantly enhance work at the grass roots level. Typical programs it assists include preparing villagers for employment in the modern sector, teaching technical skills to unemployed urban youth, and increasing smallholder agricultural production.

Some of the most effective private voluntary organizations experimenting with innovative alternative community approaches are, in fact, those connected with local church groups. One such illustrative effort is the Jesuit-initiated Savings Development Movement in Zimbabwe which is attempting to turn preexisting benevolent fraternal orders and burial societies into savings clubs where members can accumulate cash for needed agricultural inputs like fertilizer and mechanical tillage. The clubs are aimed at farmers in the so-called Tribal Trust lands whose overworked soils are only productive with such inputs, but who are often either unable to obtain credit from commercial sources or are unwilling to take the risks associated with it. Many other locally based groups exist. They are often very cost-effective but usually have little contact with one another.

The Donors and South Africa

Much of the donor activity in Southern Africa which affects the Republic of South Africa does so indirectly. Implicit in a coordinated strategy to strengthen the majority-ruled states of Southern Africa economically is the desire to weaken the hold of Pretoria's minority regime over the region. South Africa wants access to Southern African labor and markets; the creation of exclusive Southern African trading partnerships, both internal to the region and with the outside world, deprives it of that access, and thus lessens its economic dominance. As multinationals no longer find South Africa to be an investor's paradise, the lack of economic incentives may encourage them, more than moral suasion, to phase out.

Southern Africa is rich in exploitable minerals and potential industrial, hydroelectric, and agricultural resources. In addition to Zambia's copper, Zimbabwe's chrome, and Angola's oil, Botswana's output of industrial diamonds now exceeds South Africa's, and the largest uranium mine in the world is at Rossing, Namibia. Dams on the Kafoe and Cunene, and the Cabora Bassa Dam, provide water for power and irrigation, and analysts are now predicting that Southern Africa has the capacity to return to food self-sufficiency within a few years. Donor activities designed to develop the region as a rival to South Africa may have a deleterious effect on the Republic. Donors who choose a country-by-country or piecemeal approach will be less effective in that regard, whether deliberately or out of ignorance.

Most donors are unwilling to take direct action to help bring about majority rule in South Africa other than the necessarily discreet support which various church organizations and the U.N. provide to the major liberation movements, the ANC, PAC, and BCM. Because South Africa is not a developing country and because of the government's abhorrent racial policy, most donors are also understandably loath to supply assistance to South Africa, despite the widespread poverty and malnutrition which is the lot of most rural and many urban black South Africans.

There are only two areas of activity in which those funding organizations concerned about the plight of black South Africans are presently engaged: the protection and extension of their legal rights and educational opportunities. The legal work is being supported externally only by church groups and a few U.S. foundations, primarily Carnegie and Ford; the latter also provides limited assistance for education and training of black South Africans on the post-secondary levels, as do AID, one U.N. agency, UNETPSA (see below), and some Western European church groups.

Law and Social Justice

In the field of law and human rights in South Africa, Carnegie, Ford, and the Rockefeller Brothers' Fund support the Legal Resources Centre, a public interest law firm founded in 1979 in Johannesburg. The Centre has a clinic to which blacks can turn for legal assistance. Lawyers connected with the Centre try "test cases" to see if specific gains, such as winning the severance pay which a domestic is due, or the right to have her husband live with her, can set precedents for future litigation. Several internships each year enable a few recent black law graduates to hone their skills by working with the senior lawyers associated with the Centre.

A similar endeavor, the Centre for Applied Legal Studies of the University of the Witwatersrand, which combines research and scholarship, particularly on labor law, with activism, is assisted by both Ford and Carnegie. Members of the Centre produce materials on the legal rights of black workers and trade unionists and have also successfully defended blacks in pass violation and housing cases, as well as on labor issues. Decisions to support this Centre were based on the judgment that black unions, which are rapidly becoming the most effective vehicles for challenging the present system, can and should benefit from effective legal advice and defense.

While it can be argued that working within the law in South Africa only sustains a nefarious system, there are several strong arguments for this sort of endeavor. One is that it alleviates some people's suffering, however limited and short-term. Another is that it reinforces the realization in successful plaintiffs that they are not totally powerless, an awareness that can carry over into other arenas. It also demonstrates that the law itself need not always be a tool for oppression. In addition, any legal and administrative training currently provided will almost certainly prove useful in whatever post-liberation situation emerges.

Education

External educational support for black South Africans mainly takes the form of fellowship opportunities to study abroad on the post-secondary level, although some assistance is provided to students inside South Africa who are studying by correspondence. Approximately one hundred black South Africans are brought to the United

States each year for advanced-degree study. The three main funding sources, each of which supports around thirty new students annually, are (1) the United Nations Education and Training Program for Southern Africa (UNETPSA); (2) the United States government, which channels its fellowship support through several different agencies; and (3) a consortium of private foundations, companies, and universities coordinated by the Institute of International Education. An additional ten students or so are sponsored each year by church organizations, or by corporations such as IT&T and the Ford Motor Company.

UNETPSA has been in existence since 1967. It is supported by voluntary contributions of U.N. members (to which the United States contributes about $1 million annually), and offers graduate and undergraduate training to South African nationals in the United States only when comparable study is not available in Africa or other Third World countries. U.S. government fellowship funds for South Africans are administered by three different agencies, the African-American Institute, the Phelps-Stokes Fund, and the Institute of International Education.

The African-American Institute administers two programs. One, the Southern African Training Program, is funded by USAID, and was primarily designed to enable black South Africans, Zimbabweans, and Namibians to study in development-related fields. Although the several hundred students presently sponsored under this program in independent Africa or the United States will continue to be supported, the program has received no funding for new students since 1979. The African-American Institute also administers, with funds from USICA (U.S. International Communication Agency), the Southern African Student Program, which also offers post-graduate study in the United States. The majority of students assisted under this program since the early 1960s have been refugees, although only about half of those currently sponsored have refugee status. The rest are nationals who have applied from countries other than that of their origin. A committee in New York makes the final selections, based on recommendations from the UNHCR, the OAU, or an international agency, university, or liberation movement in the applicant's country of residence. USICA also subcontracts to the Institute of International Education the administration of Fulbright scholarships, of which fifteen to twenty each year now go to black South Africans. Finally, USAID monies also enable the Phelps-Stokes Fund to select, place, and support about twenty refugee black South African students annually in predominantly black undergraduate institutions in the United States.

In the fall of 1979, the Institute of International Education began a small private South African Education Program which sought tuition waivers from U.S. universities and travel and maintenance costs from corporate or foundation sources for half a dozen master's degree students annually. Since 1977 it had also administered for the Ford Foundation a similar program which enabled a number of black South African university teachers to pursue graduate degrees abroad. In 1981, the two projects were merged into an expanded program in the hope of eliciting more support from other sources and achieving more coordination in placement and administration. An Educational Opportunities Committee was established in Johannesburg in 1980 under the leadership of Bishop Desmond Tutu to rationalize the recruitment and selection of students on the South African side, and to advise on priority areas for training. Thirty new students were supported by this program in the 1981–82 academic year, and a hundred or so are planned for 1982–83.

The African Education Trust is a London-based organization which for over twenty years has performed a similar function in procuring scholarships and providing educational counsel to students from South Africa. One difficulty it has encountered, however, is that because South African educational qualifications do not match the requirements of U.K. universities most of its recent awards have been to long-term Zimbabwean or South African exiles who have acquired British educational credentials or students who have already attended a South African university for several years.

Several outside organizations also provide support for the higher education of blacks within South Africa. UNISA, the University of South Africa, is the world's largest correspondence college. It is nonracial, since its courses are taught through the mail rather than in classrooms. Since it also has no rigid hours it is ideal for working blacks, except that they often have difficulty paying the fees and understanding the printed materials by themselves. The South African Council on Higher Education (SACHED) Trust is a black-led nonprofit organization which provides "bursaries" (fellowships) and tutorials for many UNISA students. SACHED presently receives outside support from the Ford Foundation, Misereor (the German Catholic Bishops Fund), The United Church of Canada, and the Geneva-based

World University Services, which, in turn, is funded by Scandinavian governments and other European sources. Pace Commercial College, a vocational high school now being built in Soweto by the American Chamber of Commerce in South Africa, is the first major outside attempt to provide Africans with educational opportunities within South Africa on the pre-university level. It has already provoked controversy, however, with the appointment of a white headmaster.

There are those who argue that providing South African blacks with Western educational opportunities aids the Botha government in its attempt to create and "buy off" a small black urban middle class with a vested interest in preserving the status quo; others charge that it self-servingly facilitates exploitative multinationals' need for managerial personnel and new consumers to support its own system, while at the same time gaining points cosmetically for appearing to help black advancement. They thus reject support for "elite" education, maintaining that it is counterproductive and only impedes the cause of genuine liberation.

Many others, however, advocate outside educational opportunities for blacks, although they do so for a variety of motives and with variously timed scenarios for the transition to majority rule in mind. Education may be the one area concerning South Africa where Western self-interest and legitimate black needs intersect. Public and private U.S. support for the education of South African blacks was urged by Chester Crocker, President Reagan's Assistant Secretary for African Affairs, prior to his appointment.[57] (Crocker's redefinition of "constructive engagement" once in office, however, to mean closer links between Washington and Pretoria understandably raises serious questions, especially if U.S. government funds will be made available only at the expense of the previously supported training programs for South African refugees.) With a very different perspective, Bishop Desmond Tutu has courageously written from within South Africa that

> education has a pivotal role in our liberation struggle. . . . an investment in Black education will be an investment in an enterprise that is designed to change, not merely to improve the diabolically oppressive apartheid system. . . . when the new South Africa dawns we shall need all the trained personnel we can get.[58]

And in 1979 a black consciousness leader in exile in Botswana stated that outside supporters must not let the South African government thwart the then-nascent efforts to establish a black-led coordinating mechanism for overseas study, which later grew into Bishop Tutu's Educational Opportunities Committee. He was not at all worried that those who go abroad for training would be coopted, but instead stressed their contributions once they are able to return and work from within the country, arguing that the South African government would like nothing better than to marginalize all sensitized blacks by frustrating them at home or driving them into exile.

The final area in which several American foundations commit funds is the support of research and study designed to develop a deeper understanding of the nature of forces at work in South African society. Its purpose is to create a broadened array of options and, in the process, to improve the competencies of black South African scholars. The Ford Foundation, through modest grants, currently supports research at the universities of Cape Town, Natal and Witwatersrand and the Institute of Race Relations in South Africa on topics such as labor history and attitudes toward political change. It has also supported researchers in the U.K. and the United States, the latter primarily at the Yale South Africa Program which provides white and black South Africans and South Africanists with a conducive environment for a year of reflection, research, writing and exchanging ideas. Additionally, the Rockefeller Foundation has committed approximately $2 million over the past two years for a study of U.S. foreign policy options toward South Africa.

Foundation support for those activities reflects the awareness that what happens in South Africa is of great significance, not only there, but for the future of U.S. relations with the nations of independent Africa, and, ultimately, for relations between blacks and whites within the United States of America itself.

Conclusion

This chapter began with a brief discussion of two alternative models for regional economic development in Southern Africa, a "constellation" of states which would include the Republic of South Africa and the so-called independent homelands, and the SADCC approach which does not. As long as the white minority regime continues to deny citizenship to black South Africans and tries to relegate them to impoverished labor reserves, the truly independent countries of the region will try to have as little contact with the Republic as necessary.

Nevertheless, for a long time into the future the SADCC members will be forced by economic reality into continued dealings with South Africa. As of this writing, Mozambican ports could not function without South African technicians, and 80 to 90 percent of Zimbabwe's trade goes through South Africa.[59] SADCC's realistic goal, therefore, is to lessen dependence on South Africa of the independent states of the region by strengthening their ability to respond to one another's needs for fuel, food, and manufactured goods, and to enable them to trade economically with a variety of outside suppliers in the interim. Helping further that aim should be a primary purpose of all foreign assistance to the region, it is argued.

The sources of and motivations for foreign assistance vary, as this chapter has illustrated. Most of the agencies described herein, however, depend on at least some U.S. funds, public or private. USAID's total appropriation is voted annually by Congress, the United States is the largest shareholder in the World Bank, and it has made the biggest single contribution to the UNDP every year since 1959. Church groups, which are supported primarily through private contributions, are tax-exempt, as are foundations, the incomes of which are derived from investments. U.S. taxpayers thus have multiple reasons to insist that its foreign assistance support activities that are mutually beneficial to their own interests and those of people in the recipient countries. A central premise of this chapter is that such goals will be furthered through appropriate responses to SADCC priorities. Current donor-supported activities were examined for their congruence with those priorities, since it is too early to assess "responsiveness."

It is further argued that the lessons learned from previous development experience must influence the nature of new assistance to Southern Africa. On the agricultural front, for instance, any attempts to stimulate food production will have to incorporate adequate incentives and rewards for farmers, including facilities for them to obtain the credit needed to purchase technical inputs like fertilizer and improved seeds, storage facilities, access to markets, and favorable pricing policies. This means not only that constraints confronting rural farmers must be removed, but that planning ministries and marketing boards in capital cities will need staffs with talent capable of designing and implementing appropriate policies. The latter concern also implies that aid-givers be willing to contribute, on national and regional levels, to activities which take place in the mind as well as on the ground, even if out of sync with a "basic human needs" approach. Providing appropriate training opportunities and short-term technical assistance to the SADCC Secretariat in Botswana would be one obvious way of assisting those who will be creating the new strategies for regional economic cooperation.

Another conclusion which has grown out of this review of SADCC's needs and donors' capacities is the central importance of infrastructural improvements. Upgrading existing road and rail links to coastal ports and improving those ports' facilities are essential if the independent countries of the region are to trade with one another and the outside world on mutually beneficial terms and without being beholden to the Republic of South Africa. The most appropriate sources for the necessary assistance are probably bilateral aid along Marshall Plan lines and multilateral aid from the International Bank for Reconstruction and Development which, it will be remembered, was originally chartered at the end of World War II as a means of financing Europe's economic recovery. Since improving ports and roads in Mozambique is vital to the success of such an approach, however, the fact that USAID's appropriations for that country have never been spent there is unfortunate. The situation of the World Bank Group is more complex. Technically the Bank is waiting for Mozambique to join the IMF and itself, and to request a loan. The U.S. congress cannot prohibit the Bank from making loans to any particular country, but it can fail to vote an entire contribution, as it nearly did with a 1981 IDA replenishment. Given criticism of the Bank by the current administration for being too supportive of socialist experiments, U.S. officials might balk at the prospect of Bank loans to Mozambique, but probably could not thwart such assistance.

If the U.S. government were to overcome its concern with Mozambique's ideology and provide assistance directly through AID and indirectly through the Bank, that would reduce Mozambique's reliance on the Eastern block while at the same time advancing the development goals of all of the independent states of the region. On the other hand, those regional efforts will be undercut if the United States, through a policy of "constructive engagement," insists on helping South Africa maintain its economic control over its neighbors, or allows a colonial situation to continue in Namibia. Happily, some Western European countries are already assisting Mozambique individually. In the face of official U.S. intransigence, however, it is especially incumbent upon private nongovernmental organizations to assist local efforts and help strengthen talents indigenous to the region. Hoping for "spillovers" from U.S.-funded assistance to Zimbabwe is not enough.

Governments around the world provide aid bilaterally and through numerous international organizations and development banks, and individuals contribute to the development process through religious groups and other private channels. The leaders of the black-ruled states of Southern Africa have appealed for international assistance, which the various donors reviewed here are capable of providing. Their regional plan holds out strong possibilities for success, particularly in light of Zimbabwe's impressive industrial and agricultural base, its ability to serve as the focal point for integrated regional economic development, and its commitment, and that of its neighbors, to that goal. Donors admit to self-interest, and claim loftier motives as well. By responding with assistance to SADCC priorities in the areas of transport, agriculture, manpower training, industry, and energy, donors would accomplish both sets of goals.

9.

The International Moral Protest

Colin Legum

South Africa is unique in being the only country whose political system is unanimously condemned by the nations of the world—a situation without precedent in international affairs. South Africa is not the only oppressive regime in the world, nor even the only one which practices racism; its offense in the eyes of the world community is that it is the only one which has institutionalized racism, and which seeks to maintain this *status quo* by an undemocratic form of government that excludes the majority of its population from any kind of participation in the central parliament where all its laws are made. What makes this offense even greater is that this institutionalized discrimination against black peoples exists on the African continent itself. Moreover, the apartheid rule was formalized in a succession of laws at a time when the modern world community had committed itself, through the United Nations Charter and by other internationally approved declarations and conventions, against the denial of human rights.

The moral protest against apartheid has been the major reason why South Africa has come to be ostracized as a pariah state, "a skunk among nations." Even those countries which still maintain close economic and diplomatic links with Pretoria, and those political leaders who defend it against proposals to subject it to sanctions, join in condemning its system on moral grounds. For example, Major Patrick Wall, a British Conservative member of parliament and an acknowledged protagonist of South Africa, described its policies at the United Nations as "totally repugnant and morally indefensible." Dr. Kurt Waldheim, former U.N. secretary-general, added in 1978 in his address to the special meeting at the General Assembly to mark the International Anti-Apartheid Year: "Apartheid is not only immoral and inhuman, but also a grave danger to international peace and security."

The African opposition to apartheid has based itself on these precise grounds as is reflected in the seminal Lusaka Manifesto of 1969, subsequently endorsed by the Organization of African Unity (OAU). Its key passage reads:

> By this Manifesto we wish to make clear, beyond all shadow of doubt, our acceptance of the belief that all men are equal, and have equal rights to human dignity and respect, regardless of color, race, religion or sex. We believe that all men have the right and duty to participate, as equal members of the society, in their own government. We do not accept that any individual or group has any right to govern any other group of sane adults without their consent, and we affirm that only the people of a society, acting together as equals, can determine what is, for them, a good society, and a good social economic or political organization. . . . We affirm that without an acceptance of these ideals—without a commitment to these principles of human equality and self-determination—there can be no basis for peace and justice in the world.

However—and this is an important point because of the charge of double standards leveled by critics against African leaders—the Lusaka Manifesto contains this admission:

> None of us would claim that within our own States we have achieved that perfect social, political and economic organization which would ensure a reasonable standard of living for all our people and establish individual security against avoidable hardship or miscarriage of justice. On the contrary, we acknowledge that within our own States the struggle towards human brotherhood and unchallenged human dignity is only beginning. It is on the basis of our *commitments* to human equality and human dignity, not on the basis of *achieved perfection*, that we take our stand of hostility towards the colonialism and racial discrimination which is being practised in Southern Africa. It is on the basis of our commitment to these universal principles that we appeal to other members of the human race for support.

It hardly needs saying that, by no means, have all of Africa's leaders—any more than others—lived up to these fine avowals of principles—a point made with increasing frequency in recent years by Africans themselves. Thus, Tanzania's President Julius Nyerere told a meeting at Oxford University (England) in 1975: "South Africa is a tyranny. It is not the only tyrannical police state in the world, *nor even in Africa.* There are too many of them." Tanzania was one of a number of African countries which boycotted the OAU summit in Kampala in 1975 because of their refusal to bestow legitimacy on Idi Amin's rule. Explaining this stand, Nyerere's government declared: "Tanzania cannot accept the responsibility of participating in the mockery of condemning colonialism, apartheid and fascism in the headquarters of a murderer, an oppressor, a black fascist and a self-confessed admirer of fascism."

Nor are African concerns confined only to the denial of fundamental rights by the apartheid regime; this was shown by the OAU's unanimous decision in 1979 to adopt a Human Rights Charter for Africa—which is at least an acknowledgment, as Nyerere has said, that racism practiced against blacks by blacks is no more tolerable than when blacks suffer at the hands of whites.

The United Nations has provided an ideal platform from which to mount the kind of moral and political campaign against apartheid that was envisaged in the OAU's Charter and the Lusaka Manifesto, since Article I of the world body's Charter has as one of its purposes the promotion and encouragement of respect for human rights and fundamental freedoms for all, without distinction as to race, color, religion, or sex. This commitment was buttressed in 1952 by the adoption of the Declaration of Human Rights. Reflecting the American Declaration of Independence, the U.N. Declaration asserts that all human beings are "born free and equal in dignity and rights." In 1960, acting under pressure from a growing number of African member states, the General Assembly condemned "all manifestations and practices of racial, religious and national hatred in the political, economic and social, educational and cultural spheres of the life of society as violations of the U.N. Charter and the Universal Declaration of Human Rights." Three years later, in 1963, the General Assembly went a step further when it adopted the U.N. Declaration on the Elimination of All Forms of Racial Discrimination. Its first article declares such discrimination to be a denial of the U.N. Charter and a violation of the Human Rights Declaration, and stamps it as "an obstacle to friendly and peaceful relations among nations . . . capable of disturbing peace and security among peoples."

This was followed two years later, in December 1965, by an international Convention on the Elimination of All Forms of Discrimination, to which all member states were invited to adhere. Signatories of the Convention, which now number about one hundred, accept that "any doctrine of superiority based on racial differentiation is scientifically false, morally condemnable, socially unjust and dangerous; and that there is no justification for racial discrimination, in theory or in practice anywhere."

Thus, step by step, an international system of human rights has been built up, not only within the U.N. framework but also through regional organizations such as the European Economic Community and the Organization of American States, as well as the OAU, to which some reference has already been made. Although this development reflects a growing concern by the world community about human rights—and specifically about such abuses as torture in prisons, detention without trial, and impediments to travel, the question of the rights of immigrant communities, and political terrorism—the momentum, at least within the U.N. system, came from the growing opposition to, and concern over, South Africa's racial policies. Apartheid has by now become a universally recognized and utilized word for a morally repugnant theory and practice of racial and social discrimination—so much so that even the South African regime itself no longer favors it, preferring instead the safer and more beguiling political concept of separate development.

However, while the sense of moral outrage against apartheid has become almost universal, the world community has itself remained divided and ambiguous when it has come to consider what practical measures to take in combating the South African system. Resistance to full-scale sanctions has come very largely from the Western community, for reasons discussed elsewhere in this book.

Opinion diverges sharply, both about the value of moral protest in politics and in assessing the meaningfulness of what has been accomplished by international society in actively combating apartheid, as distinct from simply affirming principled opposition and expressing moral repugnance. There are those who argue that moral power is, at best, only a marginal element in the political decision-making process, as against those who claim that it is a crucial determinant of policy. On a different level, there are those who dismiss almost entirely the usefulness of the measures so far adopted by the international community against apartheid, as against those who believe that, whatever the shortcomings, the international community has indeed made a significant contribution to the anti-apartheid struggle.

While it hardly needs pointing out that the impressive level of international moral protest against apartheid has so far failed to end that system, it is hard to deny that it has made an important contribution toward the struggle to overcome it. What is clearly evident is that all the principal actors on both sides of the conflict attach considerable importance to the moral dimension of the political struggle over apartheid. Apartheid is only one example—albeit a lurid one—of the widespread phenomenon of racism. Therefore, the creation of a climate of world opinion against racial discrimination has a potential value which carries far beyond the borders of South Africa itself.

Moral protest has, however grudgingly, produced a variety of measures at the international level. In 1960, the Commonwealth of Nations decided that there was no place for an apartheid state within a multiracial organization, a decision that left the Pretoria regime with the alternative of either reforming its society or losing its place in the Commonwealth. Having elected the second option, it found itself isolated from a family of nations which, in the past, had played an important role in bolstering the morale of whites on the African continent. The process of isolating South Africa was carried an important step further in 1963 when the newly founded OAU called for a total boycott of the Pretoria regime. (This decision is discussed in an earlier chapter.) The U.N. specialized agencies and other intergovernmental organizations have subsequently excluded South Africa from any association with themselves.

A U.N. Trust Fund for South Africa was established in 1965 to assist political prisoners, to which over $5 million has already been contributed. Twice that sum has been donated to a U.N. Educational and Training Program for Southern Africa, which now administers over 1,300 scholarships. Those liberation movements in Southern Africa approved by the OAU have received official U.N. recognition, which carries with it support from UNESCO, ILO, WHO, FAO, and other specialized agencies for their nonmilitary activities. A U.N. Trust Fund for Publicity Against Apartheid was set up in 1975.

Two years earlier, in 1973, the U.N. General Assembly adopted an International Convention on the Suppression and Punishment of the Crime of Apartheid, which declared that "apartheid is a crime against humanity, and that inhuman acts resulting from its policies and practices, and of similar policies and practices of racial segregation and discrimination . . . are crimes violating the principles of international law and, in particular, the purposes and principles of the U.N. Charter, and as constituting a serious threat to international peace and security."

Although the Security Council has on a number of occasions vetoed attempts to endorse a comprehensive sanctions program against South Africa, it voted in favor of an arms embargo against the Republic in 1963. This ban was made mandatory in 1977. By far the most complete set of sanctions taken against the apartheid state has been the world boycott against South African sporting bodies. This boycott was extended in 1981 when a blacklist was opened by the U.N. of all individual sportsmen who, in defiance of the boycott, visit South Africa to participate in sporting events. The Commonwealth itself adopted the Gleneagles Agreement in 1979 which enjoins member governments to do everything possible to prevent their sportsmen from competing against Springbok national teams.

The nine member states of the European Community have collectively adopted a Code of Conduct to govern the practices of their companies operating in South Africa. A voluntary scheme of a similar character, the Sullivan Code, is supported by a number of American companies. Sweden, acting purely from a moral imperative and against its own economic interest, has enacted a law which forbids any new investment in South Africa.

This incomplete catalogue of action by the international community gives some idea of the wide range of measures so far taken against apartheid. Parallel to these decisions on the South African issue taken by the U.N. and other international organizations has been a corresponding program of punitive measures taken in respect of Namibia and, until its independence, against Rhodesia as well.

While these decisions by the international community may fall far short of what the opponents of apartheid desire, there can be no mistaking the hostility of world opinion against South Africa: a hostility that springs from a strong moral revulsion against the ideas and practices of apartheid.

Notes

Introduction

1. *New York Times*, March 9, 1980, quoted in AF Press Clips March 14, 1980, XV, no. 11, p. 3.
2. *Africa Report*, January–February 1981, pp. 7–14.

1. The Communist States and Southern Africa

1. See, for instance, Edward T. Wilson, *Russia and Black Africa Before World War II* (New York and London: Holmes & Meier, 1974); Colin Legum, "National Liberation in Southern Africa," *Problems of Communism*, XXIV, no. 1 (January–February 1975): 1–20.
2. John A. Marcum, *The Angolan Revolution*, vol. 1 (Cambridge, Mass.: MIT Press, 1969) and vol. 2 (Cambridge, Mass.: MIT Press, 1978).
3. See, for example, Legum, loc. cit.
4. See William J. Durch, *The Cuban Military in Africa and the Middle East: From Algeria to Angola*, Professional Paper no. 201 (Arlington, Va.: Center for Naval Analyses, September 1977), pp. 17–18; William M. LeoGrande, *Cuba's Policy in Africa, 1959–1980* (Berkeley: University of California Press, 1980), pp. 9–10, 13.
5. See Melvin Croan, "A New Afrika Korps?" *The Washington Quarterly*, 3, no. 1 (Winter 1980): 21–37; idem, "East Germany and Africa," in David E. Albright and Jiri Valenta, eds., *The Communist States and Africa* (Bloomington: Indiana University Press, forthcoming).
6. For detailed discussion of the evidence regarding Cuban and Soviet attitudes, see LeoGrande, op. cit., pp. 13–22; Marcum, op. cit.; Jiri Valenta, "Soviet Decision-Making on the Intervention in Angola," in David E. Albright, ed., *Communism in Africa* (Bloomington: Indiana University Press, 1980), pp. 93–117.
7. The South African intervention in the Angolan civil war toward the end of October 1975 facilitated the carrying out of this enterprise, for that intervention cast the Communist undertaking in a much more favorable light than it would otherwise have enjoyed. But the essential decisions that led to the increased involvement of Communist states in the Angolan affair clearly preceded the South African intervention. See particularly Valenta, loc. cit., pp. 102–12.

229

8. See Edward Gonzalez, "Cuban Policy Toward Africa: Activities, Motivations, and Outcomes," in Albright and Valenta, *The Communist States and Africa;* Croan, "East Germany and Africa"; Valenta, loc. cit., pp. 112–16.

9. For the texts, see *Pravda,* October 9, 1976, and Foreign Broadcast Information Service, *Daily Report: Soviet Union,* April 4, 1977, pp. H/2–5.

10. For a representative discussion of Soviet attitudes toward these parties and of Soviet contacts with them, see C. P. Nemanov, "Parties of a Vanguard Type in the African Countries of Socialist Orientation," *Narody Azii i Afriki,* no. 2 (1979): 16–28.

11. U.S. Central Intelligence Agency, *Communist Aid Activities in Non-Communist Less Developed Countries, 1979 and 1954–79*, ER 80–10318U (Washington, D.C., October 1980), p. 39. This and other documents in the series published by the CIA on Communist aid activities in non-Communist less developed countries are available through the Document Expediting Service of the U.S. Library of Congress.

12. U.S. Arms Control and Disarmament Agency, *World Military Expenditures and Arms Transfers 1969–1978* (Washington, D.C., 1980); *The Washington Post,* February 8, 1980.

13. According to the Western intelligence sources cited in *Newsweek,* July 9, 1979, the GDR had by that time taken on the function of main arms supplier of ZAPU.

14. On relations between the ANC and the Black Consciousness Movement and the attitudes of both toward the USSR, see, for example, Steven F. McDonald, "The Black Community," in Richard E. Bissell and Chester A. Crocker, eds., *South Africa into the 1980s* (Boulder, Colo.: Westview, 1979); Caryle Murphy, in *The Washington Post,* August 19, 1980.

15. *Communist Aid . . . 1979 and 1954–79*, p. 15.

16. See the annual publications on Communist aid activities in non-Communist less developed countries put out by the CIA for 1976 through 1979.

17. *Los Angeles Times,* January 1, 1980.

18. See the compilation in Gonzalez, loc. cit.

19. Durch, op. cit., pp. 31–34; LeoGrande, op. cit., pp. 53–54.

20. See, for instance, the compilation of visits of African delegations to Cuba in Gonzalez, loc. cit.

21. Croan, "East Germany and Africa."

22. See *Communist Aid . . . 1979 and 1954–79*, especially pp. 15 and 21. Unfortunately, the aggregate figures for military and economic advisers cited in the text are the only ones available.

23. Croan, "East Germany and Africa."

24. Ibid.

25. Ibid.

26. Ibid.

27. Ibid.

28. The aid and trade data were compiled from the annual publications on Communist aid activities in non-Communist less developed countries published by the CIA for 1976 through 1979; USSR Ministry of Foreign Trade, *Vneshniaia torgovlia SSSR v 1977 g.: Statisticheskii sbornik* (Moscow: Statistika, 1978); USSR Ministry of Foreign Trade, *Vneshniaia torgovlia SSSR v 1978 g.: Statisticheskii sbornik* (Moscow: Statistika, 1979). Dollar equivalents for trade figures were calculated by the author using a conversion rate of 1.4 dollars to the ruble. This was the average ruble/dollar ratio during the period under

consideration. The figure for economic technicians was derived from information in *Communist Aid . . . 1979 and 1954–79*, p. 21.

29. Croan, "East Germany and Africa"; *Statistical Pocket Book of the German Democratic Republic 1979* (East Berlin: Staatsverlag der Deutschen Demokratischen Republik, 1979); *Communist Aid . . . 1979 and 1954–79*, p. 21. East German trade statistics have not broken down trade turnover into exports and imports since 1974. Dollar equivalents for trade figures were calculated by the author in a two-step process. Foreign exchange marks were converted to rubles at the fixed rate of 4.667 foreign exchange marks to the ruble; then rubles were translated into dollars at the conversion rate of 1.4 dollars to the ruble.

30. Jorge I. Domínguez, "Cuba in the 1980s," *Problems of Communism*, XXX, no. 2 (March–April 1981): 48–59; Lawrence H. Theriot and JeNelle Matheson, "Soviet Economic Relations with Non-European CMEA: Cuba, Vietnam and Mongolia," in U.S. Congress, Joint Economic Committee, *Soviet Economy in a Time of Change* (Washington, D.C.: U.S. Government Printing Office, 1979), vol. 2, pp. 551–67; *Communist Aid . . . 1979 and 1954–79*, p. 21.

31. *The New York Times*, March 25, 1981; summary of pledges announced by Tom Mswaka, Zimbabwe Secretary for Economic Planning and Development, on March 26, 1981. Promises of aid made before the conference raised the figure for total expected aid during the first four years of independence to $2 billion.

32. The ensuing discussion draws upon David E. Albright, "The USSR, Its Communist Allies, and Southern Africa," *Munger Africana Library Notes*, no. 55, November 1980.

33. For careful weighing of the evidence with respect to Cuban interests and goals, see Durch, op. cit.; Gonzalez, "Cuban Policy Toward Africa: Activities, Motivations, and Outcomes"; idem, "Cuba, the Soviet Union, and Africa," in Albright, *Communism in Africa*, pp. 145–67; LeoGrande, op. cit. The analysis of GDR interests and goals derives from John M. Starrels, "GDR Foreign Policy," *Problems of Communism*, XXIX, no. 2 (March–April 1980), pp. 72–75; Croan, "A New Afrika Korps?"; idem, "East Germany and Africa"; personal conversations with East German diplomats.

34. See, for instance, Gonzalez, "Cuba, the Soviet Union, and Africa"; Croan, "East Germany and Africa."

35. Theroit and Matheson, loc. cit.; *Statistical Pocket Book of the German Democratic Republic*.

36. On Southern Africa's minerals and their significance, see, for example, Philip Crowson, *Non-Fuel Minerals and Foreign Policy* (London: Royal Institute of International Affairs, 1977); W.C.J. van Rensburg, "Africa and Western Lifelines," *Strategic Review*, Spring 1978; Richard E. Bissell, "How Strategic Is South Africa," in Bissell and Crocker, op. cit., pp. 216–18: Congressional Research Service, U.S. Library of Congress, prepared for the U.S. Senate Foreign Relations Committee, Subcommitee on Africa, *Imports of Minerals from South Africa by the United States and the OECD Countries* (Washington, D.C.: U.S. Government Printing Office, 1980). With respect to the sea lanes and their importance, see, for instance, Bissell, loc. cit., pp. 214–15; *Africa News*, October 13, 1980, pp. 6–7.

37. For typical illustrations, see Dimitri Volsky, "Southern Version of NATO," *New Times*, No. 36, September 1976; I.S. Ulanovskaia, *South Africa: Racism Doomed* (Moscow: Znanie, 1978), p. 20, quoted in Morris Rothenburg,

The USSR and Africa: New Dimensions of Soviet Global Power (Washington, D.C.: Advanced International Studies Institute, 1980), p. 222; Anatoly Gromyko, "Africa in the Strategy of Neo-Colonialism," *International Affairs,* November 1978, p. 84; V. Kudriavtsev in *Izvestiia,* May 4, 1979.

38. For elaboration of the evidence on the first point, see Valenta, "Soviet Decision-Making on the Intervention in Angola"; Rothenburg, *The USSR and Africa,* pp. 11–50. On the second point, see Vernon V. Aspaturian, "Soviet Global Power and the Correlation of Forces," *Problems of Communism,* XXIX, no. 3 (May–June 1980):1–18.

39. For a description of Moscow's growing capabilities for the projection of force and a detailed analysis of their meaning in the Southern African situation, see Albright, "The USSR, Its Communist Allies, and Southern Africa," pp. 15–17.

40. R. A. Ul'ianovskii, "On the Countries of Socialist Orientation," *Kommunist,* no. 11 (July 1979), p. 118. Ul'ianovskii is a deputy director of the International Department of the Central Committee of the CPSU. For an equally definitive commentary, see the book by K.N. Brutents, another deputy director of the International Department, entitled *Osvobodivshiesia strany v 70-e gody* (Moscow: Izdatel'stvo politicheskoi literatury, 1979).

41. See Albright, "The USSR, Its Communist Allies, and Southern Africa," pp. 11–13, for more extended discussion of the evidence bearing upon these priorities.

42. For elaboration, see Aspaturian, loc. cit.

43. For an excellent illustration, see the article by Anatoly Gromyko, Director of the African Institute of the USSR Academy of Sciences and the son of Foreign Minister Andrei Gromyko, entitled "Western Diplomacy vs. Southern Africa," *International Affairs,* March 1979, pp. 20–28.

44. The article by Anatoly Gromyko cited in n. 43 is typical.

45. For more detailed treatment, see David E. Albright, "Moscow's African Policy of the 1970s," in Albright, *Communism in Africa,* pp. 35–66; *Communist Aid . . . 1979 and 1954–79.*

46. For an explicit statement of this perspective with respect to Africa as a whole, see M.L. Vishvevskii, "Washington's Policy in Africa and American African Studies," *SShA,* January 1980, p. 118.

47. Soviet memorandum submitted to the United Nations by Foreign Minister Gromyko on October 4, 1976, in *Pravda,* October 5, 1976.

48. See V. Rymalov, "Newly Free Countries: Problems of Economic Development," *International Affairs,* July 1978, p. 58.

49. See, for instance, "How to Interpret the Peculiarities and Level of Development of Capitalism in Latin America," *Latinskaia Amerika,* January–February 1979, pp. 69–70.

50. For elaboration, see George T. Yu, "Sino-Soviet Rivalry in Africa," in Albright, *Communism in Africa;* Colin Legum, "The Soviet Union, China, and the West in Southern Africa," *Foreign Affairs,* 54, no. 4 (July 1976): 745–62.

51. G. Kromushin, "Ideological Struggles in Africa," *International Affairs,* June 1979, p. 55. See also Y. Semyonov, "Peking and the National Liberation Movement," ibid., January 1980, pp. 29–39.

52. V. Sofinsky and A. Khazanov, "Angolan Chronicle of the Peking Betrayal," ibid., July 1978, pp. 60–69.

53. See, for instance, Brutents, *Osvobodivshiesia strany v 70-e gody,* pp. 67–77.

54. Highly explicit reflections of this approach may be found in Gromyko,

"Africa in the Strategy of Neo-Colonialism," pp. 84–89, and especially idem, "Western Diplomacy vs. Southern Africa," pp. 20–28.

55. The following analysis of Yugoslav and Romanian activities owes much to Trond Gilberg, "Romania, Yugoslavia, and Africa: 'Nonalignment and Progressivism,' " in Albright and Valenta, *The Communist States and Africa;* Paul Gafton and the Romanian Section, "Romania's Presence in Black Africa," *Radio Free Europe Research,* Background Report no. 118, May 23, 1979; William F. Robinson, "Eastern Europe's Presence in Black Africa," ibid., Background Report no. 142, June 21, 1979.

56. Socialist Federated Republic of Yugoslavia, Federal Bureau of Statistics, *Statistički Godišnjak Jugoslavije 1977* (Belgrade, 1977). The dollar equivalent was computed by the author on the basis of a fixed rate of 17 dinar to the dollar.

57. See, for example, Valenta, loc. cit., p. 100.

58. See the list of Romanian aid commitments to Africa in Gafton et al., p. 13.

59. For a report of the opening of swapo's office in Bucharest, see Leopold Unger, *The International Herald Tribune,* March 19, 1979.

60. *Scinteia,* April 19, 1979.

61. Socialist Federated Republic of Yugoslavia, Federal Bureau of Statistics, *Statistički Godišnjak Jugoslavije 1979* (Belgrade, 1979). Dollar equivalents were calculated by the author on the basis of the average annual conversion rates for the years concerned (15.9 and 18.6 dinars to the dollar, respectively).

62. Republic of Socialist Romania, *Anuarul Statistic al Republicii Socialiste Romania* for 1977–79 (Bucharest: Directia Centrala de Statistica, 1977–79). Dollar equivalents were computed by the author, using the average annual commercial exchange rates for the given years (20.0 and 18.4 lei to the dollar, respectively).

63. Radio Bucharest, February 6, 1978; *Scinteia,* April 19, 1979.

64. *Scinteia,* April 27, 1979.

65. See, for instance, Zdenko Antic, "Yugoslavia Tries to Mobilize the Nonaligned Nations," *Radio Free Europe Research,* Background Report no. 52, March 6, 1980.

66. According to Mugabe, as reported in *The International Herald Tribune,* February 8, 1979.

67. See Radio Salisbury Domestic Service in English, March 27, 1981, Foreign Broadcast Information Service, *Daily Report: Middle East and Africa,* March 27, 1981, p. U/3; summary of pledges announced by Tom Mswaka, Zimbabwe Secretary for Economic Planning and Development, on March 26, 1981.

68. See, for example, Ceausescu's speech at a plenum of the Central Committee of the Romanian Communist Party, in *Scinteia,* August 4, 1978; *Lumea,* no. 18, April 26, 1979.

69. That the intervention of the Soviet–Cuban–East German "quasi-coalition" in Angola prompted this new activism on the part of Yugoslavia and Romania there can be little doubt. Throughout the civil war there, for example, the Romanian media refrained from publishing any information about the presence of Cuban or other foreign military forces supporting the mpla. For more explicit evidence in the Yugoslav case, see the recent book entitled *Communism's Crossroads,* written by Janez Stanic, a Slovene journalist who had served as Moscow correspondent of the Ljubljana daily *Delo* in

1964–67, and serialized in the Zagreb fortnightly *Start* at the end of 1980 and the beginning of 1981. The relevant chapter, the fourth one, appeared in *Start*, January 31, 1981. For a summary of it, see Slobadan Stankovic, "Slovene Author Attacks Soviet-Cuban Interference in Africa," *Radio Free Europe Research*, Background Report no. 33, February 9, 1981.

70. Reuters dispatch from the United Nations, February 6, 1979.

71. For assessment of the interests and goals of Yugoslavia and Romania in the African context in general, see Gilberg, loc. cit.; Gafton et al., loc. cit.; Robinson, loc. cit.

72. For the Yugoslav figures, see Laura D'Andrea Tyson and Gabriel Eichler, "Continuity and Change in the Yugoslav Economy in the 1970s and 1980s," in U.S. Congress, Joint Economic Committee, *East European Economic Assessment: Part 1—Country Studies, 1980* (Washington, D.C.: U.S. Government Printing Office, 1981), p. 183. The Romanian figures are calculated from data in Marvin R. Jackson, "Romania's Economy at the End of the 1970's: Turning the Corner on Intensive Development," in ibid., p. 274.

73. Tyson and Eichler, loc. cit., p. 187; Jackson, loc. cit., pp. 277–78.

74. The subsequent discussion of Chinese undertakings in Southern Africa, both before and after the mid-1970s, draws to some extent upon Yu, "Sino-Soviet Rivalry in Africa"; Bruce D. Larkin, *China and African 1949–1970* (Berkeley, Calif.: University of California Press, 1971); idem, "China and Africa: Politics and Constraint," in Albright and Valenta, *The Communist States and Africa*.

75. U.S. Department of State, *Communist States and Developing Countries: Aid and Trade in 1974* (Washington, D.C., February 1976); U.S. Central Intelligence Agency, *Communist Aid to the Less Developed Countries of the Free World, 1976*, ER 77–10296 (Washington, D.C., August 1977).

76. U.S. Arms Control and Disarmament Agency, *World Military Expenditures and Arms Transfers 1965–1974* (Washington, D.C.: U.S. Government Printing Office, 1976).

77. See Legum, "National Liberation in Southern Africa"; idem, "The Soviet Union, China, and the West in Southern Africa"; John Marcum, "Communist States and Africa: The Case of Angola," in Albright and Valenta, *The Communist States and Africa*.

78. For discussion of the Chinese role in the Angolan crisis, see Legum, "The Soviet Union, China and the West in Southern Africa"; Marcum, "Communist States and Africa: The Case of Angola"; Valenta, loc. cit.

79. See the annual publications on Communist aid activities in less developed non-Communist countries, put out by the CIA.

80. U.S. Arms Control and Disarmament Agency, *World Military Expenditures and Arms Transfers 1969–1978* (Washington, D.C., 1980).

81. *Communist Aid . . . 1976.*

82. *Communist Aid . . . 1979 and 1954–79*, p. 21.

83. U.S. Arms Control and Disarmament Agency, *World Military Expenditures and Arms Transfers 1969–1978.*

84. *Communist Aid . . . Less Developed Countries, 1978*, ER 79–10412U (Washington, D.C., September 1979).

85. See, for instance, Legum, "The Soviet Union, China and the West in Southern Africa"; Mugabe's comments, as reported in *The International Herald Tribune*, February 8, 1979; Mugabe's speech at Beijing University on May 13, 1981, in *Renmin Ribao*, May 14, 1981, as translated in Foreign Broadcast

Information Service, *Daily Report: People's Republic of China* (hereafter *FBIS-PRC*), May 18, 1981, pp. I/1–4.

86. On the aid commitment, see the summary of pledges announced by Tom Mswaka, Zimbabwe Secretary of Economic Planning and Development, on March 26, 1981. For the Chinese coverage of Mugabe's sojourn, see *FBIS-PRC*, May 13–18, 1981.

87. See McDonald, loc. cit., especially pp. 33–46.

88. See Deng Ziaoping's speech to the United Nations in early 1974, *Peking Review*, April 12, 1974. For a recent key restatement of this position, see "China Belongs to the Third World Forever," *Liaowang*, no. 5, 1981, in *FBIS-PRC*, pp. A/3-4.

89. For elaboration of this point, see Jonathan D. Pollack, "Chinese Global Strategy and Soviet Power," *Problems of Communism*, XXX, no. 1 (January–February 1981), pp. 54–69.

90. Editorial, *Renmin Ribao*, April 18, 1980, in *FBIS-PRC*, April 30, 1980, p. I/5.

91. Premier Hua Guofeng's speech at a Beijing banquet in honor of Zambian President Kenneth Kaunda, *Renmin Ribao*, April 10, 1980, in *FBIS-PRC*, April 16, 1980, p. I/6.

92. On these matters, see, for example, the "Quarterly Chronicle and Documentation" section of *The China Quarterly* since the beginning of 1977; Kenneth Lieberthal, "The Politics of Modernization in the PRC," *Problems of Communism*, XXVII, no. 3, (May–June 1978), pp. 1–17; Richard E. Batsavage and John L. Davie, "China's International Trade and Finance," in U.S. Congress, Joint Economic Committee, *Chinese Economy Post-Mao* (Washington, D.C., U.S. Government Printing Office, 1978), pp. 707–41; Angus M. Fraser, "Military Modernization in China," *Problems of Communism*, XXVIII, no. 5–6 (September–December 1979), pp. 34–49; Pollack, loc. cit.

93. For implicit Chinese acknowledgement of this possibility, see Radio Beijing in Mandarin, March 5, 1981, in *FBIS-CHI*, March 10, 1981, pp. I/5–6. It should be stressed, however that the Chinese have not been willing to accept all of these interests as legitimate. See the criticisms of U.S. policy toward South Africa by Radio Beijing Domestic Service in Mandarin, in *FBIS-PRC*, June 24, 1981, pp. B/3-4, and *Renmin Ribao*, September 14, 1981, in *FBIS-PRC*, September 22, 1981, pp. I/1-2.

94. See especially Donald S. Zagoria, *The Sino-Soviet Conflict, 1956–61* (Princeton, N.J.: Princeton University Press, 1962).

95. For an excellent treatment of Chinese behavior in the United Nations, see Samuel S. Kim, *China, The United Nations, and World Order* (Princeton, N.J.: Princeton University Press, 1979).

96. *Renmin Ribao*, June 29, 1980, in *FBIS-PRC*, July 9, 1980, p. I/2. For other recent commentaries on South Africa, see the articles by Sima Da and Xu Dewen in *Renmin Ribao*, April 23 and June 5, 1980, as translated in *FBIS-PRC*, May 5, 1980, pp. I/2–3, and June 11, 1980, p. I/4; Beijing Xinhua in English, March 5, 1981, in *FBIS-PRC*, March 5, 1981, pp. I/2–3; Radio Beijing in Mandarin, March 6, 1981, in *FBIS-PRC*, March 10, 1981, pp. I/5–6; Xinhua Correspondent Mei Zhenmin, Radio Beijing in English, May 20, 1981, in *FBIS-PRC*, May 21, 1981, pp. I/1–2; Xinhua correspondents from Gaborone, Radio Beijing in English, June 1, 1981, in *FBIS-PRC*, June 5, 1981, I/2–3.

97. See Hua Guofeng's speech at a Beijing banquet in honor of Zambian

President Kaunda, loc. cit., pp. I/5–7; Vice Premier Li Xiannian's speech at a banquet in honor of a visiting delegation from Botswana, as broadcast by Beijing Xinhua in English, June 24, 1980, in *FBIS-PRC,* June 26, 1980, p. I/3; Beijing Xinhua in English, March 5, 1981, in *FBIS-PRC,* March 5, 1981, pp. I/2–3.

98. International Institute for Strategic Studies, *The Military Balance 1980–81* (London, 1980).

99. See, for instance, Fraser, loc. cit.

100. For more extended discussion of this preoccupation, see Pollack, loc. cit.

101. *The Washington Post,* June 6, 1979.

102. See, for example, Xinhua interview with Mugabe, Beijing Xinhua in English, March 7, 1980, in *FBIS-PRC,* March 7, 1980, pp. I/3–4; feature by Xinhua correspondents Xia Ze and Ying Qian on the birth of the Republic of Zimbabwe, Beijing Xinhua in English, April 17, 1980, in *FBIS-PRC,* April 8, 1980, p. I/4; commentary by Xinhua correspondent, Beijing Xinhua in English, April 17, 1980, in *FBIS-PRC,* April 18, 1980, pp. I/506; Beijing Xinhua in English, March 15, 1981, in *FBIS-PRC,* March 16, 1981, p. I/1.

103. For more detailed discussion, see Yu, loc. cit.

104. Commentator article in *Renmin Ribao,* March 6, 1980, in *FBIS-PRC,* March 11, 1980, p. I/3. That the target of these gibes was the USSR, subsequent Chinese commentary made abundantly clear. See, for instance, Radio Beijing in Mandarin, March 6, 1981, in *FBIS-PRC,* March 10, 1981, pp. I/5–6.

105. For a sophisticated treatment of this strategy—though in a broader context—see Kim, op. cit.

106. *Communist Aid . . . 1979 and 1954–79,* p. 15.

107. U.S. Arms Control and Disarmament Agency, *World Military Expenditures and Arms Transfers 1969–78.*

108. Compiled from the annual volumes published by the CIA on Communist aid activities in non-Communist less developed countries. These volumes do not break down the figures for the East European states in terms of individual countries.

109. U.S. Department of State, Bureau of Public Affairs, "Mozambique," *Background Notes,* September 1980.

110. See the annual country analyses in the series *Foreign Economic Trends and Their Implications for the United States,* prepared by the U.S. Department of State and released by the U.S. Department of Commerce.

111. *Communist Aid . . . 1979 and 1954–79,* p. 21.

112 For relevant discussion of the economic problems and their repercussions, see Holland Hunter, "Soviet Economic Problems and Alternative Policy Responses," in *Soviet Economy in a Time of Change,* vol. 1, pp. 23–27; Herbert Block, "Soviet Economic Performance in a Global Context," in ibid., pp. 110–40; Seweryn Bialer, "The Politics of Stringency in the USSR," *Problems of Communism,* XXIX, no. 3 (May–June 1980): 19–33; Hartmut Zimmerman, "The GDR in the 1970's," ibid., XXVII, no. 2 (March–April 1978): 22–25; Croan, "East Germany and Africa"; Ernst Kux, "Growing Tensions in Eastern Europe," *Problems of Communism,* XXIX, no. 2 (March–April 1980): 21–37; Doris Cornelson, "The GDR in a Period of Foreign Trade Difficulties: Development and Prospects for the 1980's," in *East European Economic Assessment: Part 1—Country Studies, 1980,* pp. 299–324; Domínguez, loc. cit.; Tyson and

Eichler, loc. cit., pp. 139–214; Jackson, loc. cit., pp. 231–98; Gilberg, loc. cit.; Batsavage and Davie, loc. cit., pp. 707–24; Arthur G. Ashbrook, Jr., "China: Shift of Economic Gears in Mid–1970s," in *Chinese Economy Post-Mao*, pp. 204–35; Robert F. Dernberger, "Beijing Looks Ahead: Prospects for the Chinese Economy," *Problems of Communism*, XXVIII, no. 5–6 (September–December 1979): 1–15; Richard P. Suttmeier, "Politics, Modernization, and Science in China," ibid., XXX, no. 1 (January–February 1981): 22–36.

113. The aid figures were compiled from data in the annual volumes put out by the CIA on Communist aid activities in non-Communist less developed countries.

114. U.S. Arms Control and Disarmament Agency, *World Military Expenditures and Arms Transfers 1969–1978*.

115. Ibid.

116. International Institute for Strategic Studies, *The Military Balance 1974–1975* (London, 1974); idem, *The Military Balance 1980–1981*. To the extent that South Africa accomplished this buildup through arms purchases rather than its own internal means, the matériel came mostly from Western Europe, primarily France.

117. U.S. Arms Control and Disarmament Agency, *World Military Expenditures and Arms Transfers 1969–1978*.

118. Ibid.

119. For more detailed discussion, see Bialer, loc. cit.; Abram Bergson, "The Soviet Economy and the 1981–85 Plan," *Problems of Communism*, XXX, no. 3 (May–June 1981): 24–36.

120. For a typical illustration, see A.B. Davidson, "Where Is South Africa Going?" *Narody Azii i Afriki*, no. 2 (1978):15–17; A. Makarov, "South Africa—Mainstay of Racism and Apartheid," *International Affairs*, no. 1 (January 1981): 59–67.

121. See, for example, Domínguez, loc. cit.

122. For more detailed discussion, see LeoGrande, op. cit., pp. 63–65.

123. For elaboration, see Gonzalez, "Cuban Policy Toward Africa: Activities, Motivations, and Outcomes."

124. See, for instance, Cornelson, loc. cit.

125. For relevant analysis of constraints, see Tyson and Eichler, loc. cit.

126. See, for example, Antic, loc. cit.

127. See, for instance, Jackson, loc. cit.

128. For discussion of the readjustment of the initial program, see Dernberger, loc. cit.

2. U.S. Policy toward Southern Africa

1. For an excellent treatment of the variety of postures adopted by the United States in Southern Africa, see Donald Rothchild, "U.S. Policy Styles in Africa," in K. Oye, et al., *Eagle Entangled: U.S. Foreign Policy in a Complex World* (New York & London, 1979), pp. 304–35.

2. Ibid., p. 307–309.

3. See National Security Study Memorandum 39 (NSSM #39), reprinted in Mohamed A. El-Khawas and Barry Cohen, eds., *The Kissinger Study of Southern Africa* (New York, 1976), p. 86.

4. See Option 2 of NSSM #39, ibid., p. 105.

5. See Kissinger's statement to the Senate Subcommittee on African Affairs, Senate, Subcommittee on African Affairs, "Implications of Angola for Future U.S. Foreign Policy," January 29, 1976, p. 2.

6. John Marcum, "Angola: Perilous Transition to Independence," in Gwendolen M. Carter and Patrick O'Meara, eds., *Southern Africa: The Continuing Crisis* (Bloomington, Ind., 1979), p. 175.

7. U.S. Congress, Senate, Committee on Foreign Relations, Subcommittee on African Affairs, *U.S. Policy Toward Africa*, Hearings, March 5, 1976, p. 193.

8. See Andrew Young's statement to the Senate Subcommittee on Africa, U.S. Congress, Senate, Committee on Foreign Relations, Subcommittee on African Affairs, *Ambassador Young's African Trip*, Hearings, June 6, 1977, p. 14.

9. Thomas Karis, "United States Policy toward South Africa," in Gwendolen M. Carter and Patrick O'Meara, eds., *Southern Africa: The Continuing Crisis* (Bloomington, Ind., 1979), pp. 342–43.

10. See Rothchild, op. cit., pp. 311–28.

11. See Han Austin and Banning Garrett, "U.S. Africa Policy: Hardening the Line," *International Bulletin*, vol. 5, no. 11 (June 5, 1978): 5.

12. See Robert M. Price, *U.S. Foreign Policy in Sub-Saharan Africa*, Policy Papers in International Affairs, Institute of International Studies, University of California (Berkeley, 1978), pp. 51–58.

13. See Richard Burt, "Reagan Aides Diagnose 'Regionalitis' in U.S.-Africa Policy," *New York Times*, December 7, 1980.

14. Rowland Evans and Robert Novak, *Washington Post*, March 11, 1981, p. A23.

15. David Rees, "Soviet Penetration in Africa," *Conflict Studies* 77 (November 1976), p. 1; see also Patrick Wall, ed., *The Southern Oceans and the Security of the Free World* (London, 1977), passim.

16. See Rees, op. cit., p. 1.

17. At the end of 1979 President Kaunda of Zambia announced the purchase of weapons worth $100 million from the Soviet Union and Eastern Europe. Some 200 Zambian pilots and ground crewmen for the newly purchased fighter planes will be trained in the USSR.

18. Quoted in Evans and Novak, op. cit.

19. Subcommittee on Mines and Mining of the Committee on Interior and Insular Affairs of the U.S. House of Representatives, "Sub-Saharan Africa: Its Role in Critical Mineral Needs of the Western World," July 1980, p. 20.

20. Quoted in Henry Brandon, "The Litmus Tests for Reagan's Global Strategy," *London Times*, March 8, 1981, p. 10.

21. Colin Legum, ed., *African Contemporary Record*, 1976/77 (London, 1978): B458.

22. Barclay's Bank Group, *ABECOR Country Report: Zambia*, May 1980.

23. U.S. Congress, House Subcommittee on Mines and Mining, *Sub-Saharan Africa: Its Role in Critical Mineral Needs of the Western World*, July 1980, p. 23.

24. See *African Development*, 10, 11 (November 1976):1113.

25. See *African Business*, April 1979; and *West Africa*, July 16, 1979, p. 1288.

26. See *Africa Confidential*, 20:24 (November 28, 1979); and ibid.

27. See *African Business*, January 1980, p. 31; and *Africa Confidential*, November 28, 1979.

28. *African Economic Development*, October 10, 1980, p. 8.

29. Quoted in *Wall Street Journal,* March 30, 1981, p. 1.

30. U.S. Department of the Interior, Mining and Minerals Policy, 1977, p. 26.

31. U.S. Congress, Senate, Committee on Foreign Relations, Subcommittee on African Affairs, *Angola,* Hearings, January 29, 1976, p. 8 (emphasis added).

32. *San Francisco Chronicle,* March 11, 1981, p. 12.

33. For a more extensive analysis of the "doctrine of credibility" see Price, *U.S. Foreign Policy in Sub-Saharan Africa,* pp. 30–35.

34. See n. 31.

35. See statement by Secretary of State Alexander Haig, n. 32; see also statement by Henry Kissinger, *The Washington Post,* February 26, 1976.

36. See Leslie H. Gelb, "U.S. Seeks Angola Compromise as Price for Accord on Namibia," *New York Times,* June 1, 1981, p. 1.

37. Ibid.

38. Ibid.

39. For an argument in support of such a policy see an article by Senator, and member of the Foreign Relations Committee, Richard G. Lugar, "Help the Fight Against Imperialism in Angola," *The Washington Star,* December 15, 1980, p. 14.

40. See David Wood, "U.S. Seeks to Overturn Africa Policy Restrictions," *Washington Star,* March 12, 1981.

41. See *Africa Confidential,* 22:10, May 6, 1981, p. 7; see also Leslie Gelb, op cit.

42. See Chester A. Crocker, "Scope Paper: Your [Haig] Meeting with South African Foreign Minister Botha, May 14," *New York Times,* May 29, 1981.

43. See Gelb op. cit.

44. See statement by President Reagan made in a television interview with Walter Cronkite, quoted in *West Africa,* No. 3319, March 9, 1981, p. 475.

45. See *San Francisco Examiner,* March 22, 1981, p. 24.

46. Quoted in *To the Point,* 5:32 (August 11, 1978), p. 24.

47. See Tom Gilroy, "Black Africa Criticizes Reagan Stand on South Africa," *The Christian Science Monitor,* March 13, 1981.

48. Barclays Bank Group, *ABECOR Country Reports* (Nigeria, October 1980).

49. See Stephen D. Krasner, "U.S. Commercial and Monetary Policy: Unravelling the Paradox of External Strength and Internal Weakness," *International Organization,* vol. 31, no. 4 (Autumn 1977): 650–56.

50. See *South Africa Digest,* June 15, 1979, p. 11; see also "South Africa Plans to Boost Coal Production," *World Business Weekly,* March 9, 1981, p. 15.

51. For an extensive analysis of this point see my "Apartheid and White Supremacy: The Meaning of Government-Led Reform in the South African Context," in Robert Price and Carl Rosberg, *The Apartheid Regime* (Berkeley, 1980), 297–332.

52. Ibid., pp. 320–21.

53. See Chester A. Crocker, et al., "A U.S. Policy for the '80's" *Africa Report,* January–February 1981, p. 12; similar sentiments were frequently expressed by officials in the Carter administration. For example, U.N. Ambassador Andrew Young told a Congressional committee in 1977: "I think . . . that our policy is . . . a commitment to move as rapidly as possible to achieve a transfer to majority rule [in South Africa] without violence." See U.S. Congress, Senate, Hearings Before the Subcommittee on African Affairs of the Senate

Foreign Relations Committee, *Ambassador Young's African Trip,* June 6, 1977, p. 14.

54. Crocker, op. cit., p. 12.

55. "In South Africa . . . there are at last signs of a new pragmatism and flexibility in the policies of the P.W. Botha government that assumed power in 1978," ibid., p. 7.

56. Quoted in *West Africa,* No. 3319, March 9, 1981, p. 475.

57. See Robert M. Price, "Apartheid and White Supremacy," in Price and Rosberg, eds., *The Apartheid Regime.*

4. The Middle East Dimension

1. For surveys of Afro-Arab relations see Colin Legum, *Africa Contemporary Record (ACR)* 1973–74, 1974–75, 1975–76, 1976–77, 1977–78, 1979–80. Also see Victor T. Le Vine and Timothy W. Luke: *The Arab-African Connection, Political and Economic Realities* (Westview Press, Colorado, 1979). Anthony Sylvester: *Arabs and Africans: Co-operation for Development* (Bodley Head, London, 1981)

2. See *ACR,* 1978–79, p. B923; 1979–80, pp. B867–8.

3. *The Military Balance,* Institute of Strategic Studies, London, 1979 and 1980. Also, *Financial Mail,* Johannesburg, April 17, 1981, pp. 272–6.

6. Nigeria and Southern Africa

1. David Martin and Phyllis Johnson, *The Struggle for Zimbabwe: The Chimurenga War* (London: Faber & Faber, 1981), pp. 302–303.

2. *Address By His Excellency Alhaji Shehu Shagari, President of the Federal Republic of Nigeria to the OAU Assembly of Heads of State and Government in Freetown 1–4* July 1980.

3. Ibid.

4. *Address by President Alhaji Shehu Shagari of the Federal Republic of Nigeria to the 35th Session of the UN General Assembly on 6 October 1980.*

5. Ibid.

6. *Daily Sketch* (Ibadan), 26 November 1980.

7. See *The OAU Lome Declaration on a New Strategy for the Liberation of Namibia and the Elimination of Apartheid and Racial Segregation in South Africa* Paper PL/DEC/32 (II) 43.80/Rev. 1 1980.

8. *Daily Times* (Lagos), 17 March 1970.

9. *Long Live African Unity: Text of the Statement by His Excellency, Major General Yakubu Gowon at the Seventh O.A.U. Assembly of Heads of State and Government,* 4 September 1970.

10. For the full text of this address see the *Morning Post* (Lagos), 25 June 1971.

11. *Text of Address to the OAU Summit extraordinary session in Addis Ababa on 11 January 1976.*

12. *Report of the Committee on the Review of Nigeria's Foreign Policy Including Economic and Technical Cooperation under the Chairmanship of Professor A. Adedeji,* May 1976.

13. *President Shehu Shagari's Address to the Meeting of the National Assembly on 16 October 1979.*

14. See Shagari's Address to the UN General Assembly, 6 October 1980 op. cit.

15. See the *Daily Sketch* (Ibadan), 17 August 1978.

16. For details see Charles O. Lerche and Abdul Said, eds., *Concepts of International Politics* 2nd edition (Englewood Cliffs, N.J.: Prentice-Hall, 1970), pp. 59–77: and Theodore A. Couloumbis and James H. Wolfe (eds.) *Introduction to International Relations* (Englewood Cliffs, N.J.: Prentice-Hall, 1978) pp. 56–73.

17. *West Africa* (London), 15 September 1980.

18. *New Nigerian* (Kaduna), 20 March 1980.

19. *Daily Times,* 27 November 1980.

20. *New Nigerian* (Kaduna), 25 November 1980.

21. President Shagari speculated that this would probably happen with the launching of the ₦40 billion Development Plan in 1981. See *Daily Times,* 26 November 1980.

22. *Export Destination of Nigerian Crudes 1978–80 Nigerian National Petroleum Company* (Lagos: Govt. Printer 1981).

23. Interview, May 1981.

24. *The Military Balance* 1980/81 (London: IISS 1979), p. 53.

25. *New Nigerian* (Kaduna), 19 April 1980.

26. *New Nigerian;* also *The Puch* (Lagos), 9 December 1980.

27. For details see Gabriel O. Ijewere, *Two Decades of Independence in Nigeria with Special Reference to Nigeria in International Relations: Text of Paper presented on the occasion of the 20th independence anniversary of the Federal Republic of Nigeria,* Lagos, Ministry of External Affairs, September 1980.

28. See *The Military Balance* 1980/81 op. cit., p. 54.

29. See Gwendolen M. Carter, *Which Way Is South Africa Going?* (Bloomington: Indiana University Press, 1980), p. 114.

30. Robert S. Jaster, *South Africa's Narrowing Security Options* (London, IISS 1980), p. 47.

31. Ibid., p. 45.

32. Carter, *Which Way Is South Africa Going?* p. 126.

33. Ibid.

34. Colin Legum, *The Western Crisis over Southern Africa* (London: Africana Publishing Co., 1979), p. v.

35. *Namibia: A Trust Betrayed* (New York: UN Secretariat 1974).

36. Interview, November 1980.

37. Ibid.

38. Alaba Ogunsanwo, *The Nigerian Military and Foreign Policy 1975–79: Processes, Principles, Performance and Contradictions* (Princeton University, Research Monograph No. 45, 1980), p. 37.

39. Interview, September 1980.

40. For further details see Olajide Aluko, *Nigeria and Southern Africa* (London: *George Allen & Unwin, Ltd.*), forthcoming.

41. During the writer's visit to Southern Africa in August-September 1980, Nigerian radio could not be picked up in any Southern African countries except for Zambia, and even there only at night.

42. *The Sunday Times* (London), 9 March 1980.

43. At the 16th anniversary celebrations of SWAPO in Dar es Salaam in

August, 1980, where SWAPO dancers wore dresses sewn from materials provided by Nigeria, they sang in praise of socialist countries like the USSR, East
Germany, and Cuba, but did not mention Nigeria at all.

7. South Africa in the Political Economy of Southern Africa

1. Provisional data from the *1979 World Bank Atlas* reproduced in *Economic
Spotlight* (Volkskas Bank Ltd., January 1981), and extracted in *South African
Digest*, 27 February 1981, p. 8.

2. Ronald Hyam, *The Failure of South African Expansion, 1908–1948* (New
York: Africana Publishing, 1972); and Martin Channock, *Britain, Rhodesia and
South Africa, 1900–1945: The Unconsummated Union* (London: Frank Cass,
1977).

3. John Sprack, *Rhodesia: South Africa's Sixth Province* (London: International Defence and Aid, 1974).

4. See Kenneth W. Grundy, "Anti-Neo-Colonialism in South Africa's Foreign Policy Rhetoric," in Timothy M. Shaw and Kenneth A. Heard, eds.,
Cooperation and Conflict in Southern Africa: Papers on a Regional Subsystem (Washington, D.C.: University Press of America, 1976), pp. 351–64.

5. D. Hobart Houghton, *The South African Economy*, 4th ed. (Cape Town:
Oxford University Press), 1976, pp. 212–32.

6. See Kenneth W. Grundy, "Intermediary Power and Global Dependency:
The Case of South Africa," *International Studies Quarterly*, XX, no. 4 (December, 1976): 553–80.

7. Among the dozens of items that might be consulted, see: Bruce J. Oudes,
"Evolving American Views of South Africa," in Richard E. Bissell and Chester
A. Crocker, eds., *South Africa into the 1980s* (Boulder, Col.: Westview, 1979),
pp. 159–86; Clyde Ferguson and William R. Cotter, "South Africa: What Is to
be Done?" *Foreign Affairs*, vol. 56, no. 2 (January, 1978): 253–74; Thomas
Karis, "United States Policy toward South Africa," in Gwendolen M. Carter
and Patrick O'Meara, eds., *Southern Africa: The Continuing Crisis* (Bloomington: Indiana University Press, 1979), pp. 313–62; and the proceedings of the
International Seminar on the Role of Transnational Corporations in South
Africa, London, 2–4 November 1979. See Sem. 1–8/79 of *Notes and Documents*,
published by the United Nations, Department of Political and Security Council Affairs, Centre Against Apartheid (November, 1979–February, 1980), esp.
no. 7, Christabel Gurney, "Recent Trends in the Policies of Transnational
Corporations." In the same series, also see: Ann Seidman and Neva Makgetla,
"Transnational Corporations and the South African Military-Industrial Complex," No. 24/79 (September, 1979).

8. John Seiler, "South African Perspectives and Responses to External Pressures," *Journal of Modern African Studies*, XIII, no. 3 (September, 1975):
447–68.

9. Deon Geldenhuys, "The Neutral Option and Sub-Continental Solidarity:
A Consideration of Foreign Minister Pik Botha's Zurich Statement of 7 March
1979," *Occasional Paper* (Braamfontein: South African Institute of International Affairs, March, 1979). See also: Kenneth W. Grundy, "Anti-Neo-Colonialism," in Shaw and Heard, *Cooperation and Conflict*.

10. Like Riker's theory of coalitions, each seeks to piece together the small-
est winning combination with the fewest external side payoffs: William H.

Riker, *The Theory of Political Coalitions* (New Haven, Conn.: Yale University Press, 1962).

11. Heribert Adam and Hermann Giliomee, *Ethnic Power Mobilized: Can South Africa Change?* (New Haven, Conn.: Yale University Press, 1979).

12. Robert A. Jaster, *South Africa's Narrowing Security Options.* Adelphi Papers no. 159 (London: International Institute for Strategic Studies, 1980).

13. As reported in the *Rhodesian Herald* (Salisbury), 1 September 1969.

14. See, e.g.: Kenneth W. Grundy, *Confrontation and Accommodation in Southern Africa: The Limits of Independence* (Berkeley: University of California Press, 1973), pp. 38–40 and the footnotes therein. Fundamentally sympathetic discussion of the more recent proposals can be found in G.M.E. Leistner, "Economic Cooperation between South Africa and Black African States as a Growth-Promoting Factor," paper presented at a Conference on Economic Cooperation with South Africa as a Factor of Integration, Hamburg, Germany, 26–28 September 1979; Wolfgang H. Thomas, "South Africa and Black Africa: The Future of Economic Interaction," *Politikon*, VI, no. 2 (December, 1979): 103–18; and idem, "A Southern Africa 'Constellation of States', Challenge or Myth?" *South Africa International*, X, no. 3 (January, 1980): 113–28. More critical, yet unfortunately factually outdated, is: Timothy M. Shaw, "International Organizations and the Politics of Southern Africa: Towards Regional Integration or Liberation," *Journal of Southern African Studies*, II, no. 1 (1976): 1–19. A good bibliography and some brief analyses of the issue appear in: Willie Breytenbach, ed., *The Constellation of States: A Consideration* (Johannesburg: South Africa Foundation, 1980).

15. *Africa Research Bulletin* (hereafter cited as *ARB*), (Econ.), XVII, no. 7 (31 August 1980): 5614.

16. *ARB* (Econ.), XVII, no. 7 (31 August 1980): 5614A–B.

17. Republic of South Africa, House of Assembly, *Debates* (Hansard), 7 February 1979, cols. 248–49.

18. House of Assembly *Debates*, 19 April 1979, cols. 4456–59.

19. *ARB* (Econ.), XVI, no. 4 (31 May 1979): 5084B–C.

20. *ARB* (Pol.), XVII, no. 5 (16 June 1980): 5670–72A; and no. 7 (15 August 1980): 5743C–44B.

21. *The Quail Report, Feb 8, 80: Report of the Ciskei Commission appointed in terms of Government Notice Number 14, Ciskei Official Gazette, vol 6, no. 177, 4 August 1978* (Pretoria: Conference Associates, May 1980), esp. pp. 101–27.

22. *The Star*, (Johannesburg) WAE, 9 August 1980, pp. 8–9.

23. Ibid., pp. 12–13.

24. E.g., *Christian Science Monitor*, 23 February 1981.

25. House of Assembly *Debates*, 17 February 1981, col. 1646.

26. *Towards a Constellation of States in Southern Africa: Meeting Between the Prime Minister and Business Leaders, Carlton Centre, Johannesburg, 22 November 1979* (Pretoria: Information Service of South Africa, n.d.).

27. *The Star*, WAE, 1 November 1980, p. 2.

28. David Mitrany, *A Working Peace System* (New York: Oxford University Press, 1946). Characteristic of this sort of thinking in South Africa is: J.A. Lombard, J.J. Standler, and P.J. van der Merwe, *The Concept of Economic Cooperation in Southern Africa*, 2nd ed. (Pretoria: Econburo, 1969).

29. For example, Kenneth Kaunda's remarks: *ARB* (Pol.), XVI, no. 11 (15 December 1979): 5492C.

30. *ARB* (Econ.), XVI, no. 6 (31 July 1979): 5154C–55B.

31. See Ronald T. Libby, "The Frontline States of Africa: A Small Power Entente," unpublished paper University of Zambia, 18 May 1977, mimeo.

32. *ARB* (Econ.), XVII, no. 3 (30 April 1980): 5458A–59C.

33. *ARB* (Econ.), XVII, no. 10 (30 November 1980): 5706.

34. *ARB* (Pol.), XVII, no. 10 (15 November 1980): 5834–36.

35. *The Star*, WAE, 27 December 1980, p. 12.

36. Kenneth W. Grundy, "The Social Costs of the Armed Struggle in Southern Africa," *Armed Forces and Society*, VII, no. 3 (Spring, 1981): 445–66.

37. *The Star*, WAE, 14 February 1981, p. 1; and 21 February 1981, pp. 5 & 9; and *The Daily Telegraph* (London), 15 April 1981.

38. *ARB* (Pol.), XVII, no. 12 (15 January 1981): 5908–09.

39. *The Times*, 31 January 1981.

40. *The Star,* daily edition, 1 April 1980, pp. 30–31; and 2 April 1980, p. 3.

41. *Rand Daily Mail* (Johannesburg), 2 April 1980, p. 3.

42. Quoting President Samora Machel: *Sunday Tribune* (Durban), 6 April 1980, p. 6.

43. Harry Oppenheimer, "Constellation of States in Southern Africa," *South African Digest*, 11 April 1980, p. 8; and selected quotations in: *The Star*, daily edition, 3 April 1980, p. 2. See also the remarks by Foreign Minister Pik Botha quoted in *Rand Daily Mail*, 2 April 1980, p. 3.

44. *ARB* (Econ.), XVII, no. 1 (29 February 1980): 5388B–C; and XVIII, no. 1 (28 February 1981): 5797B.

45. Ibid., no. 9 (31 October 1980): 56858B–C.

46. Ibid., 5672C–5673A.

47. Ibid., no. 6 (31 July 1980): 5566C–67.

48. Ibid., no. 8 (30 September 1980): 5640–42.

49. Ibid., XVIII, no. 1 (28 February 1981): 5797A–B.

50. Ibid., XVII, no. 11 (31 December 1980): 5733–74A; and *Financial Times* (London), 27 November 1980.

51. *African Development* (London), January 1981.

52. *ARB* (Econ.), XVIII, no. 3 (30 April 1981): 5873B–75A; *New York Times*, 28 March 1981; *The Times*, 28 March 1981; and *Financial Times*, 30 March 1981.

53. Speech to the Second Southern African Development Coordination Conference, 27 November 1980, Maputo, as quoted in *ARB* (Econ.), XVII, no. 11 (31 December 1980): 5733A.

54. For example, the general manager of Mozambique Railways once described the southern Mozambique ports as "the natural ports of the Transvaal." Quoted in *To the Point* (Johannesburg), 27 April 1979, p. 10. Similarly reassuring to Pretoria are remarks like those of the Mozambique Minister of Planning: "South Africa needs the port of Maputo and cannot avoid it. We also want the port to be used. We will not close it." *The Star*, WAE, 8 November 1980, p. 7. More complete discussion of these relationships in the post-independence period can be found in: Mario J. Azevedo, " 'A Sober Commitment to Liberation?': Mozambique and South Africa, 1974–1979," *African Affairs*, vol. 79, no. 317 (October, 1980): 567–84.

55. *Financial Times*, 2 May 1979.

56. *The Guardian*, 11 March 1981.

57. *The Star*, WAE, 14 March 1981, p. 7.

58. The 1980 figures from: House of Assembly *Debates*, 26 February 1981, Q. cols. 294–96.

59. On the politics of construction, see: Keith Middlemas, *Cabora Bassa: Engineering and Politics in Southern Africa* (London: Weidenfeld & Nicolson, 1975).

60. *ARB* (Pol.), XVIII, no. 1 (15 February 1981): 5921B.

61. *African Economic Development*, 3 October 1980.

62. There are, of course, differences among these countries. The literature on the subject is voluminous. For starters, see the chapters by E. Philip Morgan, Richard Weisfelder, Absolom Vilakazi, and Kenneth W. Grundy in Carter and O'Meara, eds., *Southern Africa*, pp. 223–312. See also: Francis d'A. Collings et al., "The Rand and the Monetary Systems of Botswana, Lesotho, and Swaziland," *Journal of Modern African Studies*, XVI, no. 1 (March, 1978): 97–121.

63. *ARB* (Econ.), XVII, no. 3 (30 April 1980): 5461A–B.

64. Ibid., XVIII, no. 1 (28 February 1981): 5799A–B.

65. Leonard T. Kapungu, *The United Nations and Economic Sanctions Against Rhodesia* (Lexington, Mass.: D.C. Heath, 1973), esp. pp. 1–19; and Harry R. Strack, *Sanctions: The Case of Rhodesia* (Syracuse, N.Y.: Syracuse University Press, 1978).

66. *Financial Times*, 11 March 1981. These data exclude petroleum and gold which, if added, would make proportions even higher.

67. *ARB* (Econ.), XVII, no. 2 (31 March 1980): 5428B; and no. 6 (31 July 1980): 5572B.

68. *The Star*, WAE, 10 January 1981, p. 19: and *ARB* (Econ.), XVIII, no. 3 (30 April 1981): 5863B–64A.

69. *The Star*, WAE, 10 May 1980, p. 19.

70. A report produced by the Catholic Institute for International Relations in London as reported in *Financial Times*, 18 April 1980, p. 16. Since UDI, however, South Africa has begun to supplant the U.K. as Rhodesia's chief source of new investment capital and credit. See the discussion in Sprack, *Rhodesia*, pp. 51–61; and Harold D. Nelson et. al., *Area Handbook for Southern Rhodesia* (Washington, D.C.: Government Printing Office, 1975), pp. 252–58.

71. *ARB* (Econ.), XVII, no. 6 (31 July 1980): 5572B.

72. *The Star*, WAE, 31 January 1981, p. 4.

73. *The Times* (London), 10 March 1981.

74. *ARB* (Econ.), XVI, no. 7 (31 August 1979): 5193C.

75. Ibid., XVII, no. 8 (30 September 1980): 5624A–B.

76. Ibid., XVI, no. 7 (31 August 1979): 5194A.

77. Thomas M. Callaghy, "Absolutism and Apartheid: Relations Between Zaire and South Africa." Paper prepared for a Conference on "South Africa in Southern Africa," The Pennsylvania State University, 13–14 October 1980.

78. Early aid practices are discussed in: G.M.E. Leistner, *South Africa's Development Aid to African States* (Pretoria: Africa Institute, 1970) and in Grundy, *Confrontation and Accommodation*, pp. 72–77. Recent aid is described in the propaganda release, "South Africa: Good Neighbor in Africa," *Backgrounder* No. 10/81 (December 1981), Washington, D.C.: The Minister (Information), South African Embassy.

79. "We Must Set Our People Free," interview with Robert Mugabe, *Africa*, no. 104 (April, 1980), p. 17.

80. Robert O. Keohane and Joseph S. Nye, *Power and Interdependence: World Politics in Transition* (Boston: Little, Brown & Co., 1977).

8. The Role of Donor Agencies in Southern Africa

1. Address by P.W. Botha, Carlton Centre, Johannesburg, South Africa, November 22, 1979.

2. "Southern Africa: Toward Economic Liberation," A Declaration by the Governments of Independent States in Southern Africa Made at Lusaka on the 1st of April 1980.

3. The first meeting of SADCC was held in July 1979 at Arusha, Tanzania, but viable economic cooperation was not possible until after Zimbabwe's independence.

4. Matthew Rothchild, "Southern Africa's Black States Strive for Economic Coordination," *Multinational Monitor*, vol. 1, no. 5, June 1980, pp. 16–19.

5. See, for instance, Guy Arnold, *Aid in Africa* (London: Kogan Page, 1979); or Frances Moore Lappé, Joseph Collins, and David Kinley, *Aid as Obstacle: Twenty Questions about our Foreign Aid and the Hungry* (San Francisco: Institute for Food and Development Policy, 1980).

6. Francis X. Sutton, "The Role of Foundations in Development," speech delivered at Texas A&M University, September 19, 1980, p. 6.

7. E.F. Schumacher, *Small Is Beautiful: Economics as if People Mattered* (London: Blond and Briggs, 1973).

8. Uma Lele, "Rural Africa: Modernization, Equity, and Long-Term Development," *Science*, Vol. 211, February 1981.

9. "Surviving a Cold Shoulder from the North," *South*, January 1981.

10. Leonard Silk, "McNamara Warns U.S. of Perils in Reducing Aid to World's Poor," *New York Times*, Sunday, June 21, 1981, p. 46.

11. David Jones, *Aid and Development in Southern Africa* (London: Croon Helm, 1977).

12. See also ch. 1.

13. The World Bank, *Rural Development: Sector Policy Paper* (Washington, D.C.: 1975), p. 61.

14. The World Bank, *World Development Report*, 1980 (Washington, D.C.: 1980), p. 111.

15. "Poverty's Strange Bedfellows," *South*, June 1981, p. 9.

16. *The New York Times*, June 21, 1981, p. 46.

17. *World Bank Annual Report*, 1979, p. 32.

18. These percentages are drawn from World Bank figures for "Eastern Africa," comprising 11 countries, 6 of which are SADCC members.

19. *World Bank Annual Report*, 1978, p. 40.

20. Lappé, Collins, and Kinley, p. 90. Their reference is to a speech by Vance to the National Convention of the League of Women Voters, May 1, 1978, entitled "Foreign Assistance and U.S. Foreign Policy."

21. See Arnold, p. 206.

22. *World Bank Annual Report*, 1978, p. 80.

23. The World Bank, *Rural Development: Sector Policy Paper* (Washington, D.C.: February 1975), p. 6.

24. Ibid.

25. *U.S.A.I.D. Congressional Presentation FY 1980*, p. 39.

26. "An overview of UNICEF policies, organization and working methods," U.N. Economic and Social Council, E/ICEF/670, March 1980, p. 44.

27. *FACTS*, Division for Economic and Social Information, Department of Public Information, United Nations, May 1979.

28. "Programme Implementation, Country and Inter-Country Programming and Projects, U.N. Decade for Transport and Communications in Africa 1978–1988, Report of the Administrator," UNDR/459, March 1980, p. 3.

29. Ibid., p. 6.

30. UNDP Country Programme for Mozambique (DP/GC/MOZ/R.I), April 1979, Appendix I.

31. Country Programme for Malawi (DP/GC/MCW/R.2), February 1980.

32. Country Programme for Lesotho (DP/GC/LES/R.2), September 1976, p. 5.

33. Country Programme for Zambia (DP/GC/ZAM/R.2), February 1977, p. 17.

34. Ibid., p. 45.

35. *U.S.A.I.D. Congressional Presentation FY 1980*, Main Volume, p. 19.

36. Ibid.

37. "He now prefers the softer phrase 'tool for peace and stability,' " reported the *Christian Science Monitor*, March 6, 1981, p. 12.

38. *U.S.A.I.D. Congressional Presentation FY 1980*, Main Volume.

39. Ibid.

40. $785 million for Israel and $750 million for Egypt out of a proposed total of $1,995 million. Ibid., p. 30.

41. Ibid.

42. The African Bibliographic Center's AID-funded SADEX project (Southern African Development Information/Documentation Exchange) has now become the U.S. repository for materials on SADCC.

43. Testimony by Goler T. Butcher, Assistant Administrator for Africa, USAID Hearings, Foreign Assistance and Related Programs, Appropriations for 1980, U.S. Congress, House, Sub-committee on Foreign Operations of the House Appropriations Committee, 96th Congress, 1st Session, 1979, Part 4, p. 200.

44. *U.S.A.I.D. Congressional Presentation, FY 1980*, Annex I, Africa, pp. 506–507.

45. See, for instance, the Agriculture, Rural Development and Nutrition program summary in the *USAID Congressional Presentation, FY 1980*, Main Volume, p. 35, "A.I.D. seeks to promote land and tenure reform and other LDC economic policies."

46. See Joyce Moock, "Future Trends in Donor Agency Support of Higher Education for Development," Rockefeller Foundation Inter-Office Correspondence, October 31, 1979. See also Lane E. Holdcraft, "The Role of External Aid," *Africa Report*, July–August, 1981, which indicates that responsible AID officials are aware of the importance of sophisticated training for African agriculturists involved in planning and policy analysis.

47. *U.S.A.I.D. Congressional Presentation, FY 1982*, Annex I, Africa, pp. 520–29. Figures given are from an early (Carter administration) draft of the 1982 presentations, and are subject to revision.

48. *U.S.A.I.D. Congressional Presentation, FY 1980*, Activity Data Sheet for Lesotho.

49. "Lesotho: Stronger Links with Pretoria?" *Africa Confidential*, February 25, 1981, p. 8.

50. *U.S.A.I.D. Congressional Presentation, FY 1980*, Activity Data Sheet for Lesotho.

51. *The New York Times*, March 24, 1981, p. 1.

52. Edward H. Berman, "Foundations, United States Foreign Policy and African Education 1945–1975," *Harvard Education Review,* no. 2, 1979.

53. IITA is the International Institute for Tropical Agriculture. Others went to ICIPE, the International Centre of Insect Physiology and Ecology in Kenya; IIRI, the International Rice Research Institute in the Philippines; and CIAT, the International Center of Tropical Agriculture in Colombia.

54. "A Report of Assistance to and with African Refugees by the Lutheran World Federation" prepared for Phelps-Stokes Fund, by Lutheran World Ministries, New York, August 1980. Figures given included actual expenditures for 1978 and 1979 and authorized figures for 1980.

55. Christina Held, "Status Report on CDS Projects up to December 31, 1980," The Lutheran World Federation, 1980.

56. Frank Taylor, "A Brief Report on Pelagano Village Industries, January 1974 to December 1980," Gaborone, 1980, p. 1. Donors listed include the Botswana Christian Council, the United Methodist Church (USA), Church World Service (USA), Presbyterian Church (USA), Unitarian Service Committee (Canada), National Council of Churches (USA) and the North Scituate Baptist Church (USA).

57. Chester Crocker, "South Africa: Strategy for Change," *Foreign Affairs* (Winter 1980/81), especially pp. 347–49.

58. Statement of Bishop Desmond Tutu, General Secretary, South African Council of Churches, September 18, 1980.

59. See John Borrell, "Need Ties Black Foes to South Africa," *The Wall Street Journal,* July 30, 1981, and Jay Ross, "Mugabe Says U.S. Can Force Change," *The Washington Post,* August 4, 1981.

Glossary

ANC	African National Congress (South Africa)
BCM	Black Consciousness Movement (South Africa)
BLS countries	Botswana, Lesotho, and Swaziland
CMEA, also COMECON	Council for Mutual Economic Assistance (the Soviet-East European answer to the EEC)
Contact Group	The five-nation team engaged in negotiations with South Africa over Namibia: Britain, Canada, France, the United States, and West Germany
DTA	Democratic Turnhalle Alliance (Namibia)
EEC, also EC	European Economic Community, consisting of Belgium, Britain, Denmark, France, Greece, Ireland, Italy, Luxembourg, the Netherlands, and West Germany
ECOWAS	Economic Community of West African States
FNLA	National Front for the Liberation of Angola
FRELIMO	Mozambique Liberation Front
Front Line States	Angola, Botswana, Mozambique, Tanzania, Zambia
HNP	Herstigte Nasionale Party [Reconstituted National Party] (South Africa)
ICRISAT	International Crops Research Institute for the Semi-Arid Tropics (Hyderabad, India)
MPLA	Popular Movement for the Liberation of Angola
MRM	Mozambique Resistance Movement
NPN	National Party of Nigeria
NPP	Nigerian People's Party
OAU	Organization of African Unity
PAC	Pan-Africanist Congress (South Africa)
PFP	Progressive Federal Party (South Africa)
SADCC	Southern African Development Coordination Conference, composed of Angola, Botswana, Lesotho, Malawi, Mozambique, Swaziland, Tanzania, Zambia, and Zimbabwe
SADF	South African Defense Force

249

SWAPO   South-West African People's Organization (Namibia)
UDI   Unilateral Declaration of Independence (Rhodesia, 1965)
UKSATA   United Kingdom South Africa Trade Association
UNITA   National Union for the Total Independence of Angola
ZANU   Zimbabwean African National Union
ZAPU   Zimbabwean African People's Union
ZIMCORD   Zimbabwe Conference on Reconstruction and Development (March 1981)

Selected Currency Rates*

Country	Rate per Dollar	Name of Currency
Angola	.0325	Kwanza
Botswana	1.2150	Pula
France	.1754	Franc
Kenya	.1110	Kenya Shilling
Lesotho	1.0380	South African Rand
Mozambique	.0350	Mozambique Escudo
Nigeria	1.5770	Niara
South Africa	1.0380	Rand
Swaziland	1.0380	Lilangeni (plural, Emalengeni)
Tanzania	.1240	Shilling
United Kingdom	1.9140	Pound
West Germany	.4465	Mark
Zaire	.1850	Zaire
Zambia	1.2300	Kwacha
Zimbabwe	1.5025	Rhodesian Dollar

*Rates quoted as of December 31, 1981, from Chase Manhattan Bank, New York.

Contributors

DAVID E. ALBRIGHT is Senior Text Editor for the journal *Problems of Communism* in Washington, D.C. He is editor of *Communism in Africa* (Bloomington: Indiana University Press, 1980), and coeditor of the forthcoming *The Communist States and Africa,* as well as author of "The U.S.S.R., Its Communist Allies and Southern Africa," *Munger Africana Library Notes,* vol. 55 (1980).

OLAJIDE ALUKO is Professor, Faculty of Administration, University of Ife, Nigeria. He is author of *Ghana and Nigeria 1957–1970: A Study of Inter-African Discord* (New York: Barnes & Noble, 1976); *Foreign Policies of African States* (London: Hodder & Stoughton, 1977); and "Britain, Nigeria, and Zimbabwe," *African Affairs* (1979).

GWENDOLEN M. CARTER is coeditor of this volume and of *Southern Africa: The Continuing Crisis* (2nd ed., Bloomington: Indiana University Press, 1982) and Professor of Political Science, Indiana University. She was formerly Melville J. Herskovits Professor of African Affairs and Director of the Program of African Studies at Northwestern University. She is author of *The Politics of Inequality: South Africa since 1948* (New York: Praeger, 1958, 1959), and of *Which Way Is South Africa Going?* (Bloomington: Indiana University Press, 1980), and coauthor of *South Africa's Transkei: The Politics of Domestic Colonialism* (Evanston, Ill.: Northwestern University Press, 1967).

KENNETH W. GRUNDY is Professor of Political Science, Case Western Reserve University, Cleveland, Ohio, and is the author of *Confrontation and Accommodation in Southern Africa: The Limits of Independence* (Berkeley: University of California Press, 1973) and numerous articles on Southern Africa.

CHRISTOPHER R. HILL is Director of the Centre for Southern African Studies at the University of York, England. He is the author of *Bantustans: The Fragmentation of South Africa* (London: Oxford University Press, 1964), and editor of *Rights and Wrongs: Some Essays on Human Rights* (Baltimore, Md.: Penguin, 1969), as well as other publications.

251

RICHARD A. HOROVITZ received a doctorate in African history from Northwestern University. He has written on the economic history of the Ivory Coast, and is currently working on a comparative study of East and West Africa. He served as a training director for Peace Corps programs in francophone Africa, and is now a program officer with the Ford Foundation.

COLIN LEGUM was Associate Editor of *The Observer, London,* and is widely regarded as the outstanding journalist writing about Africa. He is the editor of *Africa Contemporary Record: Annual Survey and Documents* (New York: Africana Publishing Company, annual, 1968–   ) and of *Africa Currents,* and author of *Africa in the 1980s: A Continent in Crisis* (New York: McGraw-Hill, 1979) and numerous pamphlets and articles.

PATRICK O'MEARA is coeditor of this work and of *Southern Africa: The Continuing Crisis* (2nd ed., Bloomington: Indiana University Press, 1982). He is Professor of Political Science and Professor, School of Public and Environmental Affairs, and Director of the African Studies Program, Indiana University. He is the author of *Rhodesia: Racial Conflict or Coexistence?* (Ithaca, N.Y.: Cornell University Press, 1975).

ROBERT M. PRICE is Associate Professor of Political Science at the University of California, Berkeley. He is author of *United States Foreign Policy in Sub-Saharan Africa: National Interest and Global Strategy* (Berkeley: University of California Institute of International Studies, 1978) and coeditor of *The Apartheid Regime: Political Power and Racial Domination* (Berkeley: University of California Institute of International Studies, 1980).

Bibliography

Compiled by DAVID L. EASTERBROOK

The purpose of this bibliography is both to indicate sources in African studies which document materials relevant to this book and to provide access to major relevant works previously published, primarily those which would be accessible in most academic libraries. It is not intended, therefore, to serve as a general background to published materials on Southern Africa.*

The bibliography is divided into two major sections; the first lists only bibliographies and include references to both serial and subject bibliographies; the second lists published books, journal articles, and official documents arranged to relate specifically to individual chapters of this book.

Bibliographies

Serial Bibliographies

Current Bibliography on African Affairs. 1962–   ; quarterly.
Compiled by the African Bibliographic Center, Washington, D.C. and published by the Baywood Publishing Co., Farmingdale, N.Y.

International African Bibliography. 1971–   ; quarterly.
Compiled at the School of Oriental and African Studies, University of London, in association with the International African Institute, and published by Mansell, London.

SADEX: The Southern Africa Development Information/Documentation Exchange. 1979–   ; bimonthly.
Compiled and published by the African Bibliographic Center, Washington, D.C. This bibliography is especially useful for its documentation of publi-

---

*For such a bibliography, Jean E. M. Gosebrink's "Sources for Contemporary South Africa" in *Southern Africa: The Continuing Crisis,* 2nd ed., Gwendolen Carter and Patrick O'Meara, eds. (Bloomington: Indiana University Press, 1982), should be consulted.

cations relating to the Southern African Development Coordination Conference (SADCC).

Subject Bibliographies

Danaher, Kevin. *South Africa and the United States: An Annotated Bibliography.* Washington, D.C.: Institute for Policy Studies, 1979. 26 pp.
_____. "U.S. Policy Options Toward South Africa: A Bibliographic Essay," *Current Bibliography on African Affairs*, Vol. 13 (1980–81), pp. 2–25.
Delancey, Mark. *African International Relations: An Annotated Bibliography.* Boulder, Col.: Westview Press, 1981. 365 pp.
_____. "The International Relations of Southern Africa: A Review of Recent Studies," *Genève-Afrique*, Vol. 15 (1976), pp. 82–135.
El-Khawas, Mohamed A. *American-Southern African Relations: Bibliographic Essays.* Westport, Conn.: Greenwood Press, 1975. 188 pp.
El-Khawas, Mohamed A., and Hope, Constance Morris. "A Bibliographical Essay on U.S. Diplomatic Relations with South Africa," *Journal of Southern African Affairs*, Vol. 4 (1979), pp. 81–116.
Fasehun, Orobola. "Selected Bibliography on the Foreign Policy of Nigeria, 1970–1977," *Current Bibliography on African Affairs*, Vol. 12 (1970–80), pp. 166–69.
Nzuwah, Mariyawanda. "An Index of Selected Resolutions, Documents, and Declarations of the United Nations on Southern Africa," *Journal of Southern African Affairs*, Vol. 4 (1979), pp. 187–247.
Rogaly, Gail L. *South Africa's Foreign Relations, 1961–1979: A Select and Partially Annotated Bibliography.* Braamfontein, South Africa: South African Institute of International Affairs, 1980. 462 pp.
Schoeman, Elna. *South Africa and the United Nations: A Select and Annotated Bibliography.* Braamfontein, South Africa: South African Institute of International Affairs, 1981. 244 pp.
Skurnik, W.A.E. *Sub-Saharan Africa: A Guide to Information Sources.* Detroit: Gale Research Company, 1977. 130 pp.
Vineberg, R.A. *Africa and the Middle East: A Bibliography.* Jerusalem: Hebrew University, 1977. 255 pp.
Zoghby, Samir M. *Arab-African Relations, 1973–1975: A Guide.* Washington, D.C.: African Section, Library of Congress, 1976. 26 pp.

Books, Articles, and Official Documents

Soviet Union

Albright, David E. "The U.S.S.R. and Africa: Soviet Policy," *Problems of Communism*, Vol. 27, No. 1 (1978), pp. 20–37.
_____. "The U.S.S.R., Its Communist Allies, and South Africa," *Munger Africana Library Notes*, Vol. 55 (1980), pp. 4–29.
Albright, David E., ed. *Communism in Africa.* Bloomington: Indiana University Press, 1980. 277 pp.
Brayton, Abbot A. "Soviet Involvement in Africa," *Journal of Modern African Studies*, Vol. 17 (1979), pp. 253–69.
Breyer, Karl. *Moskaus Faust in Afrika.* Stuttgart: Seewald, 1979. 290 pp.

Fountain, Roger W. "Cuban Strategy in Africa: The Long Road of Ambition," *Strategic Review*, Vol. 6 (Summer 1978), pp. 18–27.

Fullerton, John. "Projecting Soviet Power," *South African Journal of African Affairs*, Vol. 9 (1979), pp. 56–62.

Hallett, Robin. "Cuba and Africa," *International Affairs Bulletin*, Vol. 4, No. 2 (1980), pp. 44–55.

Legum, Colin. "The Soviet Union, China and the West in Southern Africa," *Foreign Affairs*, Vol. 54 (1975–76), pp. 754–62.

LeoGrande, William. *Cuba's Policy in Africa, 1959–1980*. Berkeley: Institute of International Studies, University of California, 1980. 82 pp.

Luce, Phillip A. *The New Imperialism: Cuba and the Soviets in Africa*. Washington, D.C.: Council for Inter-American Security, 1979. 71 pp.

Mestri, Ezzedine. *Les Cubains et L'Afrique*. Paris: Karthala, 1980. 239 pp.

Pope, R.R. "Soviet Views on Black Africa," *International Journal of Politics*, Vol. 6 (1976–77), pp. 3–105.

Rees, David. *Soviet Strategic Penetration of Africa*. London: Institute for the Study of Conflict, 1976. 20 pp.

Rothenberg, Morris. *The U.S.S.R. and Africa: New Dimensions of Soviet Global Power*. Washington, D.C.: Advanced International Studies Institute, 1980. 280 pp.

Walker, Walter. *The Bear at the Back Door: The Soviet's Threat to the West's Lifeline in Africa*. Sandton, South Africa: Valiant House, 1978. 255 pp.

United States

Bender, Gerald J. "Angola, the Cubans, and Americans Anxieties," *Foreign Policy*, No. 31 (1978), pp. 3–30.

Bierman, Werner, "U.S. Policy Towards Southern Africa in the Framework of Global Empire," *Review of African Political Economy*, No. 17 (1980), pp. 28–42.

Crocker, Chester A. "South Africa: A Strategy for Change," *Foreign Affairs*, Vol. 59 (1980–81), pp. 323–51.

Curry, Robert L. "U.S.-A.I.D.'s Southern Africa Program," *Journal of Southern African Affairs*, Vol. 5 (1980), pp. 183–97.

El-Khawas, Mohamed A., and Cohen, Barry, eds. *The Kissinger Study of Southern Africa: National Security Memorandum 39 (Secret)*. Westport, Conn.: L. Hill, 1976. 189 pp.

Goshen, Carolyn J. *Southern Africa: A Select Guide to U.S. Organizational Interests*. Washington, D.C.: African Bibliographic Center, 1979. 74 pp.

Lemarchand, René, ed. *American Policy in Southern Africa: The Stakes and the Stance*. Washington, D.C.: University Press of America, 1978. 450 pp.

Ofuatey-Kodjoe, W. "The United States, Southern Africa, and International Order," *Journal of Southern African Affairs*, Vol. 1 (1976), pp. 111–24.

Oye, Kenneth A., et al. *Eagle Entangled: U.S. Foreign Policy in a Complex World*. New York: Longman, 1979. 365 pp.

Price, Robert M. *U.S. Foreign Policy in Sub-Saharan Africa: National Interest and Global Strategy*. Berkeley: Institute of International Studies, University of California, 1978. 69 pp.

Qoboza, Percy. *The United States and South Africa: Three South African Perspectives*. Johannesburg: South African Institute of International Affairs, 1977. 15 pp.

Samuels, Michael A., et. al. *Implications of Soviet and Cuban Activities in Africa for U.S. Policy.* Washington, D.C.: Center for Strategic and International Studies, Georgetown University, 1979. 73 pp.

Stockwell, John. *In Search of Enemies: A CIA Story.* New York: Norton, 1978. 285 pp.

Study Commission on United States Policy Toward Southern Africa. *South Africa: Time Running Out.* Berkeley: University of California Press, 1981. 517 pp.

U.S. House. Committee on Foreign Affairs. *U.S. Policy Toward South Africa: Hearings April 30–June 16, 1980 Before the Subcommittee on International Economic Policy and Trade, on Africa and on International Organizations.* 96th Congress, 2nd Session. (Y4.F 76/1:Un35/19) 912 pp.

Walker, Gary A. *South African Interdependencies and Their Implications for U.S. Policy Development.* Washington, D.C.: Aurora Associates, 1980. 78 pp.

Whitaker, Jennifer S., ed. *Africa and the United States: Vital Interests.* New York: New York University Press, 1978. 255 pp.

Western Europe

All Africa Conference of Churches. *The Nuclear Conspiracy.* Nairobi: All Africa Conference of Churches, 1977. 116 pp.

Alting von Geusau, Frances A.M. *The Lomé Convention and a New International Order.* Leyden: Sijthoff, 1977. 249 pp.

Anglin, Douglas G., et. al. *Canada, Scandinavia and Southern Africa.* Uppsala: Scandinavian Institute of African Studies, 1978. 190 pp.

Anglin, Douglas G., Shaw, Timothy M., and Widstrand, Carl G., eds. *Conflict and Change in Southern Africa: Papers from a Scandinavian-Canadian Conference.* Washington, D.C.: University Press of America, 1979. 269 pp.

Asmal, Kader. *Policies of the European Economic Community Towards South Africa.* New York: United Nations Centre Against Apartheid, 1979. (Notes and Documents, 11/79) 12 pp.

Bley, Helmut. *Afrika und Bonn: Versaumnisse und Zwänge Deutscher Afrika-Politik.* Hamburg: Rowohlt Taschenbuch Verlag, 1978. 347 pp.

Bouvier, Paule. *Europe et la Coopération au Développement: Un Bilan, la Convention du Lomé.* Brussels: Éditions de l'Université du Bruxelles, 1980. 191 pp.

Brandt, Hartmut, et. al., eds. *Perspectives of Independent Development in Southern Africa.* Berlin: German Development Institute, 1980. 183 pp.

Cervenka, Zdenek. "West Germany's Role in Africa in 1977: An Economic Super-Power on the Move," *Africa Contemporary Record,* Vol. 10 (1977–78), pp. A117–A124.

Cervenka, Zdenek, and Rogers, Barbara. *The Nuclear Axis: Secret Collaboration between West Germany and South Africa.* London: Julian Friedmann, 1978. 464 pp.

Commission of the European Communities. Information Directorate. *The European Community and Southern Africa.* Brussels: Information Directorate, Commission of the European Communities, 1977. (Information, 166/77 E) 18 pp.

Frey-Wouters, Adele E. *The European Community and the Third World: The Lomé Convention and its Impact.* New York: Praeger, 1980. 290 pp.

Hall, K.B., and Chopra, H.S., eds. *The E.E.C. and the Third World.* London:

Hodder and Stoughton in Association with the Overseas Development Institute and the Institute for Development Studies, 1981. 500 pp.

Huisman, Ruurd. *The Role of South African Coal in the Benelux Countries.* New York: United Nations Centre Against Apartheid, 1981. (Notes and Documents, 13/81) 23 pp.

Hull, Galen. "The French Connection in Africa: Zaire and South Africa," *Journal of Southern African Studies,* Vol. 5 (1979), pp. 220–33.

Hurwitz, Leon. "The EEC and Decolonization: The Voting Behaviour of the Nine in the United Nations General Assembly," *Political Studies,* Vol. 24 (1976), pp. 435–47.

Jones, David. *Aid and Development in Southern Africa: British Aid to Botswana, Lesotho and Swaziland.* London: Croom, Helm, 1977. 313 pp.

Langa, A. "Africa's Links with the EEC Lead to Dependence," *African Communist,* No. 82 (1980), pp. 44–50.

McQueen, Matthew. *Britain, the E.E.C. and the Developing World.* London: Heinemann, 1977. 119 pp.

Owen, David. "The Importance of Negotiated Settlements in Southern Africa," *International Affairs Bulletin,* Vol. 2 (1979), pp. 47–54.

Ripkin, Peter. "West German Options in Southern Africa," *Journal of Southern African Affairs,* Vol. 3 (1978), pp. 133–51.

Taillefer, Bernard. *Le Dernier Rempart: France-Afrique du Sud.* Paris: Sycomore, 1980. 259 pp.

United Nations. Centre Against Apartheid. *International Conference on the European Economic Community and South Africa.* New York: United Nations Centre Against Apartheid, 1979. (Notes and Documents, 9/79) 11 pp.

Von Bothmer, Lenelotte. *Opposition to Apartheid in the Federal Republic of Germany.* New York: United Nations Centre Against Apartheid, 1981. (Notes and Documents, 6/81) 16 pp.

Middle East

Arab Bank for Economic Development in Africa. *La Coopération Arabo-Africaine: Les Étapes Importantes.* Khartoum: Banque Arabe pour le Développement Économique en Afrique, 1978. 38 pp.

"The Israeli-South African Axis," *Africa Report,* Vol. 25 (November/December 1980), pp. 8–22.

LeVine, Victor T., and Luke, Timothy W. *The Arab-African Connection: Political and Economic Realities.* Boulder, Col.: Westview Press, 1979. 155 pp.

Shaw, Timothy M. "Oil, Israel, and the OAU: An Introduction to the Political Economy of Energy in Southern Africa," *Africa Today,* Vol. 23 (1976), pp. 15–26.

Stevens, Richard P., ed. *Israel and South Africa: The Progression of a Relationship.* New York: New World Press, 1976. 214 pp.

Sylvester, Anthony. *Arabs and Africans: Cooperation for Development.* London: Bodley Head, 1981. 251 pp.

United Nations. Centre Against Apartheid. *Relations between Israel and South Africa: Report of the United Nations Special Committee Against Apartheid.* New York: United Nations Centre Against Apartheid, 1977. (Notes and Documents, 5/77) 22 pp.

Organization of African Unity

Andemichael, Berkanykun. *The OAU and the UN: Relations Between the Organization of African Unity and the United Nations.* New York: Africana, 1976. 331 pp.

Cervenka, Zdenek. *The Unfinished Quest for Unity: Africa and the OAU.* London: Julian Friedmann, 1977. 251 pp.

El-Ayouty, Yassin. *The OAU after 10 Years: Comparative Perspectives.* New York: Praeger, 1975. 262 pp.

El-Khawas, Mohamed A. "Southern Africa: Challenge to the OAU," *Africa Today,* Vol. 24 (1977), pp. 25–41.

Mugomba, Agrippah T. *The Foreign Policy of Despair: Africa and the Sale of Arms to South Africa.* Nairobi: East African Literature Bureau, 1977. 355 pp.

Shaw, Timothy M. "Oil, Israel, and the OAU: An Introduction to the Political Economy of Energy in Southern Africa," *Africa Today,* Vol. 23 (1976), pp. 15–26.

Thomas, Wolfgang H. "South Africa and Black Africa: The Future of Economic Cooperation," *Politikon,* Vol. 6 (1979), pp. 103–18.

Wolfers, Michael. *Politics in the Organization of African Unity.* London: Methuen, 1976. 229 pp.

Nigeria

Akinyemi, A. Bolaji, ed. *Nigeria and the World: Readings in Nigerian Foreign Policy.* Ibadan: Oxford University Press for the Nigerian Institute of International Affairs, 1978. 152 pp.

Aluko, Olajide. "Britain, Nigeria, and Zimbabwe," *African Affairs,* Vol. 78 (1979), pp. 91–102.

―――. *Essays in Nigerian Foreign Policy.* London: G. Allen & Unwin, 1981. 296 pp.

Aluko, Olajide, ed. *The Foreign Policies of African States.* London: Hodder & Stoughton, 1977. 243 pp.

Ogunsanwo, Alaba. *Nigerian Military and Foreign Policy, 1975–1979: Processes, Principles, Performance and Contradictions.* Princeton: Center for International Studies, Woodrow Wilson School of Public and International Affairs, Princeton University, 1980. 86 pp.

South Africa

Baffoe, Frank. "Some Aspects of the Political Economy of Cooperation and Integration in Southern Africa: The Case of South Africa and the Countries of Botswana, Lesotho, and Swaziland," *Journal of Southern African Affairs,* Vol. 3 (1978), pp. 327–42.

Barratt, John. *Eyes on the Eighties: The International Political Outlook for Southern Africa.* Braamfontein, South Africa: South African Institute of International Affairs, 1979. 17 pp.

Bissell, Richard E. *Apartheid and International Organizations.* Boulder, Col.: Westview Press, 1977. 231 pp.

―――. *Southern Africa and the World: Autonomy or Interdependence?* Philadelphia: Foreign Policy Research Institute, 1978. 67 pp.

Bissell, Richard E., ed. *South Africa into the 1980s.* Boulder, Col.: Westview Press, 1979. 254 pp.

Breytenbach, Willie. *The Constellation of States: A Consideration.* Johannesburg: South Africa Foundation, 1980. 81 pp.

Burgess, Julian. *Interdependence in Southern Africa: Trade and Transport Links in South, Central and East Africa.* London: Economist Intelligence Unit, 1976. 95 pp.

Carter, Gwendolen M., and O'Meara, Patrick, eds. *Southern Africa: The Continuing Crisis.* Bloomington: Indiana University Press, 1982 revised edition.

Clifford-Vaughn, F. McA., ed. *International Pressures and Political Change in South Africa.* Cape Town: Oxford University Press, 1978. 109 pp.

Clough, Michael. *Regional Cooperation in Southern Africa: Promises and Pitfalls.* Salisbury: Zimbabwe Economic Society, 1980. 36 pp.

————. *A Transatlantic Symposium—Where is South Africa Heading? June 6–8, 1980, Seven Springs Center: A Report.* Mount Kisco, N.Y.: Seven Springs Center, 1980. 48 pp.

Cobbe, James H. "Integration among Unequals: The Southern African Customs Union and Development," *World Development,* Vol. 8 (1980), pp. 329–36.

Collings, Francis d'A. "The Rand and the Monetary Systems of Botswana, Lesotho, and Swaziland," *Journal of Modern African Studies,* Vol. 16 (1978), pp. 97–121.

Crocker, Chester A. "South Africa: Strategy for Change," *Foreign Affairs,* Vol. 59 (1980–81), pp. 323–51.

Egeland, Leif. *Interdependence in Southern Africa.* Braamfontein, South Africa: South African Institute of International Affairs, 1978. 4 pp.

Geldenhuys, Deon. "Regional Cooperation in Southern Africa: A Constellation of States?" *International Affairs Bulletin,* Vol. 2 (1979), pp. 36–72.

Green, Reginald H. "Constellation, Association, Liberation: Economic Coordination and the Struggle for Southern Africa," *Africa Contemporary Record,* Vol. 12 (1979–80), pp. A32–A45.

————. "Toward Southern African Regionalism: The Emergence of a Dialogue," *Africa Contemporary Record,* Vol. 11 (1978–79), pp. A40–A49.

Grundy, Kenneth. "Regional Relations in Southern Africa in the Global Political Economy," in Delancey, Mark W., ed., *Aspects of International Relations in Africa.* Bloomington: African Studies Program, Indiana University, 1979, pp. 90–125.

Guelke, Adrian. "Southern Africa and the Super Powers," *International Affairs,* Vol. 56 (1980), pp. 648–64.

Jaster, Robert S. *South Africa's Narrowing Security Options.* London: International Institute for Strategic Studies, 1980. 51 pp.

Kgarege, Aloysius, ed. *SADCC 2-Maputo: The Proceedings of the Second Southern African Development Coordination Conference.* London: SADCC, 1981. 288 pp.

Kornegay, Francis A. "Lusaka and Regional Cooperation in Southern Africa, Part I: The Zimbabwe Connection," *SADEX,* Vol. 2, No. 3 (1980), pp. 1–16.

————. "Lusaka and Regional Cooperation in Southern Africa, Part II: The South African Dilemma," *SADEX,* Vol. 2, No. 4 (1980), pp. 1–14.

————. "Namibia's Transition and Regional Cooperation in Southern Africa," *SADEX,* Vol. 3, No. 1 (1981), pp. 1–25.

Legum, Colin. "The Continuing Crisis in Southern Africa," *Africa Contemporary Record,* Vol. 11 (1978–79), pp. A3–A24.
_____. *Southern Africa: The Secret Diplomacy of Detente.* New York: Africana, 1975. 91 pp.
_____. "The Southern African Crisis," *Africa Contemporary Record,* Vol. 10 (1977–78), pp. A3–A32.
_____. *The Western Crisis over Southern Africa: South Africa, Rhodesia, and Namibia.* New York: Africana, 1979. 260 pp.
Leistner, G.M.E. "Can Southern Africa Get It Together?" *South African Journal of African Affairs,* Vol. 9 (1979), pp. 84–91.
_____. *Towards a New Order in Southern Africa: A Collection of Papers Bearing on Economic Development, Regional Interdependence and Closer Union in Southern Africa.* Pretoria: Africa Institute of South Africa, 1979. 51 pp.
Loubser, J.G.H. *Transport Diplomacy with Special Reference to Southern Africa.* Sandton, South Africa: Valiant House, 1980. 29 pp.
McCrystal, Lawrence. "Economic Liaison in Southern Africa," *South African Journal of African Affairs,* Vol. 9 (1979), pp. 76–81.
Makgetla, Neva, and Seidman, Ann W. *Outposts of Monopoly Capitalism: Southern Africa in the Changing Global Economy.* Westport, Conn.: L. Hill, 1980. 370 pp.
Metrowich, F.R. *South Africa's New Frontiers.* Sandton, South Africa: Valiant House, 1977. 160 pp.
Mkandawine, P. Thandika. "Reflections on Some Future Scenarios for Southern Africa," *Journal of Southern African Affairs,* Vol. 2 (1977), pp. 427–39.
Mosley, Paul. "The Southern African Customs Union: A Reappraisal," *World Development,* Vol. 6 (1978), pp. 31–43.
Nsekela, Amon J., ed. *Southern Africa: Toward Economic Liberation.* London: Rex Collings, 1981. 274 pp.
Price, Robert M., and Rosberg, Carl G. *The Apartheid Regime: Political Power and Racial Domination.* Berkeley: Institute of International Studies, University of California, 1980. 376 pp.
Prinsloo, D.S. *Revolutions and Railways in Southern Africa.* Pretoria: Foreign Affairs Association, 1978. 28 pp.
Rotberg, Robert I. *Suffer the Future: Policy Choices in Southern Africa.* Cambridge: Harvard University Press, 1980. 311 pp.
Rotberg, Robert I., and Barratt, John, eds. *Conflict and Compromise in Southern Africa.* Lexington, Mass.: Lexington Books, 1980. 212 pp.
Schlemmer, Lawrence. *Change, Reform and Economic Growth in South Africa.* Johannesburg: Ravan Press, 1978. 244 pp.
"Second Southern African Development Coordination Conference (SADCC 2), Maputo, November 1980: A Perspective," *SADEX,* Vol. 3, No. 2 (1981), pp. 1–6.
Seiler, John, ed. *Southern Africa Since the Portuguese Coup.* Boulder, Col.: Westview Press, 1980. 252 pp.
Shaw, Timothy M. "International Organizations and the Politics of Southern Africa: Towards Regional Integration or Liberation," *Journal of Southern African Studies,* Vol. 2 (1976), pp. 1–19.
_____. "International Stratification in Africa: Sub-Imperialism in Southern and Eastern Africa," *Journal of Southern African Affairs,* Vol. 2 (1977), pp. 145–65.
Shaw, Timothy M., ed. *Cooperation and Conflict in Southern Africa: Papers on a*

Regional Subsystem. Washington, D.C.: University Press of America, 1977. 479 pp.

Slater, Charles C. *Easing Transition in Southern Africa: New Techniques for Policy Planning.* Boulder, Col.: Westview Press, 1979. 183 pp.

Spandau, Arndt. *Economic Boycott Against South Africa: Normative and Factual Issues.* Cape Town: Juta, 1979. 200 pp.

Ström, Gabriele W. *Development and Dependence in Lesotho, the Enclave of South Africa.* Uppsala: Scandinavian Institute of African Studies, 1978. 186 pp.

Thomas, Wolfgang H. "A Southern African 'Constellation of States': Challenge or Myth," *South Africa International,* Vol. 10 (1980), pp. 113–28.

Uppsala. Universitet. Southern Africa Research Group. *Studies on South African Imperialism.* Uppsala: Uppsala University Department of Peace and Conflict Studies, 1977. 103 pp.

Van der Merwe, Hendrik, ed. *African Perspectives on South Africa: A Collection of Speeches, Articles and Documents.* Stanford: Hoover Institution Press, 1978. 612 pp.

Van der Merwe, Nikolass, ed. *Perspectives on South Africa's Future.* Rondebosch, South Africa: Centre for African Studies, University of Cape Town, 1979. 187 pp.

Van Zyl Slabbert, Frederik. *South Africa's Options: Strategies for Sharing Power.* New York: St. Martin's Press, 1979. 196 pp.

Van Zyl Slabbert, Frederik, and Opland, Jeff, eds. *South Africa: Dilemmas of Evolutionary Change.* Grahamstown, South Africa: Institute of Social and Economic Research, Rhodes University, 1980. 248 pp.

Venter, Denis. *South Africa and Black Africa: Some Problem Areas and Prospects for Rapprochement.* Pretoria: Africa Institute of South Africa, 1980. 40 pp.

Voluntary Organizations

Arnold, Guy. *Aid in Africa.* New York: Nichols Publishing Co., 1979. 240 pp.

Betts, T. F. "Development Aid from Voluntary Agencies to the Least Developed Countries," *Africa Today,* Vol. 25 (1978), pp. 49–68.

Collins, Michael, ed. *Commonwealth African Aid Directory of Aid Agencies, Charities, Trusts, Foundations, and Official Bodies Offering Assistance in Commonwealth Countries in Africa.* London: Commonwealth Foundation, 1979. 124 pp.

Kaplan, Jacob J. *International Aid Coordination: Needs and Machinery.* St. Paul, Minn.: West Publishing Co., 1978. 58 pp.

Morgan, E. Philip. "Managing Development Assistance: Some Effects with Special Reference to Southern Africa," *SADEX,* Vol. 2, No. 1 (1980), pp. 1–17.

Technical Assistance Information Clearing House. *U.S. Non-Profit Organizations in Development Assistance Abroad.* New York: Technical Assistance Information Clearing House, 1979. 525 pp.

Index

263